DESIGNERS' SELFIMAGE

An International Showcase of Identity Graphics

BASED ON AN ISRAEL MUSEUM EXHIBITION

The Library of Applied Design
PBC INTERNATIONAL
New York

Distributor to the book trade in the United States and Canada:

Rizzoli International Publications Inc.
300 Park Avenue South
New York, NY 10010

Distributor to the art trade in the United States:

PBC International, Inc.
One School Street
Glen Cove, NY 11542
1-800-527-2826
Fax 516-676-2738

Distributor to the art trade in Canada:

Letraset Canada Ltd.
170 Duffield Drive
Markham, Ontario, L6G 1B5 Canada

Distributed throughout the rest of the world:

Hearst Books International
105 Madison Avenue
New York, NY 10016

Copyright © 1991 by
PBC INTERNATIONAL, Inc.
All rights reserved. No part of this book may be reproduced
in any form whatsoever without written permission of the
copyright owner, PBC INTERNATIONAL, INC.,
One School Street, Glen Cove, NY 11542.

Library of Congress Cataloging-in-Publication Data
Marcus, Joshua.
    Designers' self image : an international showcase of identity
graphics / Joshua Marcus with the Israel Museum.
      p.   cm.
    Includes index.
    1. Self-presentation in art—Exhibitions. 2. Visual
communication—Exhibitions. 3. Commercial art—
Exhibitions. 4. Graphic arts—History—20th century—
Exhibitions. I. Muze'on Yiśra'el (Jerusalem) II. Title.
NC997.A4J46 1991
741.6'09'048074569442--dc20   90-26650
  ISBN 0-86636-134-0   CIP

*CAVEAT—Information in this text is believed accurate, and
will pose no problem for the student or casual reader.
However, the author was often constrained by information
contained in signed release forms, information that could
have been in error or not included at all. Any
misinformation (or lack of information) is the result of failure
in these attestations. The author has done whatever is
possible to insure accuracy.*

The editors regret that due to page limitations all entries
submitted could not be included in this publication. All
those who submitted work are listed in the Appendix.

Color separation, printing and binding by
Toppan Printing Co. (H.K.) Ltd. Hong Kong

Typography by
TypeLink, Inc.

10 9 8 7 6 5 4 3 2 1

ACKNOWLEDGMENTS

To produce any publication requires a vast amount of talent, resources, cooperation and coordination. There are many who played a role in the production of this book and I express my gratitude to them all:

— *To Izzika Gaon and the Israel Museum, the creators of the "SELF-IMAGE" exhibition.*

— *To Motoo Nakanishi, whose support and influence over the years has been a great inspiration to the international design and management community and to the editor's own personal growth.*

— *To Rafael Figueroa, whose creativity added to the success of this publication. In his spare time he contributed himself and his talents.*

— *To Penny Sibal-Samonte, Kevin Clark, Susan Kapsis, Richard Liu, Marylin Eisen, Conny Korrel, Emanuel Jay, Alvin Milton and always to my wife Andrea Leah. Their belief in this project and their exceptional effort have made this publication a reality.*

PREFACE

IZZIKA GAON
Senior Curator, Design Department
The Israel Museum, Jerusalem

In The Israel Museum's archaeological collections, among the Eynan artifacts from the Natufian period (over 10,000 years ago), there is an exhibit I'm particularly attached to—a basalt pestle and pebbles arranged to signify a human being—probably one of the first works of art made in this part of the world. After carefully observing his own and his colleagues' bodies, our prehistoric creator analyzed the formal components, and then selected a material and medium to work in. The resulting well-balanced composition was easily identifiable and understood by the artist's community, as it is by us today.

We can trace a similar process in the way contemporary designers work. Confronted with a problem, they manipulate shapes, colors and images in order to create a new representation. Later on, hammered into our memory, this image "automatically" will signify orders, ideas and products, to all of us, the consumers of visual communication.

In our homes, at work, and at leisure, we are surrounded and motivated by a turbulent sea of man-made images aimed at influencing our opinions. All of us have surely asked ourselves at least once, "Who is *behind* all this? Who are the 'image-smiths' active simultaneously all over the globe—those creative people who are able to express themselves in different media, exploit super-sophisticated, contemporary technologies and still, at the same time, use good, old block printing with originality?" Moreover, their unique personalities and temperaments always seem to filter through, despite the rigid limits of visual conventions.

Through our network of professional connections in the design world, we became acquainted with the work of a large number of graphic designers. I was often amused and excited by the wild originality of their personal and business stationery. The idea of "studying" the artists from this angle, rather than through the work they were commissioned for, began to intrigue me. "SELF-IMAGE" presented an opportunity for designers to be themselves, netto, or, to be, in professional lingo, their own "clients."

The Design Department requested stationery and explanations from hundreds of graphic designers and later decided to expand the scope and collect other self-promotional material as well. A fascinating array of pamphlets, cards, calendars, books and exhibition posters began to arrive in personalized rolls, envelopes and packages from five continents.

The more narcissistic types among them naturally chose their self-portraits as representative, while many others struggled with the problem, stretching their imagination to search for a unique image. "Mirror, mirror on the wall, who is the fairest of them all?..." In tune with a constantly changing world, they can alter their graphic identities at any opportunity, starting with a change in address. Equipped with trained eyes and communication sensitivities, graphic designers send critical messages about themselves and how they would like to be seen by others. The essential information is transmitted with color, paper and type.

The material we received illustrated how experience and knowledge in visual communication enabled these professionals to achieve the desired impression. We should not forget that this same expertise allows them to control and even limit information about themselves. If we had a way to look deeper and further, we would have liked to extend our investigations to the designers' office space and home environment.

We decided to turn our exciting collection into a show and to exhibit almost all the items designers had chosen to send to us. After discussing whether one should group the material in various categories, we decided to purposefully arrange the exhibition in such a way that the individual viewer could "process" the information through his/her own personal perception. In the center of the exhibition area, we created an enormous "cloud" of stationery in transparent envelopes "floating" from the ceiling and hung to eye level. Thus, the visitor could wander through the "cloud," meet old and make new "friends." Other small printed material was exhibited in a long glass showcase. The original "SELF-IMAGE" exhibition covered 4,000 square feet and opened in early July 1989 at the Palevsky Design Pavilion, The Israel Museum, Jerusalem.

Without entering into detail, in our opinion, there is one very clear phenomenon in this graphic opus which we can call a "return-to-roots." The observer will note a great deal more handwriting, scribbling and collages, a phenomenon of particular interest in our computerized era.

Is it possible
that after the field of computer graphics is mastered,
the hand-drawn line will be rediscovered?

September 25, 1990

The Israel Museum

Founded in 1965, today the Israel Museum ranks among the world's major arts institutions of international scope. Spanning a ridge on Jerusalem's Hill of Tranquility, the vast museum complex provides a source of inspiration to over one million visitors annually. Among its many structures are the Bezalel Museum of Fine Arts, the five-acre Billy Rose Art Garden designed by Isamu Noguchi, and the newly-completed Nathan Cummings 20th Century Art Building.

Renowned for its outstanding archaeological collections, the Israel Museum is increasingly well-known for its commitment to international and Israeli contemporary art and design. In the words of Director Martin Weyl, "the museum's mission is to engage an international public, as well as the local Israeli community, in an ongoing exploration of how artists express their many cultures and address the questions of our world."

In keeping with that mission, the museum has expanded its expertise in ancient symbology to include modern-day symbology of identity, providing the conceptual basis for "SELF-IMAGE," a show that premiered in the museum in July 1989 and which provided the genesis for this book.

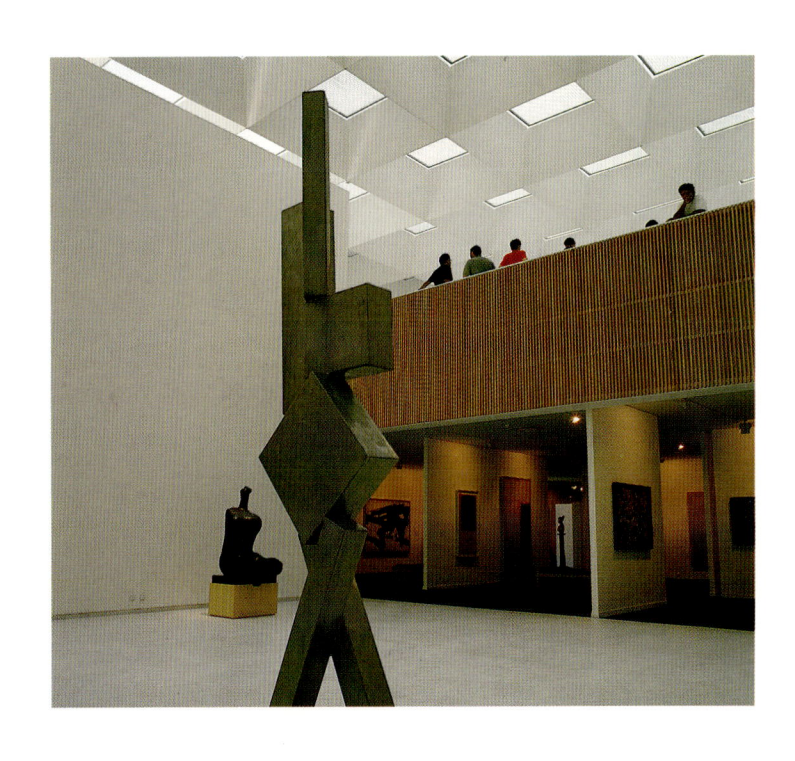

CONTENTS

PREFACE 6

INTRODUCTION 8

NORTH AMERICA 11

EUROPE 83

MIDDLE EAST 165

FAR EAST 177

AUSTRALIA 203

APPENDIX 217

INDEXES 223

JOSHUA S. MARCUS
President
PAOS New York

INTRODUCTION

The concept of identity has existed since the beginning of civilization when man began to use symbols to identify his world and reality. The past fifty years have seen a dynamic change in our perspective of identity. Identity making is now a major industry. Designers and design firms are common on the American business landscape. Every day these designers tackle identity problem solving for clients. What better way to explore this industry than to have the designers who make up the creative part of this industry present their own professional identity solutions.

The origin of this book stems from an Israel Museum exhibition called "SELF-IMAGE," which premiered in the museum in July 1989, and has since traveled to Tokyo and will open in London in summer 1991. We selected samples from the exhibition to depict and represent the variety and diversity of work that has made up this wonderful expression of designers' self identity.

As I reviewed the manifold self image solutions, I was prodded to ask: What is identity? Surely identity is more than just the abstract design of an individual. Identity is the result of what we are, after we have figured out who we are and what our purpose is and will be for existing. Identity development, then, should be more than just the design of pretty or sophisticated symbols. It should be the result of a careful analysis conducted by a consultant who knows how to ask the right questions and probe the inner depths of the client he or she is working with. Surely, many of the designers presented here asked themselves these questions as they moved to demonstrate and illustrate their own image.

A well-known designer, who is responsible for many familiar designs on our landscape, recently told me that his stationery was simple and uncomplicated and yet it required the most intricate creativity. It powerfully represents him and his philosophy while speaking to a variety of clients with different identities and styles. The challenge for the designer then, is to establish his or her own identity without alienating or prejudicing clients. At the same time, the designer must give clients enough information to convey talent and ability to successfully complete an identity or design solution.

Within these pages are examples of how designers throughout the world are addressing this challenge. From the upbeat designs of Rick Tharp, to the simplicity of Jacques Garamond and subtlety of Motoo Nakanishi, designers express themselves and their work differently.

Before proceeding, I must thank the designers, all of whom went to the trouble to send us their work. It is difficult to present some of the world's most outstanding designers in such an abrupt and condensed manner. Regrettably, we could not include everyone, but we made every effort to present an international sampling of some of the best. From the work we selected, you will see a panorama of identity solutions generated by some of the world's most renowned identity makers.

The success of the "SELF-IMAGE" exhibition is attributed to Izzika Gaon, Senior Curator, and Elaine Varady, Associate Curator of Design at the Israel Museum. Thanks to their vision, affection and hard work, the museum continues to grow in the area of contemporary exhibitions and to be a source of inspiration to artists and visitors throughout the world.

I am pleased to see the State of Israel taking a leading role in the identity industry. What starts today with company identity may evolve tomorrow into new developments in country identity solutions. My grandfather, Jesse Eisen, imbued me with a dream to see the State of Israel become a leader in design, culture, manufacturing and religious study. The dream he envisioned is coming alive today throughout Israel and in the Israel Museum.

Joshua Marcus is president of PAOS NEW YORK, a member of the PAOS Group, that provides corporate identity consulting to international clientele. PAOS has developed identity programs for such companies as Mazda, Kenwood, Bridgestone, Kirin Brewery, Nippon Telegraph and Telephone, Ricoh, Sumitomo Bank, and Kawasaki Steel.

NORTH AMERICA

CHERMAYEFF & GEISMAR ASSOCIATES
Ivan Chermayeff, *Partner*
New York, New York, USA

"**I** design letterheads for myself which are modest, hopefully elegant, not too showy, printed on decent paper in a typeface which is both modern and classical, and then get out of the way."

"I include my family as extensions of myself; Umbra is my daughter, Tulip is my son-in-law, Jane is my wife."

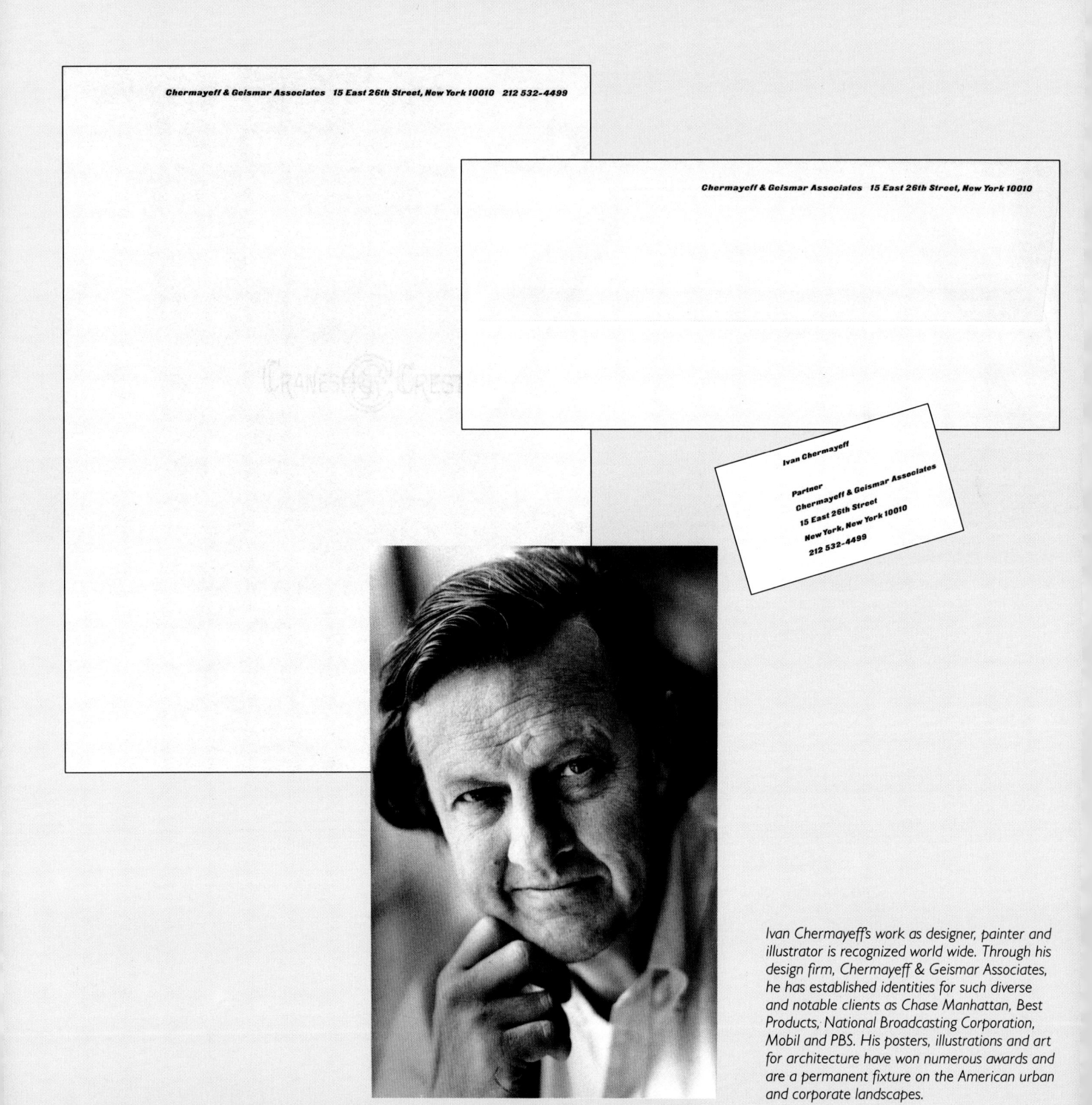

Ivan Chermayeff's work as designer, painter and illustrator is recognized world wide. Through his design firm, Chermayeff & Geismar Associates, he has established identities for such diverse and notable clients as Chase Manhattan, Best Products, National Broadcasting Corporation, Mobil and PBS. His posters, illustrations and art for architecture have won numerous awards and are a permanent fixture on the American urban and corporate landscapes.

Umbra Editions, Inc.
288 West Street
New York, N.Y. 10013
212 219-8140
Fax 212 925-3309

May Castleberry
Catherine Chermayeff
Karen Marta
Nan Richardson

JANE CLARK CHERMAYEFF
140 EAST 81 PH W NEW YORK
NY 10028 (212) 744 3970

Tulip Films, Inc.
Penthouse
145 Sixth Avenue
New York, N.Y.
10013
Tel: 212.366.5096
Fax: 212.645.6232

Jonathan David

Chermayeff. 347 E. 62nd St. Iyfc. 21

IVAN CHERMAYEFF—1984 MOHAWK GRAPHICS COLLECTION

IVAN CHERMAYEFF—1984 MOHAWK GRAPHICS COLLECTION

15

DALY & DALY, INC.
Morgan and Rita Daly, *Principals*
Brookline, Massachusetts, USA

"**O**ur objectives in designing our new image and stationery were to identify Daly & Daly as a design firm without using words, and to project the image of a 'strong idea' firm that is deft at handling complex graphic (two-dimensional) and environmental (three-dimensional) design projects. The firm's logo is a trompe l'oeil, accomplished through the use of form, shade and shadow. It is illustrated on a flat, two-dimensional surface, but it creates the illusion of a three-dimensional design.

PROMOTIONAL MAILER

The Dalys graduated from Pratt Institute and worked for several design firms in New York and Boston. In 1978 they founded Daly & Daly, Inc. to specialize in corporate, institutional and retail identity through graphics and environmental design. Within the firm, Morgan's focus is environmental design, from signage and exhibitions to interior and exterior design. Rita's focus is graphic design, including annual reports, print advertising, magazines and communication material.

TURQUOISE DESIGN, INC.
Mark Timmings, *Art Director*
Hull, Quebec, Canada

"Turquoise's visual communications theme has always revolved around water. The colored band at the top of our stationery is a graphic expression of the relaxed, colorful atmosphere of the beach: yellow sand blends to blue sea to create turquoise."

"Business stationery is more than a vehicle for information; it is also an important public relations tool. With the addition of the image of a bottle on the beach, our letterhead becomes a communiqué which we can send to the media, clients and friends to announce new developments in our company."

Canadian designer Mark Timmings founded Turquoise Design with his partner in 1980 and has gone on to win sixteen design competitions across North America. He was also named Visual Communications Chairman for the 1990 ICOGRADA Congress in Montreal. As art director of Turquoise Design, Timmings has worked hard to promote the graphic design industry, with special attention to environmental concerns and social issues.

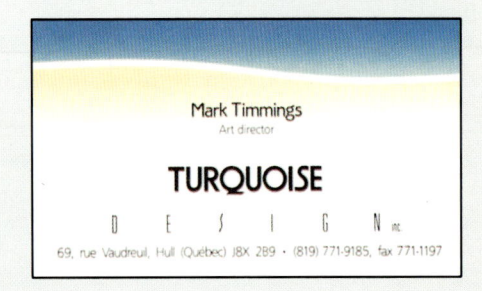

Mark Timmings
Art director

TURQUOISE
D E S I G N inc.
69, rue Vaudreuil, Hull (Québec) J8X 2B9 • (819) 771-9185, fax 771-1197

COMMUNIQUÉ

TURQUOISE inc.
2-44, rue Laval, Hull (Québec) J8X 3G7 • (819) 771-9185
D E S I G N

TURQUOISE
D E S I G N inc.
69, rue Vaudreuil, Hull (Québec) J8X 2B9 • (819) 771-9185, fax 771-1197

SUPON DESIGN GROUP, INC.
Supon Phornirunlit, *President*
Washington, District of Columbia, USA

"Supon Design Group fills a very specific niche in conservative Washington, D.C.—providing design services to organizations that generally resist change. We've designed our identity package to both support and deter that impression. Note the ways in which our logo plays with positives and negatives, the unexpected use of yellow solids, and the subtle ribbing of our stationery. A small twist on the norm. A new way of doing the everyday."

"Our overall philosophy is that good, quality design does not have to be excessive."

President of his own design firm, Supon Phornirunlit is currently on the board of directors of the Art Directors Club of Metropolitan Washington and is project director of Washington Trademark Design's International Logo Competition. He has earned over fifty awards from organizations such as the Art Directors Club of both Washington and New York, the Type Directors Club and American Corporate Identity. He has also received the DESI Award and has been recognized in PRINT'S Design Annual.

PAUL DAVIS STUDIO
Paul Davis, Owner
New York, New York, USA

"One of my stationery designs is meant to suggest a stack of letters, a trompe l'oeil play on the way papers pile up on one's desk every day. The design also emphasizes that paper is one of the prime media of graphic designers. In another design I used a spatter effect to suggest painting and experimentation, deliberately avoiding an overly neat look. Perhaps I was too successful in this regard—some recipients thought coffee and ink had been spilled on their letters."

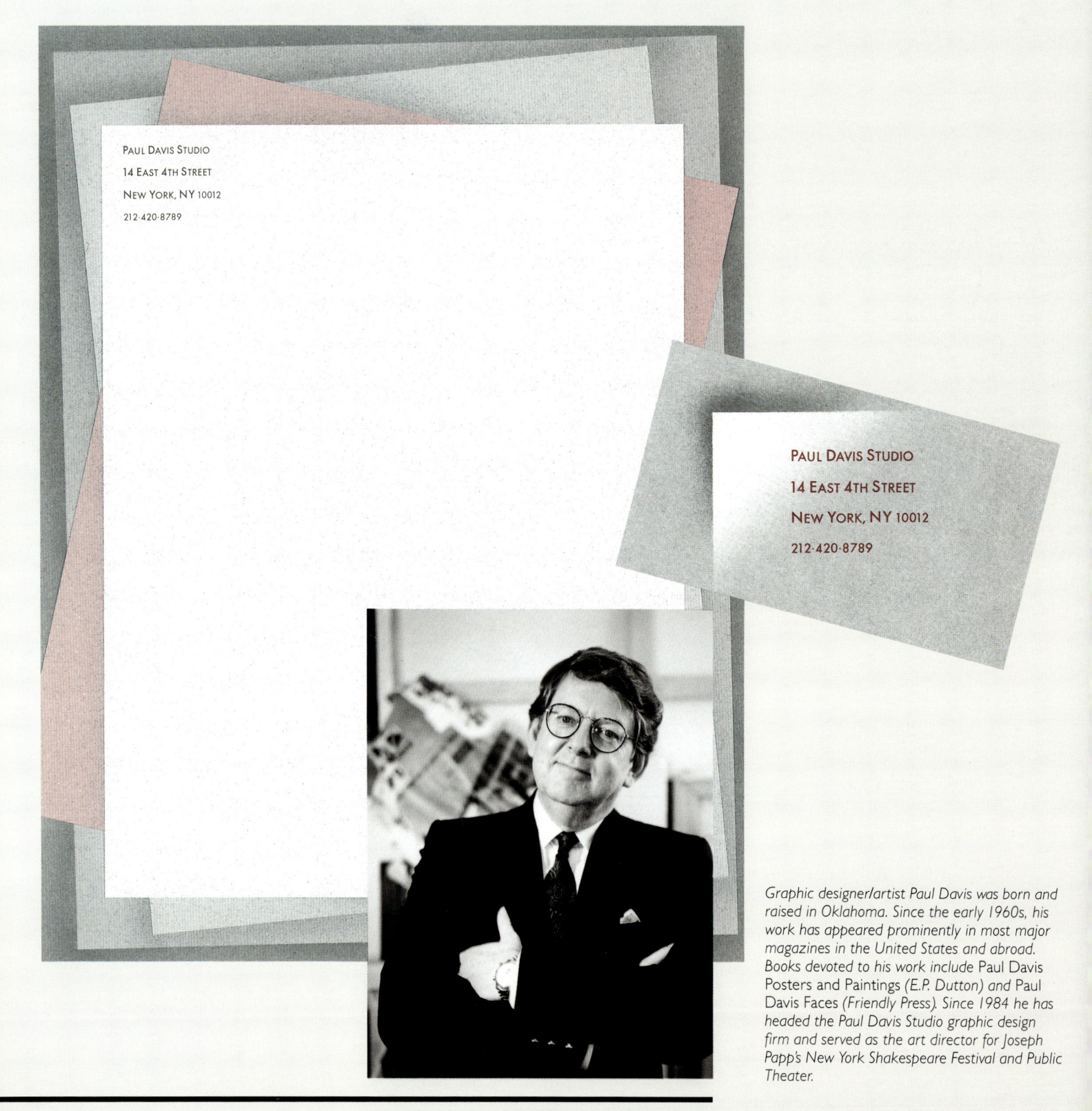

PAUL DAVIS STUDIO
14 EAST 4TH STREET
NEW YORK, NY 10012
212-420-8789

PAUL DAVIS STUDIO
14 EAST 4TH STREET
NEW YORK, NY 10012
212-420-8789

Graphic designer/artist Paul Davis was born and raised in Oklahoma. Since the early 1960s, his work has appeared prominently in most major magazines in the United States and abroad. Books devoted to his work include Paul Davis Posters and Paintings *(E.P. Dutton) and* Paul Davis Faces *(Friendly Press). Since 1984 he has headed the Paul Davis Studio graphic design firm and served as the art director for Joseph Papp's New York Shakespeare Festival and Public Theater.*

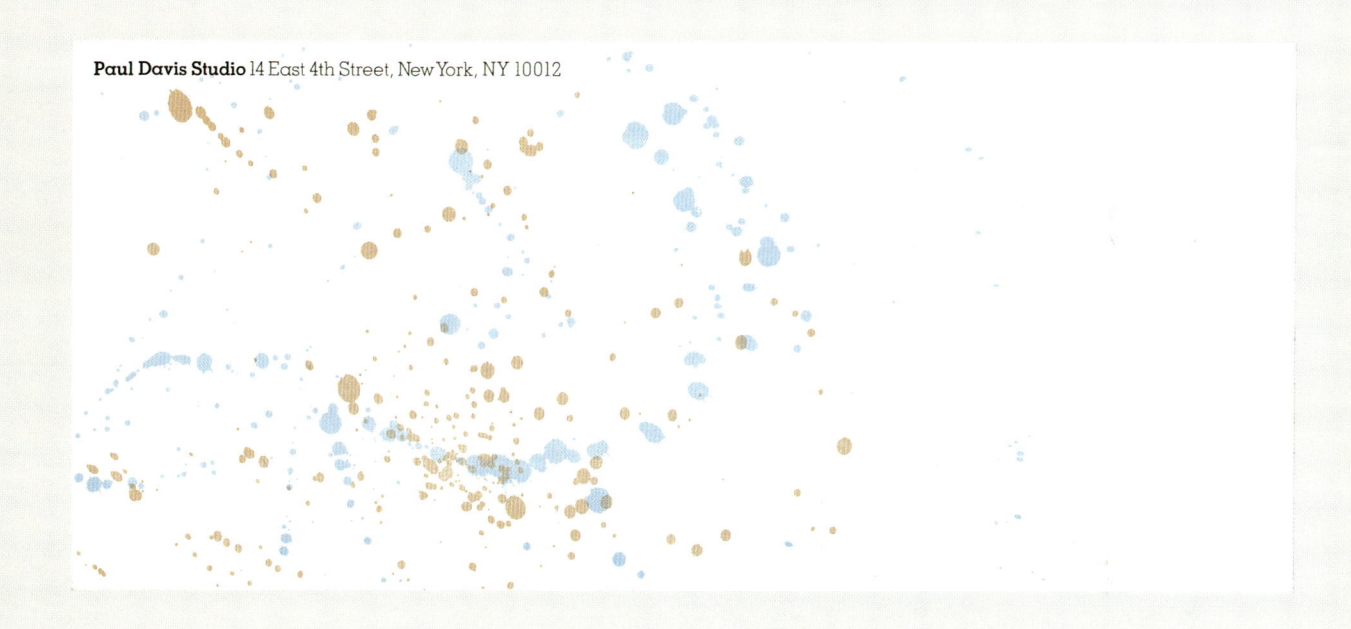

PAUL DAVIS STUDIO
14 EAST 4TH STREET
NEW YORK, NY 10012

Paul Davis Studio 14 East 4th Street, New York, NY 10012

Paul Davis Studio

14 East 4th Street, New York, NY 10012, (212) 420·8789

Myrna Davis
14 East 4th Street
New York, NY 10012
212 674·5708

AARON MARCUS AND ASSOCIATES
Aaron Marcus, *Principal*
Berkeley, California, USA

"**W**hen I started my firm almost eight years ago, I wanted a letterhead design that seemed serious (with a touch of playfulness), corporate, oriented to high technology and professional. The vertical bars, to my thinking, connote code bars, scan lines, or some other indicator of computer technology and telecommunication. A blue color was selected for its traditional association with stability, fidelity and reserve."

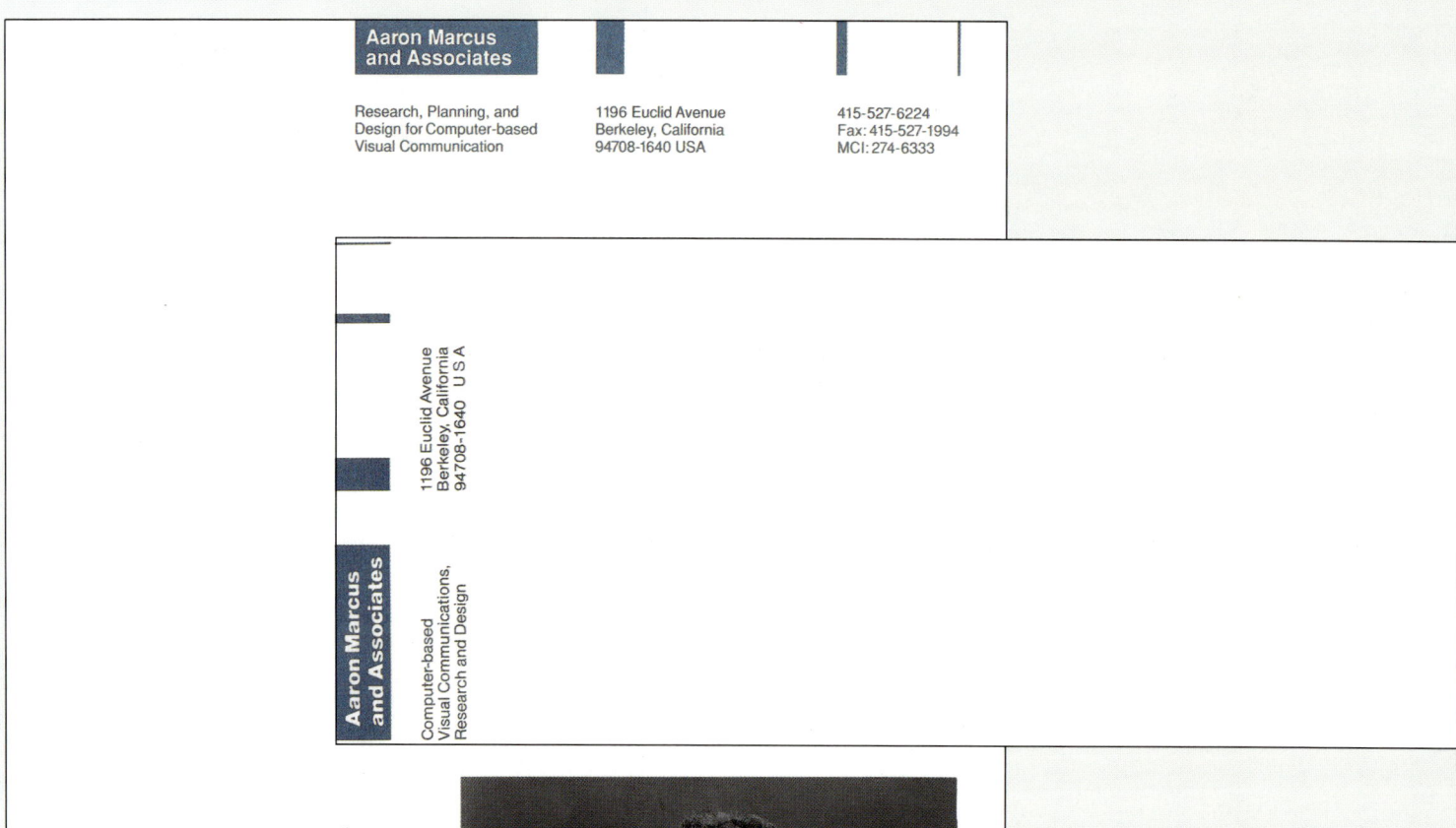

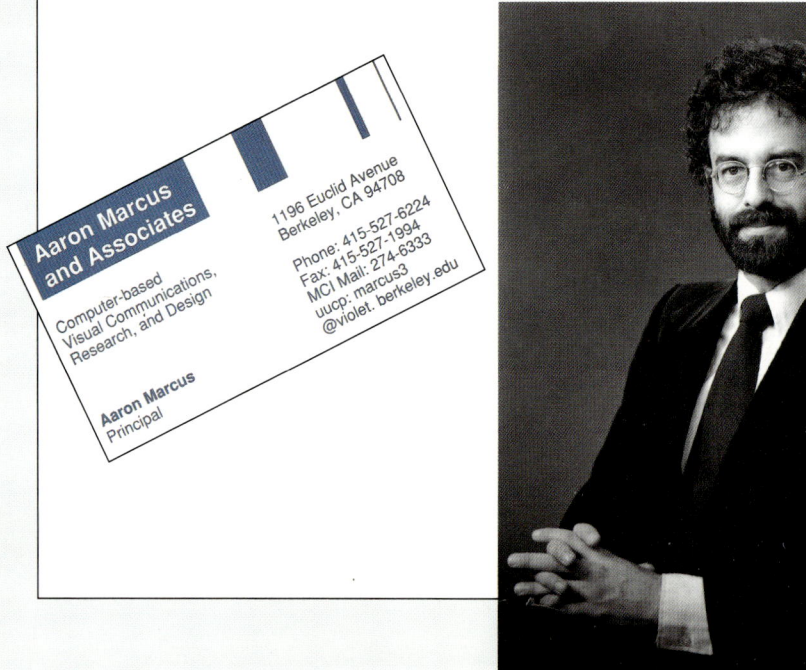

Born in Omaha, Nebraska, Aaron Marcus is a management consultant specializing in user interface design, electronic publishing and information graphics for a broad base of applications. One of the first computer graphics professionals to recognize the significance of graphic design for successful computer graphic systems, he founded his firm in 1982 providing consulting services to both users and suppliers of computer graphics equipment and services.

MILTON GLASER
President, **Milton Glaser, Inc.**
New York, New York, USA

"It's hard to determine exactly why this stationery came about. I wanted to do something odd. At the time, I was also momentarily interested in Russian design of the twenties and thirties. All in all, there was nothing very thoughtful about how I went about doing this. Perhaps it's time to change it, in any case."

Born in New York City, Milton Glaser was a co-founder of Push Pin Studios and ranks among those who have revolutionized design in America. The impact of his work is seen in a wide range of disciplines: advertising campaigns ("I Love New York"); magazines (New York Magazine); posters (Bob Dylan silhouette); supermarkets (Grand Union); and restaurants (Rockefeller Center's Rainbow Room restoration). His firm does exhibitions and architectural and interior design, as well as corporate identity programs. Glaser's work is in the permanent collections of the Museum of Modern Art, New York; the Israel Museum, Jerusalem; and the Smithsonian Institution, Washington, D.C.

MILTON GLASER: POSTERS, POSTCARDS

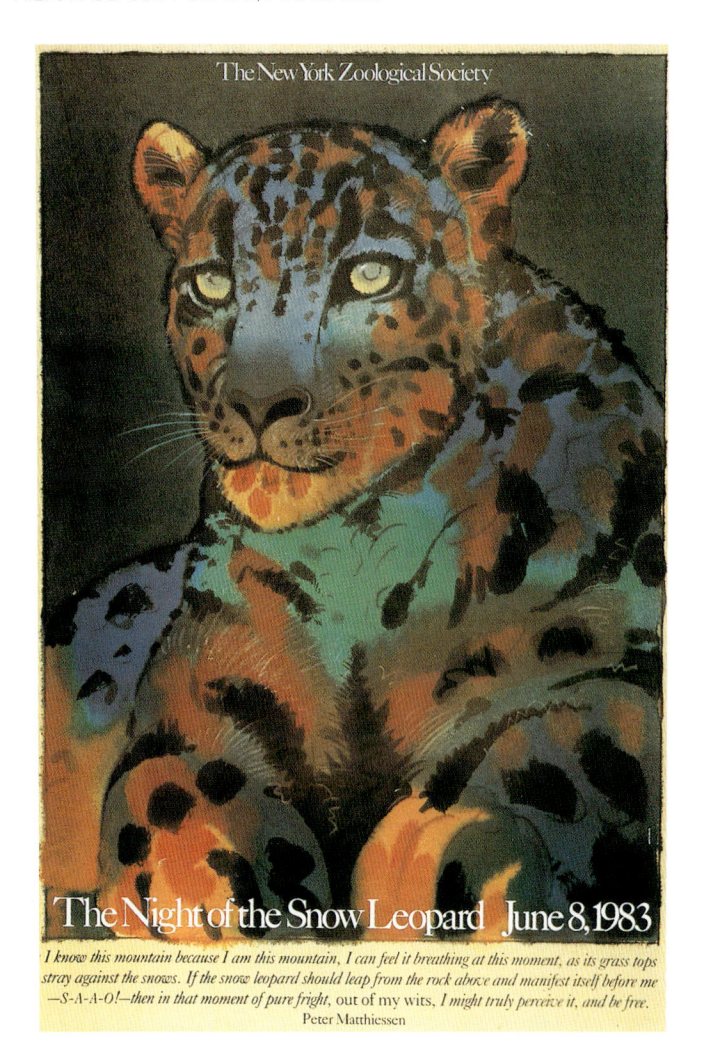

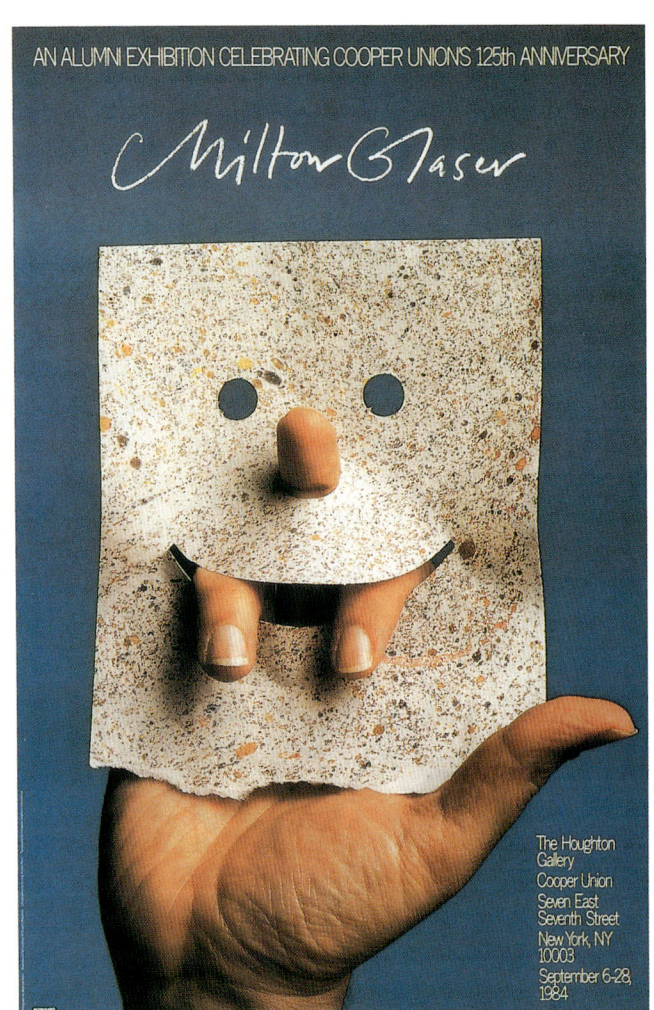

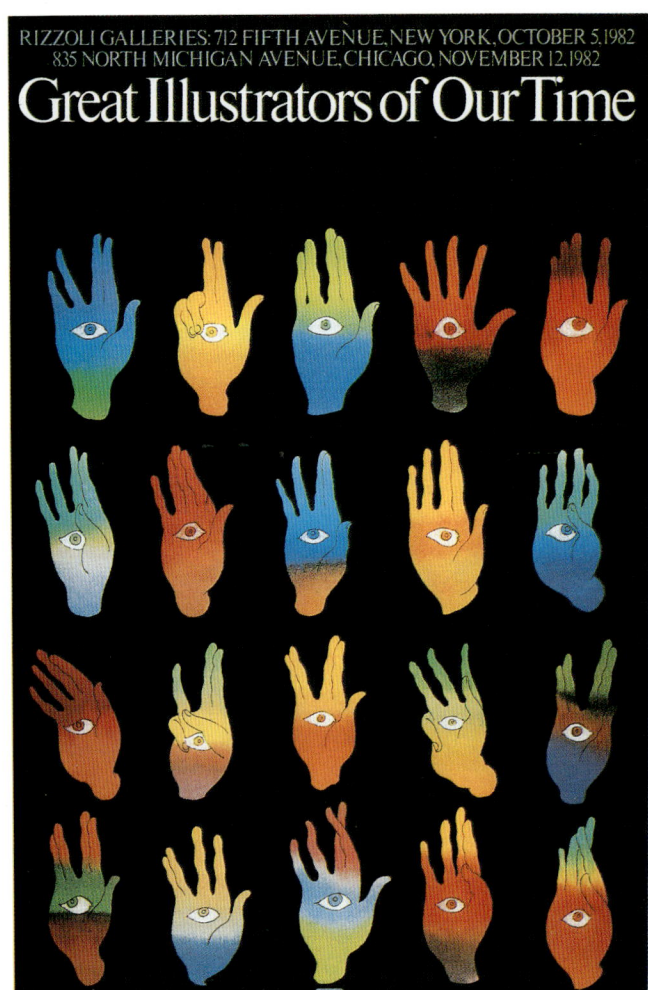

MILTON GLASER: POSTERS, POSTCARDS

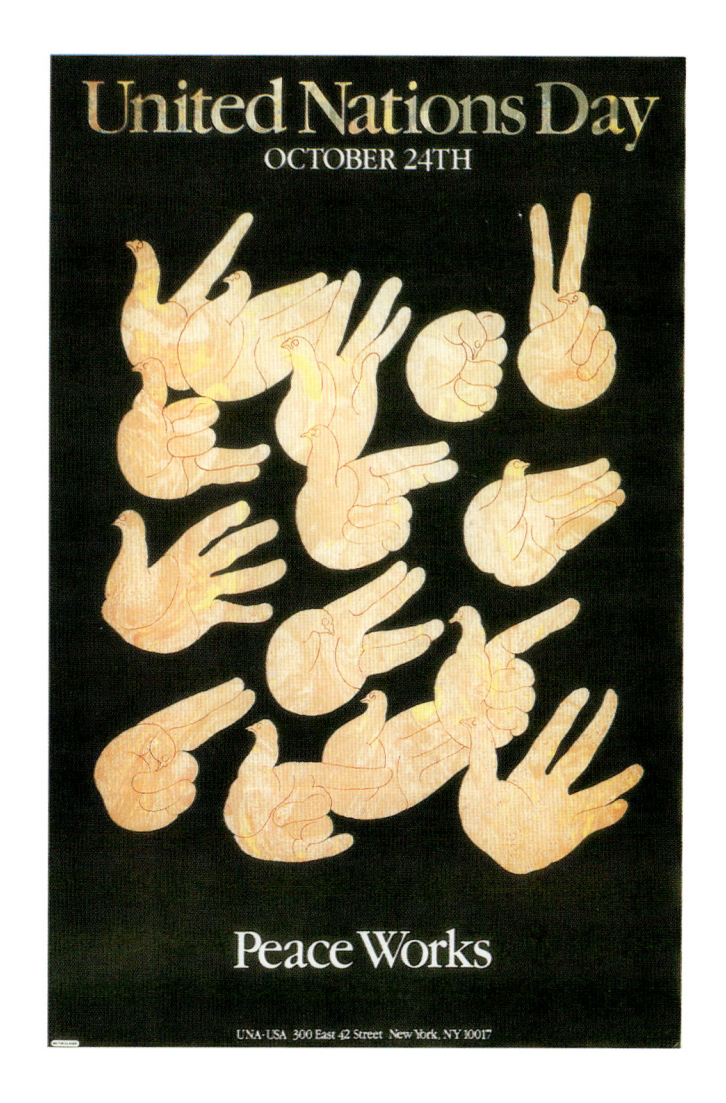

MILTON GLASER: POSTERS, POSTCARDS

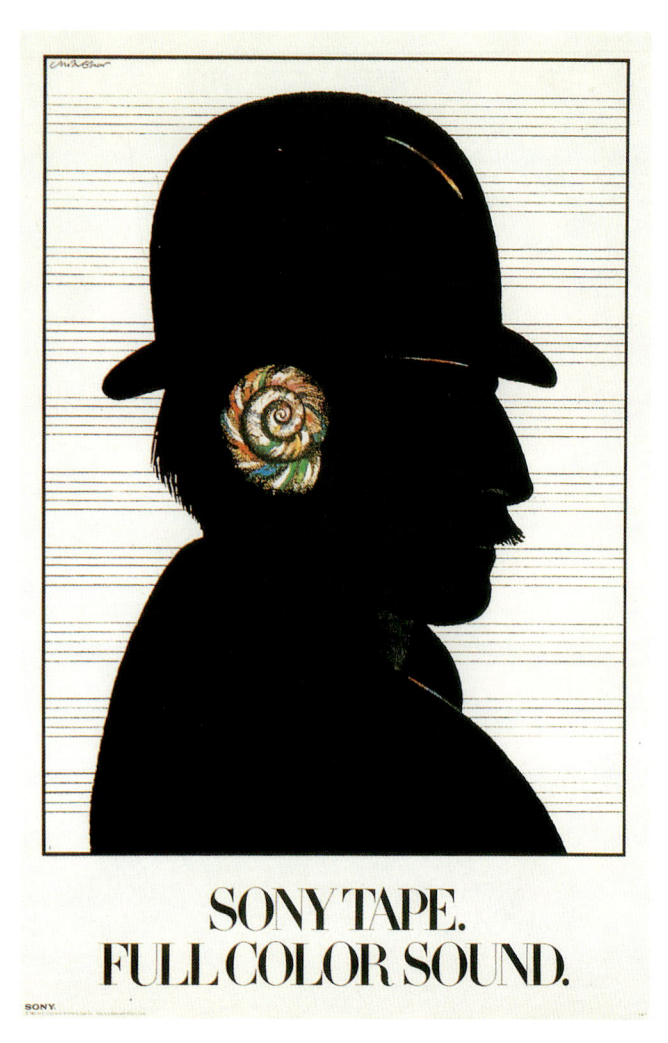

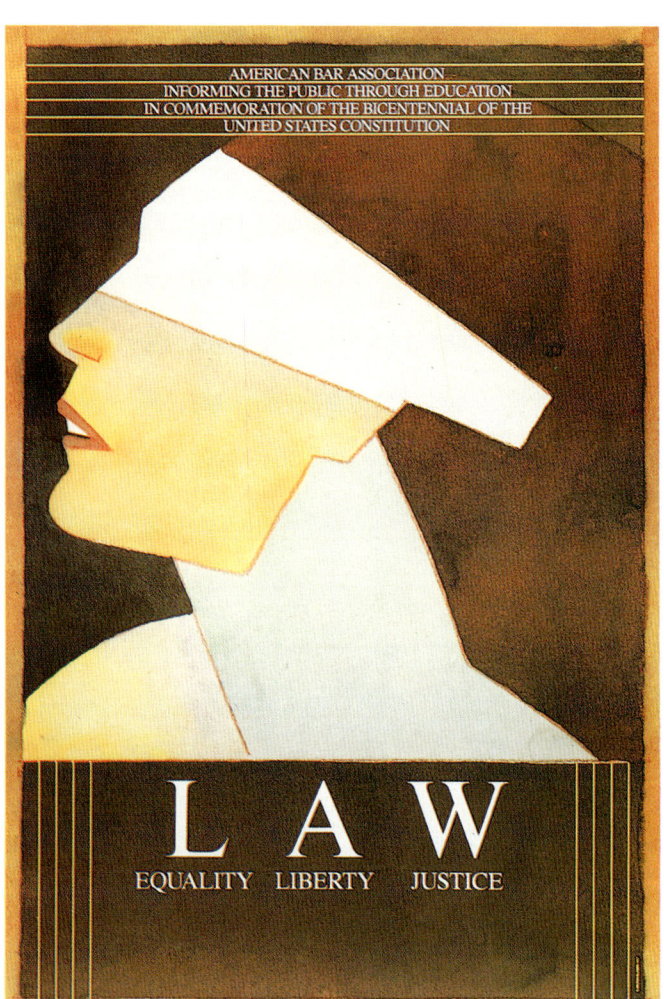

MIHO
Chairman, **Graphic Design and Packaging**
Art Center College of Design at Pasadena
Pasadena, California, USA

"My letterhead design is based on a sticker system that can be applied to any paper from any part of the world. Since I travel a lot and collect paper samples as a matter of course, I designed a system that would look good on any paper—from America to Zambia. The form and colors of the letterhead system change each time we move: from a square in Chicago, to a rectangle in New York, to a black rectangle in Connecticut, to a circle in Pasadena."

Born in Gridley, California, Miho was creative director at Needham Harper and Steers and president of his own company. He is now chairman of graphic design and packaging at the Art Center College of Design in Pasadena, California.

THARP DID IT

Rick Tharp, *Art Director/Designer*
Los Gatos, California, USA

"**W**e designed a stationery system that would not interfere with or dominate the work we present to clients. The absence of color keeps our own identity at bay while the subtle blind embossing gives a serious, low-profile, professional tone to our correspondence. This lack of superfluous design treatment is characteristic of much of the marketing material we create for our clients."

Rick Tharp established Tharp Did It in 1975. Working mainly in corporate, retail and restaurant visual identity and packaging design, the firm focuses on what Tharp refers to as "permanent" rather than "promotional" design—work that leaves a lasting impression on the product or business. Tharp Did It's clients include BRIO/Scanditoy, The Seagram Classics Wine Company, Oasis Laundries Franchise, Mirassou Vineyards, and Sebastiani Vineyards.

SIDNEY DID IT
And Make No Mistake About It

EACH PERSON IN THE STUDIO HAS HER OWN PERSONAL NOTE PADS.

THARP DID IT • DESIGN • LOS GATOS 408.354.6726 • SAN FRANCISCO 415.362.4494

NOTEPAD

I SWEAR I DIDN'T DO IT!!!!!!!!!!!!!!!!

POSTCARD

DON'T BEND IT

RUBBER STAMP

THARP *and Jana* DID IT

FIFTY UNIVERSITY AVENUE

SUITE NUMBER TWENTY ONE

LOS GATOS, CALIFORNIA 95030

408.354.6726, FAX 408.354.1450

SAN FRANCISCO 415.362.4494

THARP *and kim* DID IT

FIFTY UNIVERSITY AVENUE

SUITE NUMBER TWENTY ONE

LOS GATOS, CALIFORNIA 95030

408.354.6726, FAX 408.354.1450

SAN FRANCISCO 415.362.4494

SAUL BASS
Chairman, **Bass/Yager & Associates**
Los Angeles, California, USA

"When I was first asked, 'What is your creative philosophy?' I had no quick answer. Then it occurred to me that my unease with the question probably was the clue to the answer. For as long as I can remember I've worked as a designer. And through all the years, I've always spelled designer with a lower case 'd.' I like doing design. I believe it is useful work. It can solve communication problems, it can enhance our environment, it can enliven our imagination. Sometimes it can even provide an insight into our lives. For me design is a 'craft.' And I try very hard to be a good craftsman. Come to think of it, maybe that's my creative philosophy."

Saul Bass   7039 Sunset Boulevard, Los Angeles, CA 90028

Designer Saul Bass has developed trademarks and corporate identification systems, packages for familiar products like Quaker Oats and Wesson Oil, and symbols for over sixty motion pictures. His corporate clients include AT&T and the Bell System. In addition to designing titles for over forty celebrated motion pictures ("The Seven Year Itch," "Psycho"), Bass had directed his own award-winning short films, receiving an Academy Award for "Why Man Creates" in 1968.

PROMOTIONAL PUBLICATION

Bass/Yager & Associates

The Company

Bass/Yager is an international design and marketing consulting firm based in Los Angeles. Graphic design is at the firm's center with special emphasis on corporate identification programs, packaging, retail architecture, and film.

The Point of View

All design starts with situation analysis. We isolate and define marketing issues and then focus the design process to lead to optimum visual solutions. The primary basis for evaluation of designs is the degree to which they satisfy project objectives.

The Outcome

We are proud of the quality and longevity of our work and our client relationships. Bass/Yager & Associates has been honored by numerous awards and, more importantly, by contributing to the success our clients have achieved in the marketplace of products, services and ideas.

↓ *United Airlines: A crisp, efficient and friendly identity system with powerful marketing value for the largest domestic airline.*

↑ *Bell System: One of the world's best-known trademarks. Even after divestiture, it is widely used by Bell Companies.*

↑ *AT&T: The breakup of the Bell System required the surviving entity to redefine itself. A new trademark was needed to describe the transition of the U.S. phone company from regulated monopoly to international telecommunications company.*

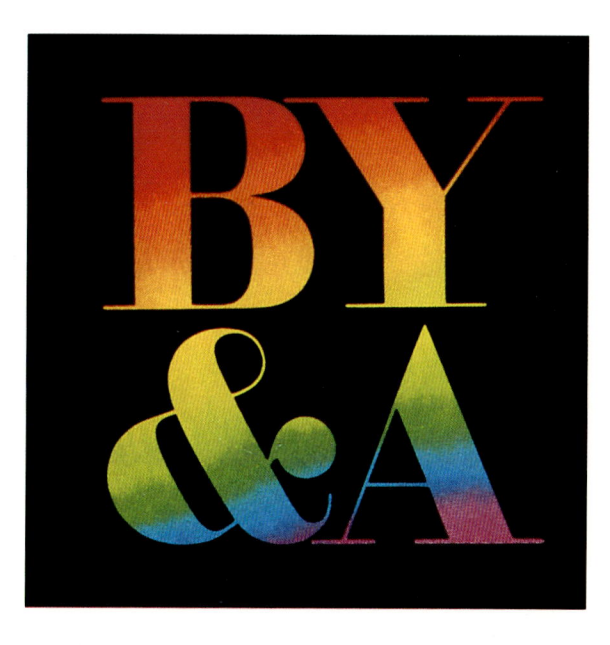

LOGO

31

PROMOTIONAL PUBLICATION

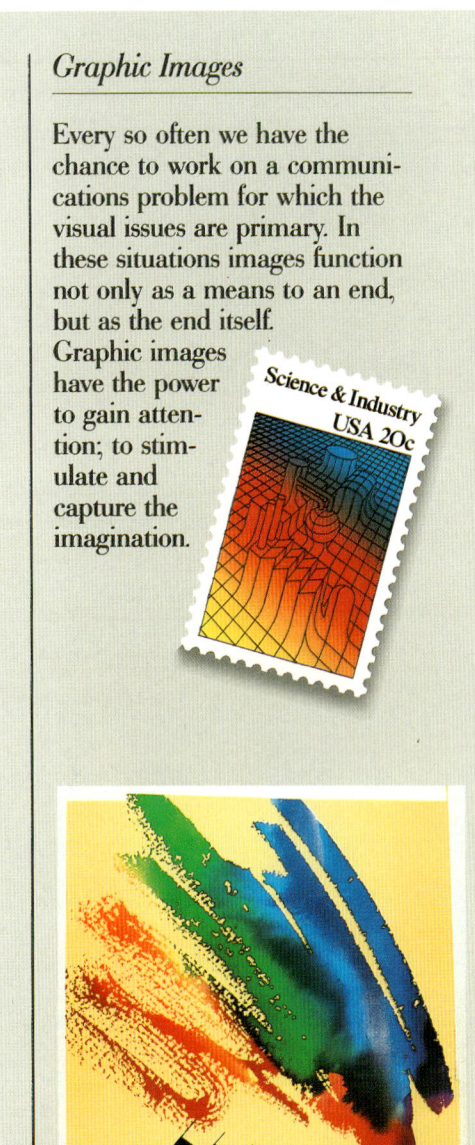

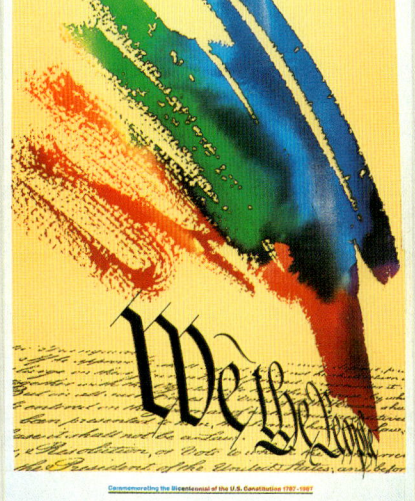

Graphic Images

Every so often we have the chance to work on a communications problem for which the visual issues are primary. In these situations images function not only as a means to an end, but as the end itself. Graphic images have the power to gain attention; to stimulate and capture the imagination.

HOLIDAY CARD

FILM SYMBOLS

32

PROMOTIONAL PUBLICATION

↓ **United Way:** *No words are needed to identify America's largest, best known and most respected charitable organization; just this familiar, and long-lasting symbol.*

↑ **General Foods:** *A visual metaphor both for the company's core businesses and the corporate commitment to continued growth.*

→ **Rockwell International:** *The new identity for merging companies involved in space age technology and industrial manufacturing.*

← **Girl Scouts:** *An American institution redefines its role in serving a new generation of young women while maintaining a connection with tradition.*

FILM SYMBOLS

MAGAZINE COVER

33

FILM SYMBOLS

HOLIDAY CARD

MAY THE NEW YEAR BRING PEACE & HAPPINESS

SAUL BASS / HERB YAGER & ASSOCIATES

PROMOTIONAL PUBLICATION

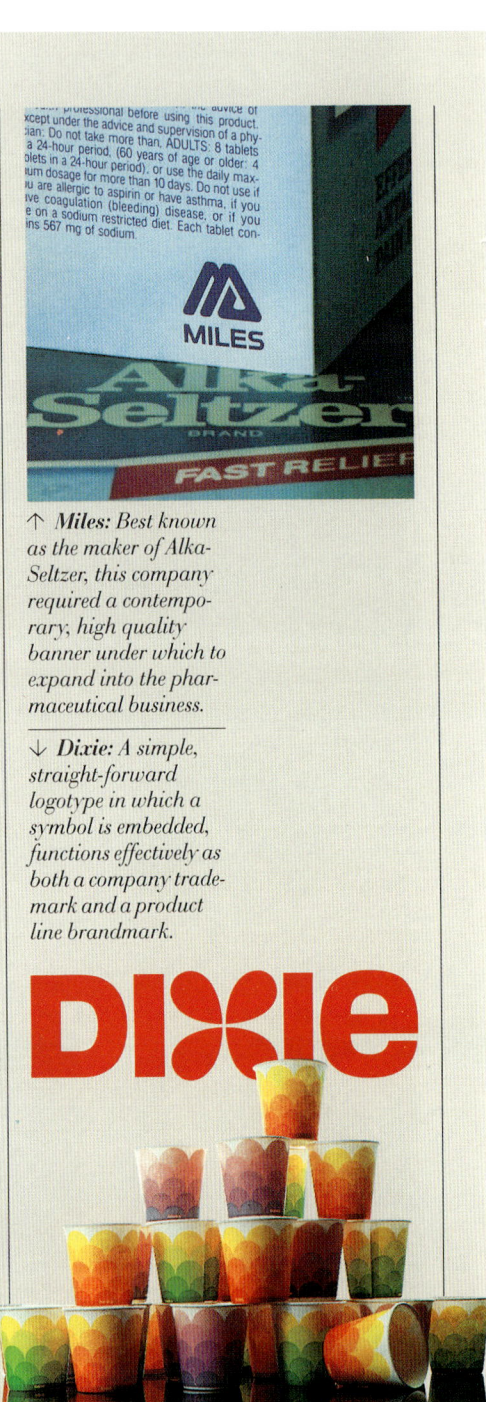

MINOLTA

↓ **Alcoa:** Updating, upgrading and repositioning a company with the help of a new name and symbol. Designed almost 30 years ago; still hard at work today.

ALCOA

↑ **Minolta:** A symbol which is effective in both very small size as on a camera, or very large as on a billboard while visually representing the elements of a lens. Particularly useful on packaging and sales promotion materials.

↑ **Miles:** Best known as the maker of Alka-Seltzer, this company required a contemporary, high quality banner under which to expand into the pharmaceutical business.

↓ **Dixie:** A simple, straight-forward logotype in which a symbol is embedded, functions effectively as both a company trademark and a product line brandmark.

Dixie

34

HOLIDAY CARD

FILM SYMBOLS

PROMOTIONAL PUBLICATION

← *Corporate TV Tags:* Most of us would agree that television is the most powerful selling medium of all. Typically, trademarks are conceived as two dimensional designs. Yet if they are to make the impact clients expect, they must translate to kinetic media as well as print. A characteristic of the more successful TV tags is that the trademarks on which they are based were conceived with those relationships in mind.

35

HENRY WOLF PRODUCTIONS, INC.
Henry Wolf, President
New York, New York, USA

"**I** like this stationery because most of my letters are unimportant and this one looks like it had already been thrown out!"

Born in Vienna, Henry Wolf arrived in the United States in 1941 where he began his career as an art director for various magazines and businesses. In 1971 he formed Henry Wolf Productions, a photography, film and design firm. Currently, Wolf is president of the Art Directors Club of New York where he was inducted into the Hall of Fame in 1980.

Felix Beltran
President, **Felix Beltran & Asociados**
Apartado de Correos, Mexico

"**I** designed my personal stationery in 1973, and the main purpose was to evoke the tendency of my work, where the sense of proper synthesis is unavoidable in the process of communication. The letter *B* is the initial of my surname, and I constructed it with lines to differentiate the initial in an attractive manner."

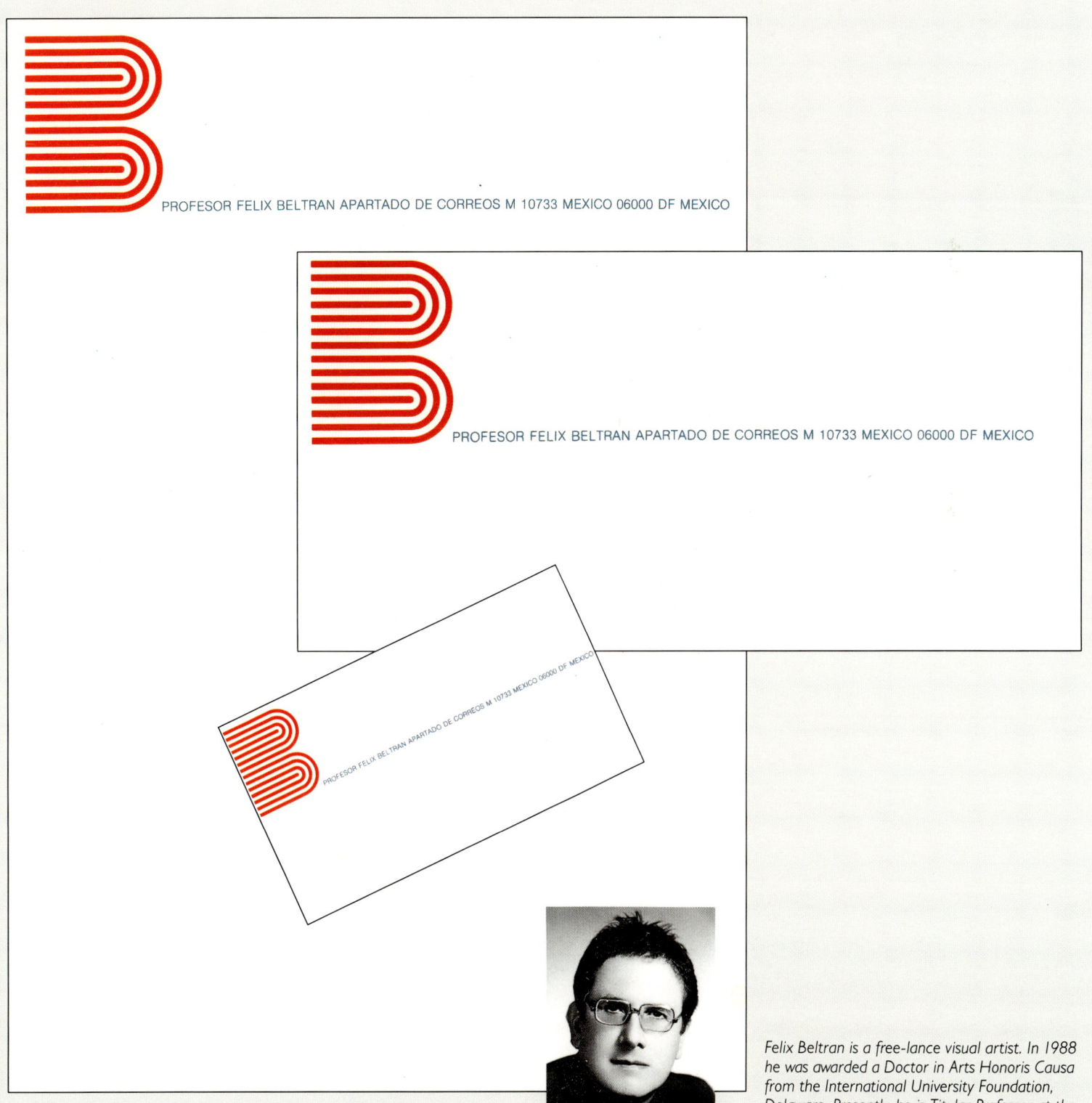

Felix Beltran is a free-lance visual artist. In 1988 he was awarded a Doctor in Arts Honoris Causa from the International University Foundation, Delaware. Presently, he is Titular Professor at the Unversidad Ibero Americana Mexico.

SKOLOS, WEDELL + RAYNOR, INC.
Nancy Skolos, *Principal*
Charlestown, Massachusetts, USA

"**O**ur stationery is illustrative of our studio's capabilities. That is to say, the complexity of elements found in the stationery may also be found in our design and photography. For example, the die-cutting and embossing are representative of our interest in bringing a three-dimensional aspect to a piece that typically is considered two-dimensional. Furthermore, the graduated areas of color suggest the subtle light and shadow which is the hallmark of our photographic style."

Skolos/Wedell, Inc. is an interdisciplinary design and photographic studio whose clients include Digital Equipment Corporation, EMI Music Publishing, James River Corporation, Steelcase and The Walker Art Center. Skolos received her B.F.A. from the Cranbrook Academy of Art and her M.F.A. from Yale University's School of Art and Architecture. She established her practice with Thomas Wedell in Boston in 1980. Together, Skolos and Wedell create illusory compositions incorporating elements of design and photography. They are known for their integration techniques of graphic collage, multiple exposures and graduated papers to create three-dimensional, often surreal images. Their posters are in the graphic design collections of the Museum of Modern Art and the Metropolitan Museum of Art.

Oscar Fernández
Design Director, **Wexner Center for the Visual Arts**
Hilliard, Ohio, USA

"The verbal environment is most confusing. And it seems designers are as much to blame by generating typographic solutions that lack any clues or aids to the content's hierarchy. Knowing my stationery would serve as evidence of my approach to design and prospective work, I produced a document recognizing its primary function, correspondence. Typewritten text falls into either the white area, for the formal, or onto the blue horizontal bars for the actual communication. By applying this simple visual treatment, clarity of purpose is reinforced."

Since receiving his MFA in Graphic Design from Yale University, Fernández, has free-lanced, taught and lectured in Ohio, Texas, Maine and Montana on a regular basis. In 1990, he became the Design Director at the Wexner Center for the Visual Arts in Columbus, Ohio. He received Awards of Excellence from the Type Directors Club of New York and the Society of Typographic Arts of Chicago in 1988, and he secured the Award of Excellence from the American Institute of Graphic Arts in New York in 1986.

WHITNEY SHERMAN
Proprietor
Baltimore, Maryland, USA

"**R**ider wanted to know which way the road went so she jumped on board not sure if she was ready for the unknown, but sure she'd have an adventure along the way.... Self image being elusive, a story is a good way to begin. And besides, the type was so beautiful."

Whitney Sherman has been a designer/illustrator for fifteen years. She has worked for F.E. Worthington as Vice President/Creative Director and for the Barton-Gillet Co. Her illustration work has been published by Business Week, Ms., the Boston Globe, San Francisco Focus, the New York Times, the Washington Post, the Los Angeles Times, Mother Jones, Vancouver Magazine, St. Martin's Press, Pentagram Design and others. Presently she is on the faculty at the Visual Communications Department of the Maryland Institute.

PROMOTIONAL BROCHURE: *EXCERPTS 1*

Whitney Sherman
ILLUSTRATION
5101 Whiteford Avenue
Baltimore, Maryland 21212

TELEPHONE 301 435 2095
FAX 301 435 8834

Illustrations © W. Sherman, 1989.

EXCERPTS 1

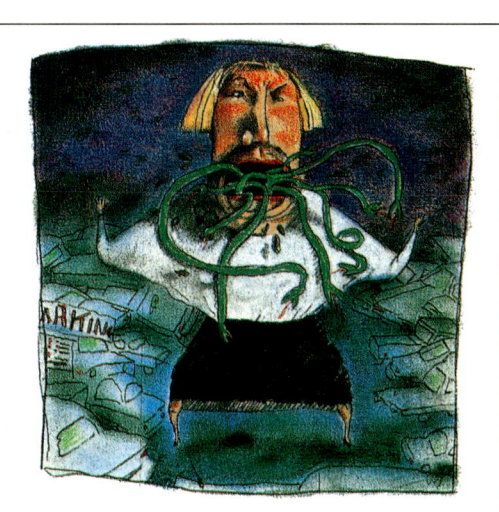

"...Stortz said, 'Boy, I'll tell you something. When I get out of this navy I'd like to manage that guy. I have no idea who he is, but he's sure wasting his time in the navy...he could be a star.'"

"The sound of glass falling fills her ears with wind chimes...Tiny knives cling to her wrist..."

"I'm alone in this. It's finally hit home. They were there. We shared the same venue but...But not the same experience. Never the same experience."

"'Spic' she said to him in a voice loud enough that everyone could hear. 'You dirty little spic.'"

41

SEYMOUR CHWAST
President and Creative Director, **The Pushpin Group**
New York, New York, USA

"The stationery for my studio projects an image that is almost totally neutral. Because of the wide range of design and variety of styles that I work in, a logo or layout that has character would be misleading. My interests go further than the decorative design and illustration that Pushpin built its reputation on. The only element that might be considered eccentric is the use of purple instead of gray, the color most used by design firms to express their serious intent."

Born in New York City, Seymour Chwast is a founding partner of Push Pin Studios (re-named The Pushpin Group in 1985), whose distinct style has had worldwide influence on contemporary visual communication. Chwast's original designs and illustrations are widely disseminated in advertising, animated films, corporate and environmental graphics, record covers, books, magazines, posters and packaging. A retrospective of his work, The Left-Handed Designer, was published by Harry N. Abrams in 1985.

BOOK JACKET

Seymour Chwast The Left-Handed Designer

BOOK JACKET

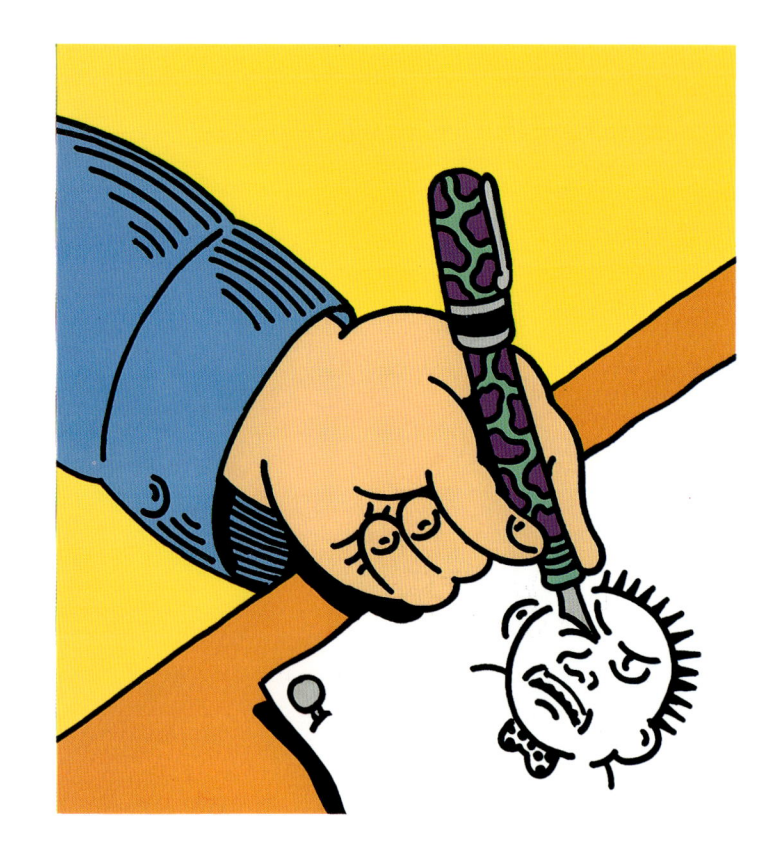

POSTER

BOOK JACKET

POSTER

POSTER

45

BOOK JACKET

0-8109-1289-9

POSTER

POSTER

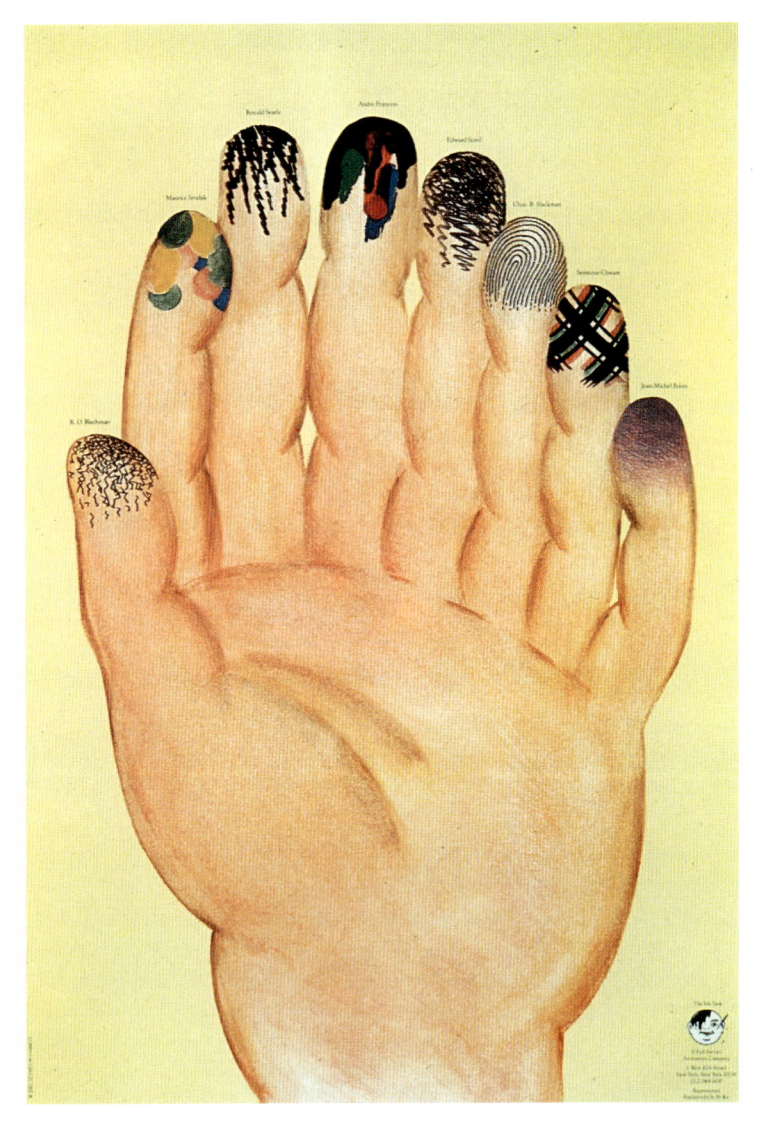

POSTER

POSTER

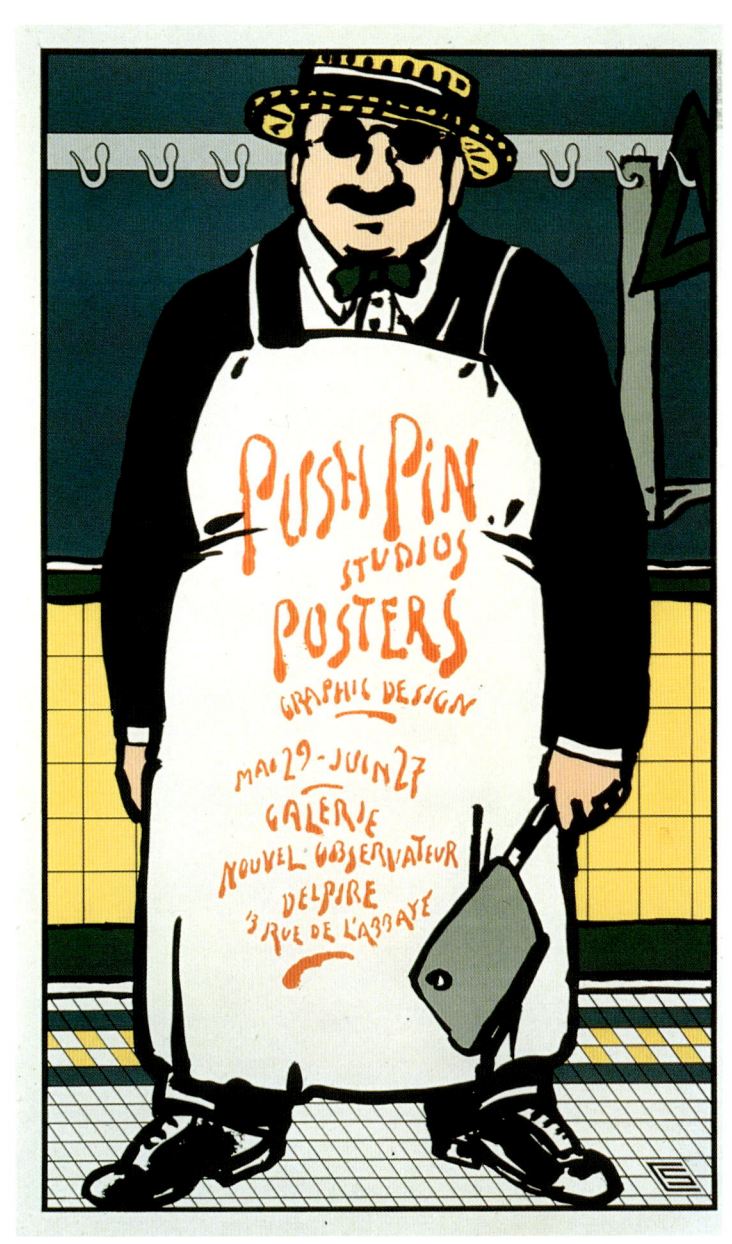

47

M&M Graphic Design
Marianne Friedman, Owner
Oakland, California, USA

"Ten years ago, when we opened our graphic design business, we agonized over our self image trying to decide whether to be serious or humorous, to use one color or two, or just throw reason to the wind! It became obvious rather quickly that Marianne and Margareta made a double M, and somehow we knew we had to capitalize on that fact. It was logical to think of M&M candies and to end up as M&M Graphic Design. When all was said and done, we chose humor over seriousness and four colors over frugality. Our desire for simplicity called for Helvetica on Bright White Strathmore Writing with high gloss white business cards to make the candies pop out. Red M&Ms no longer existed and the color brown wasn't much fun, so we chose yellow, green and orange."

Owned by Marianne Friedman, a graphic artist and writer, M&M has won awards of excellence from AdMark and East Bay Advertising and Marketing. Her former partner was Margareta Bergman Slutzkin, an artist and illustrator from Sweden. Clients include: the University of California, Berkeley (Friedman's alma mater); 17th International Conference on the Physics of Semiconductors, San Francisco; American Cancer Society and Clorox, Oakland, California.

MARGARETA BERGMAN SLUTZKIN, MARIANNE FRIEDMAN (RIGHT)

FRÉDÉRIC METZ
Director, **Centre Design UQAM***
Montreal, Quebec, Canada

"**W**hen I designed my personal letterhead in 1969, I realized that I did not like any of the mechanical typesettings available at the time, so I chose to use Letraset Cable Heavy (Stempel). What I did like was the moderate cost of black and white, so I made that my image and the two of us never parted company…we never needed to."

**Design Center of the University of Quebec at Montreal*

PROMOTIONAL CARD

Currently serving as Director of the University of Quebec's Design Center, Frédéric Metz is a veteran guest speaker, as well as a jury member for many Canadian graphic and design shows. In his own work he has covered traditional graphic image design, as well as global hotel design. He is a consultant to many firms, and his work can be found in museums throughout the world.

PRAXIS Design and Consultation
Roberto A. Dosil, *Partner*
Vancouver, British Columbia, Canada

"**P**raxis believes that in today's competitive business environment, leadership is a marketing necessity. A reinforcement of specific qualities is required to position a company in the marketplace. We believe that communication and design should be an extension of business strategy."

"The application of color, the choice of type and selection of stocks all respond to the same objective: trying to achieve a balance between interesting solutions while at the same time imparting a sense of disciplined design practice."

Roberto A. Dosil is a partner in PRAXIS Design and Consultation, a Canadian-based design firm whose specialty is corporate design. Their published reports and promotional materials reflect their commitment to design as an overall extension of business strategy. Dosil's work has been exhibited in Spain, Israel, Canada and Czechoslovakia, and has also been widely published.

COMMUNICATION PORTFOLIO

Crestbrook Forest Industries Ltd. meets the challenges of building an integrated forest company head-on. Central to the mission statement is coherent, factual reporting of operations.

Portraits of management personnel, highlighted by direct quotations are set against tightly framed, carefully detailed studio photos to create a rich identity. The impact of large photo pages is a counterpoint to smaller location shots addressing multiple use of forest lands.

British Columbia Telephone Company, in charting a course for the next decade, highlights the benefits of technological change that will impact on the company and its customers.

Communicating technological strength by positioning products and services within a real-world environment makes them understandable and desirable. Attention to detail in writing, page design, and particularly in graphic arrangement of the financial statements, support this theme in a clear and appealing manner.

LOGOS

BC BUSINESS

51

LOGOS

Requirements for promotional design can be balanced against the need for informative content. The 1st Avenue kit for a Wesbild development handily fulfills the function of a leasing brochure to attract the tenant mix required for a successful development.

Design treatment of technical promotions can be compatible with the human psyche. Through design and colourful illustration, a persuasive warmth builds Infosat's market image while clearly explaining a technical product.

COMMUNICATION PORTFOLIO

52

LOGOS

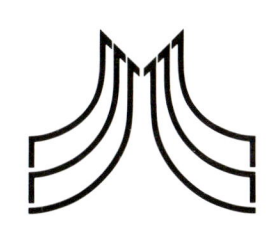

Good graphic solutions are readily accepted by the consumer, and result in sales. Fitzwright's Bare Sportswear catalogue fulfilled the need to quickly generate a favourable response in a highly competitive market.

Industrial technical promotion requires a special vision to rise above the mundane. Ulstein Z-Drive promotions consistently use good design to communicate effectively.

COMMUNICATION PORTFOLIO

53

DANIEL PELAVIN
Daniel Pelavin, *Principal*
New York, New York, USA

"**T**he shapes that I use represent the geometric aspect of my work in design, illustration and lettering. I chose the hues, values and number of colors to balance and interact with each other in a rich and varied manner. The type is hand-drawn and pays respect to classical Roman letterforms, the basis for much contemporary typography. I selected Mohawk Superfine paper, a premium stock chosen for its lack of imitation texture and its natural, pure color. The intended effect is that of a lavish and expressive, yet precisely controlled, graphic image."

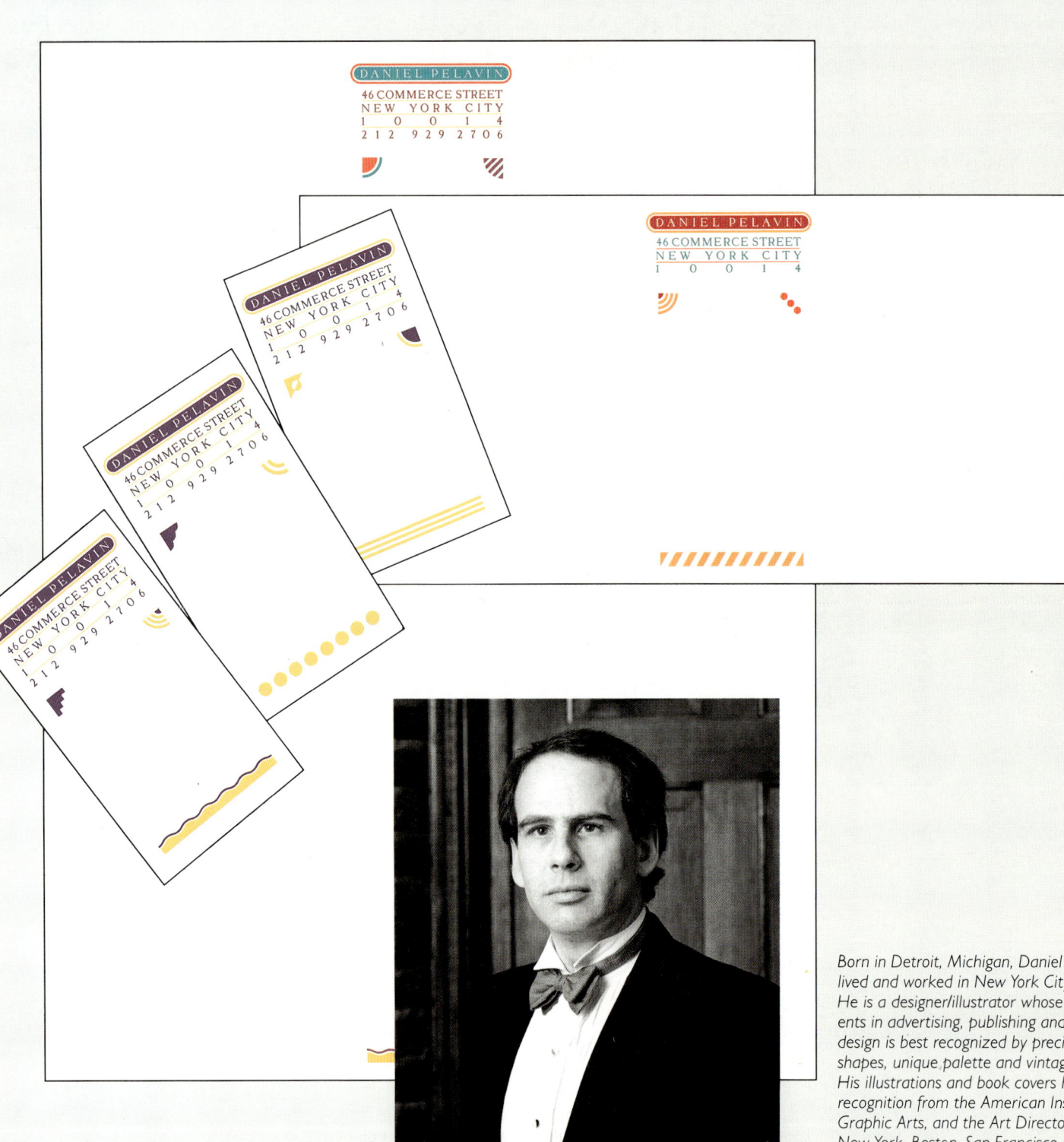

Born in Detroit, Michigan, Daniel Pelavin has lived and worked in New York City since 1979. He is a designer/illustrator whose work for clients in advertising, publishing and graphic design is best recognized by precisely drafted shapes, unique palette and vintage typography. His illustrations and book covers have earned recognition from the American Institute of Graphic Arts, and the Art Directors Clubs of New York, Boston, San Francisco and Washington, D.C. He has recently completed work on an alphabet soon to be released by International Typeface Corporation.

H. L. Chu & Company
Hoi L. Chu, *President*
New York, New York, USA

"**W**hen I started my business, one of the earliest decisions I faced was what to call my fledgling enterprise. I decided to use my name and a personal symbol on the company letterhead. The symbol is based on Pacioli, da Vinci and Durer's study of the geometric construction of Roman letters. But, instead of a Roman capital letter, I did it on my Chinese surname—Chu—thus, communicating the concept of graphic design and my Chinese heritage at the same time."

Since he founded H. L. Chu & Company in New York in 1979, Hoi Chu has designed identity and graphics programs for Chase Manhattan Bank, Danskin, Daiwa Bank, Ltd., and Key Coffee. His work has received awards from AIGA, IABC, NYAD and Bienale Uzite Grafiky and has appeared in numerous publications including CA Annuals, Graphis, ID Magazine, Print Case Books, Progressive Architecture, and Kodansha's World Graphic Design Now.

PROMOTION PIECE

PROMOTIONAL PAMPHLET

GREETING CARD

May the new year   bring you soaring happiness   and peace.

H.L.Chu & Company

PROMOTIONAL PAMPHLET

Key Coffee
Corporate and Brand Identification Program

Since its founding in Yokohama in 1920, Kimura Coffee Company has been a pioneer in the Japanese coffee industry, and "Key" brand – an Anglicized name for Kimura – has developed into one of the most recognized and respected consumer brands in Japan. Its ubiquitous symbol, a skeleton key, has been seen all over Japan – from tiny hamlets to major metropolis.

To strengthen its market identity for future international growth and to more clearly communicate to its current public, the company adopted the name "Key Coffee Inc." and underwent an update of its symbol mark.

Recognizing the inherent advantage of a universal pictogram, we recommended that the important elements, the Key illustration and the wording "Key Coffee" be retained. We further enhanced the equity of these elements by completely redrawing the key and fusing it into the letter "K" of the logotype. Thus the two items become integral parts of one another, yet can still be used separately. A secondary color, yellow, was introduced to take advantage of modern media and lend more visual excitement to the symbol.

At left, the Key Coffee logotype prior to its redesign. Above, a photo of Kimura Coffee Company, circa 1920, from the Key Coffee archives.

57

GREETING CARD

PROMOTIONAL PAMPHLET

Superior Scientific, Inc.
Corporate Identification Program

As one of the fastest growing bio-medical instrumentation service companies in the field, its original "mom and pop" identification system was no longer appropriate.

The job was to mold a program to enhance the company's marketing posture and project for it a more established image.

Central to the program is a symbol which graphically portrays the company's business. It combines the snake of Caduceus and the image of an oscilloscope, communicating medicine and technology.

It also forms the initials of the company.

GREETING CARD

58

GEORGE HARTMAN DESIGN CONSULTANT
George Hartman, President
New York, New York, USA

"**W**hen I opened my own business, I needed an image that would appear contemporary, exciting and current. I chose gray to subtly distinguish the paper from the usual run-of-the-mill white stock, and red to 'jump' from the page and arrest the eye. I selected the angle both to set the design apart and to reflect the frequent use of diagonals in my work. The type is modern, bold and strong, yet classic in intent—a professional image-carrier."

Born in Chicago in 1928, George Hartman studied at the Institute of Design, Chicago with Buckminster Fuller and Walter Gropius, among others. Formerly an art director of several magazines, he is currently an independent graphic design consultant. He has received both the Art Directors Club Award and the Publication Designers Merit Award several times.

PROMOTION PIECE

GEORGE hartman
GRAPHIC DESIGN CONSULTANT

fashion...beauty...

decorating...food...features...

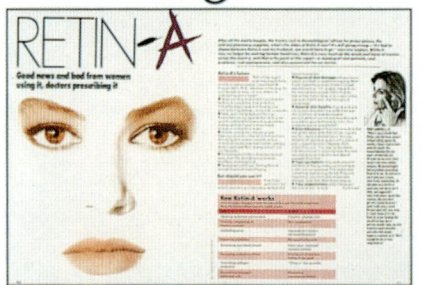

editorial (start-up or re-design)...

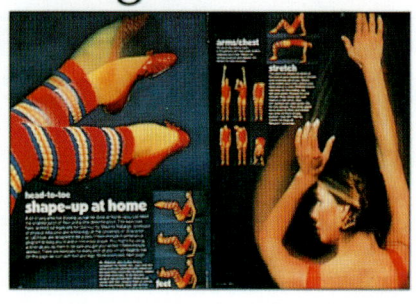

catalogs...

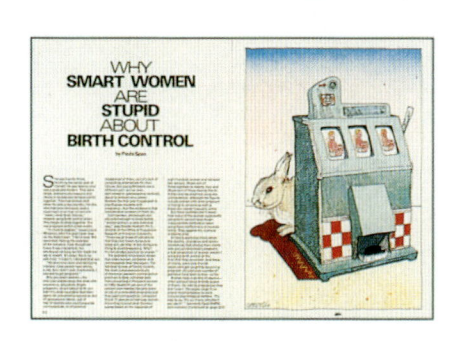

304 EAST 45TH ST.
3RD FLOOR
NEW YORK 10017
212•880•6933
212•753•0734

CROSS ASSOCIATES
James A. Cross, *President*
Los Angeles, California, USA

"**W**e designed our stationery to accommodate a number of variations which comprise the Siegel & Gale design network of ten design offices in eight countries. The image we project is businesslike which speaks to the needs of our clients who want intelligent and responsible design solutions for their corporate communications. Our business forms are designed to make documentation of each project more efficient and to ensure all necessary information is recorded and transmitted to our staff and clients."

A graduate of UCLA, James Cross began his career as a corporate art director, achieving his national reputation for innovations in annual reports, collateral materials, and corporate identification systems. In 1963 he formed Cross Associates, now an affiliate of Siegel and Gale. Cross is international president of Alliance Graphique, and his work has been featured in design publications throughout the United States, Europe and Japan.

PROMOTIONAL PUBLICATION

PROMOTIONAL PUBLICATION

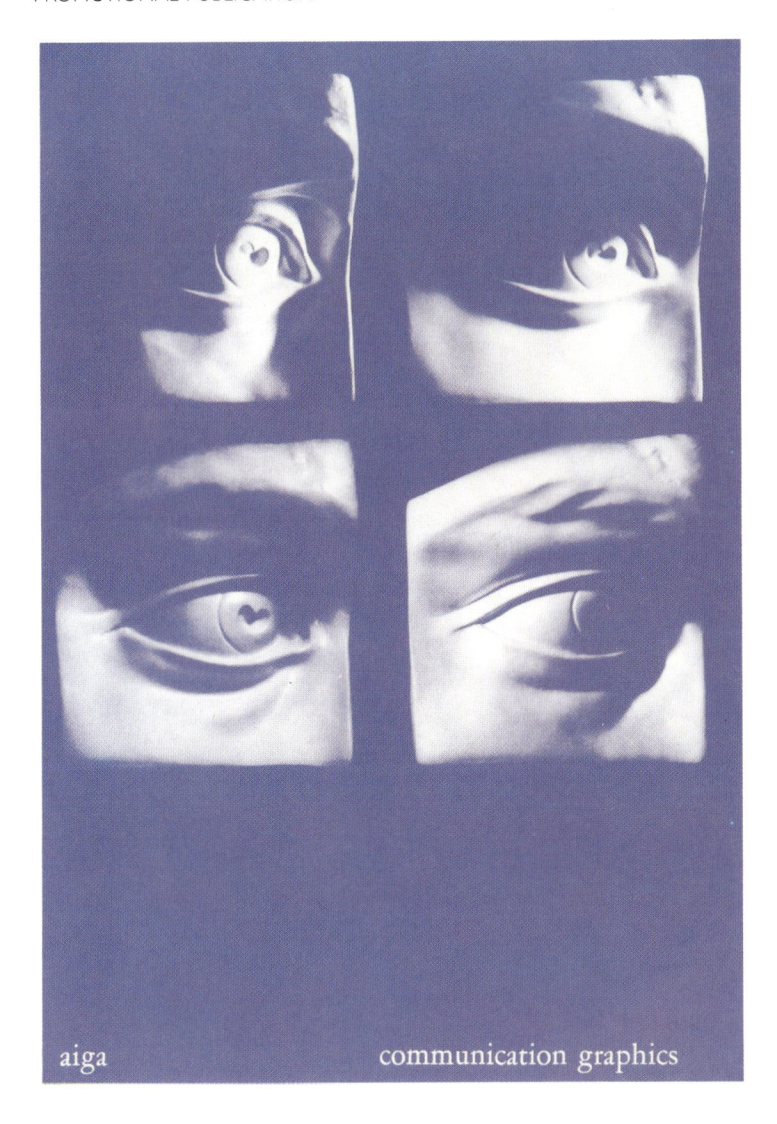

PROMOTIONAL PUBLICATION

LOGO

ADLA

PROMOTIONAL PUBLICATION

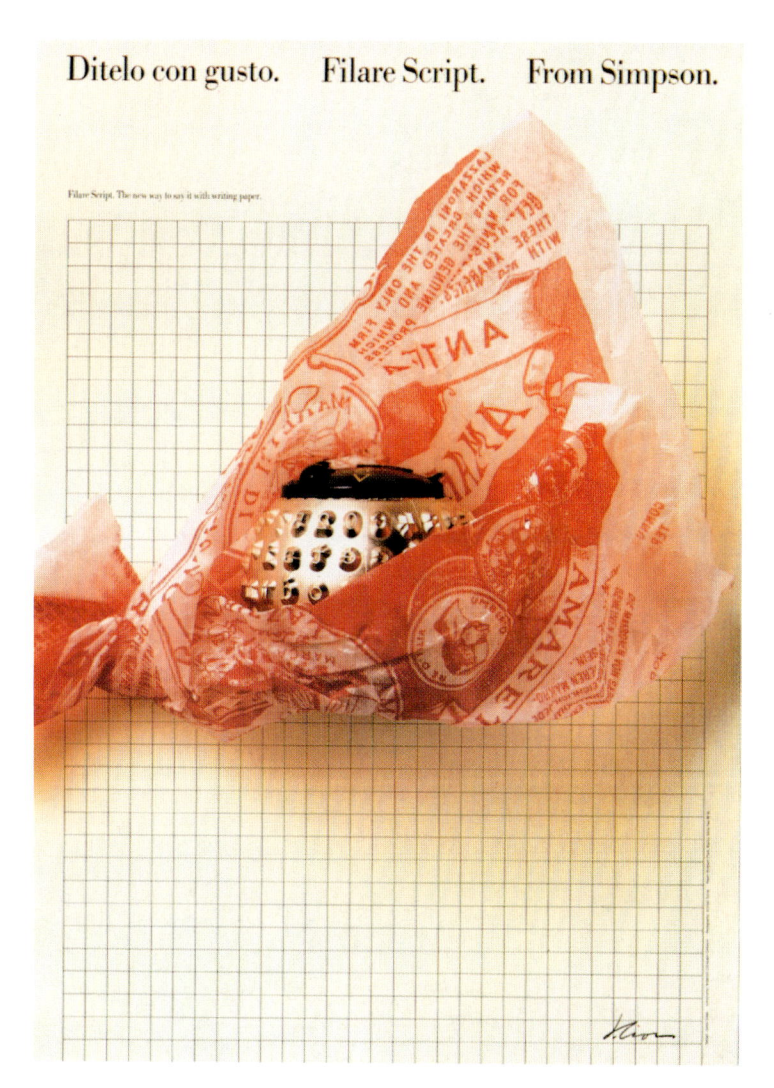

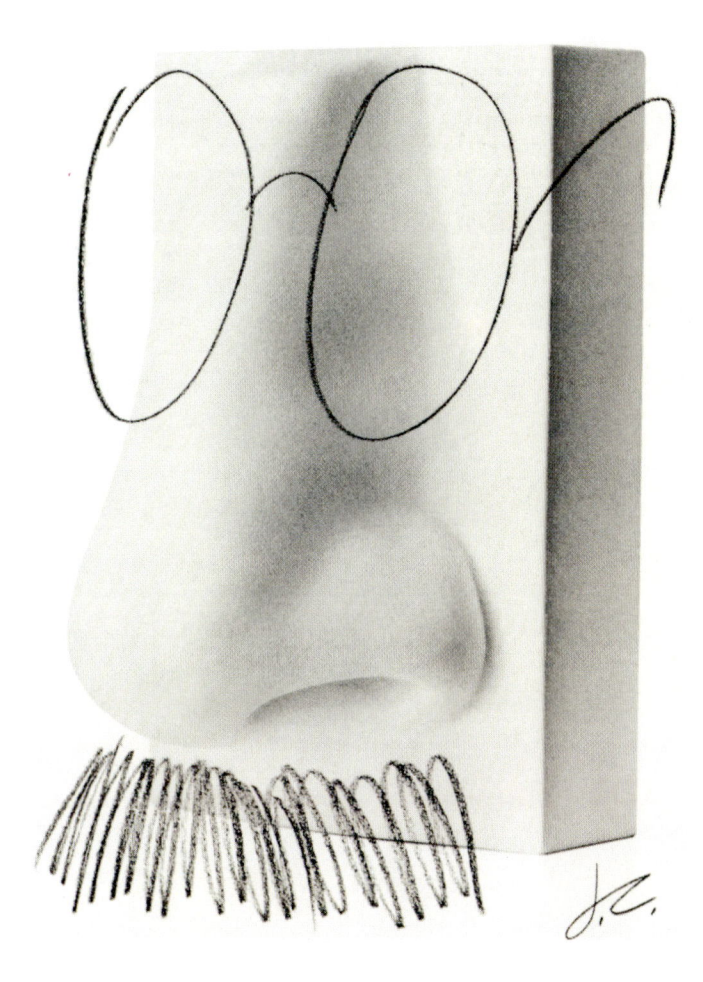

PROMOTIONAL PUBLICATION

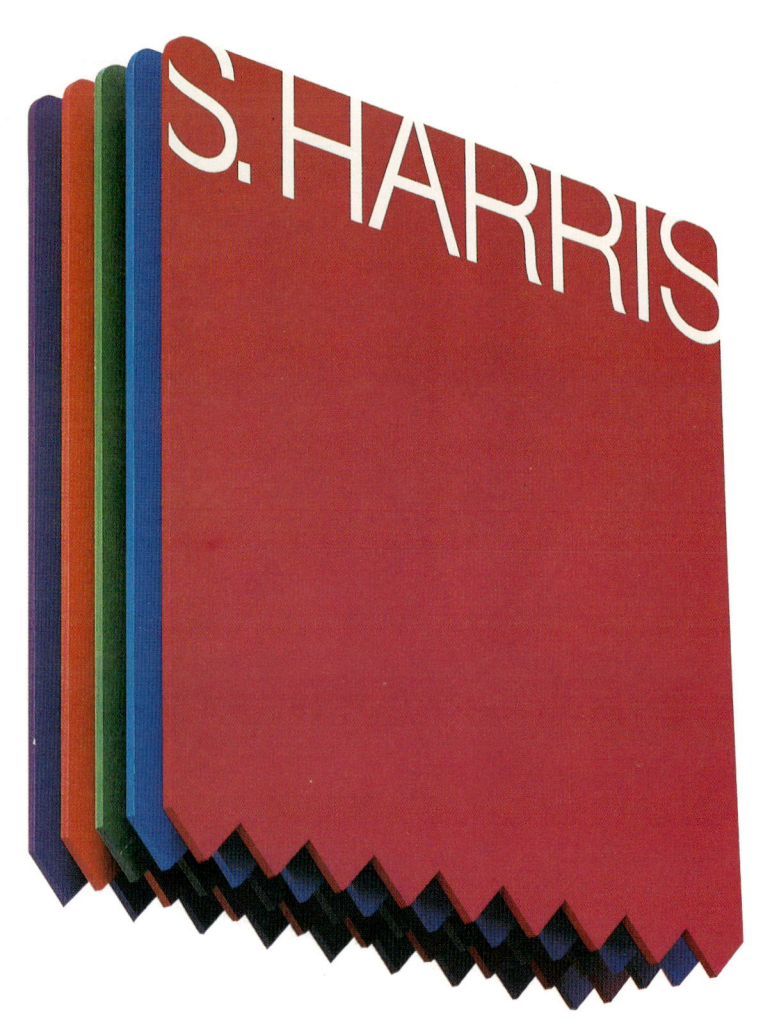

SEVENTEENTH STREET STUDIOS
Randall Goodall, *Partner*
Oakland, California, USA

"**O**ur principal image is a miniature city scene made up of old type ornaments and punctuation. Since much of our business is cover and book design for publishers, my idea was to make a logo that alluded to the fine printing tradition of book making. I'm interested in the similarity of typographic and architectural ornamentation in a given historical period. We work in a downtown area that has many superbly decorated examples of early twentieth-century architecture, including our studio, and these ornate structures are very much like the book design of the same period. I thought it would be fun and worthwhile to try to make this complicated series of connections in a single graphic device."

PROMOTIONAL BROCHURE

Born in Baltimore, Maryland, Randall Goodall began a book design business in the mid-1970s. Several years ago he formed Seventeenth Street Studios in Oakland, California, with two partners, Lorrie Fink and Naomi Schiff. Known for his upbeat approach, Goodall designs handsome books and has won numerous awards.

PROMOTION PIECE

Seventeenth Street Studios

Design & Publishing Services
415-835-1717
455 Seventeenth Street
Oakland, California 94612

LOGOS

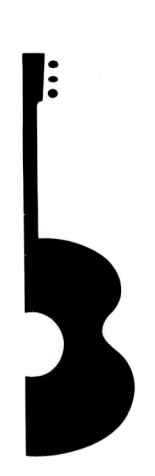

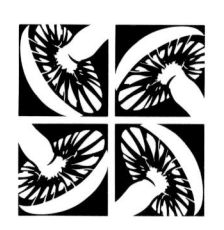

Pentagram

New York, New York; San Francisco, California, USA; and London, England

"The sixteen Pentagram partners generate an extensive program of publications and other communications ranging from the academic to the curious. The firm's self-promotional materials provide a unique outlet for the partners' creativity, as well as opportunities to maintain contact with clients, friends and acquaintances. A *Pentagram review* is published periodically as a portfolio of recent work and is used as a capabilities brochure. Other self-promotional projects include *Puzzlegrams* and *Pentagames, Living by Design* and *Ideas on Design* which are intended to be educational and informative portfolios of Pentagram's work, and the annual Christmas books and *Pentagram Papers* which allow the firm to contact existing and potential clients where a commercial approach would be inappropriate."

Pentagram Design
Services Inc
212 Fifth Avenue
New York NY 10010
Telephone (212) 683 7000
Fax (212) 532 0181

Colin Forbes
Pentagram
212 Fifth Avenue
New York NY 10010
212 683 7000

Pentagram

Pentagram Design
Services Inc
212 Fifth Avenue
New York NY 10010

New York

Michael Bierut
Colin Forbes
Peter Harrison
Etan Manasse
Woody Pirtle
Associates:
Harold Burch
Michael Gericke
Susan Hochbaum

San Francisco

Kit Hinrichs
Linda Hinrichs
Neil Shakery

London

Theo Crosby
Alan Fletcher
Kenneth Grange
David Hillman
Mervyn Kurlansky
John McConnell
John Rushworth
Peter Saville
Associates:
Pedro Guedes
Johan Santer

Pentagram is a design partnership: a reputation, a collective and a resource. Sixteen partners with individual styles, skills, strengths—and their own design teams—operate freely in a constituted federal system. They all subscribe to the culture of this constitution because they created it. Their work is accommodated, supported, organized, administered and communicated in and by the framework which is Pentagram. So, Pentagram represents a plurality of reputations, yet has a reputation all its own.

PENTAGRAM PORTFOLIO

There are eight partners in the London office where it all began, and five partners in the New York office where Pentagram first opened in America. The three partners in the San Francisco office joined the partnership in 1986.

The three-office system has catalyzed Pentagram's potential. Now there is a fluidity of work between the partners, their offices and the markets in which they operate. The individual freedom of the partners has also become a concerted freedom. Pentagram's Anglo-American axis added another dimension to the character of the partnership's output, which is demonstrable.

ACM Siggraph
Computer graphics convention

PENTAGRAM PORTFOLIO

Elektra

Elektra Entertainment
Record and entertainments company

The Children's Museum
Discovery centre

71

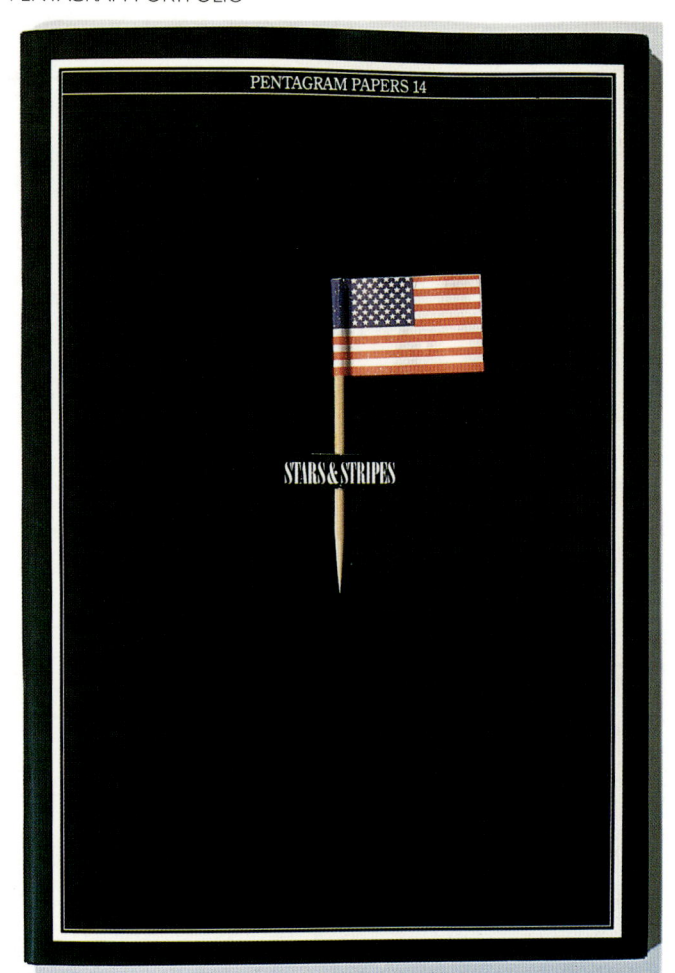

PENTAGRAM PORTFOLIO

Canned asparagus from California, c.1930.

David Edwards
Furniture manufacturer

72

PENTAGRAM PORTFOLIO

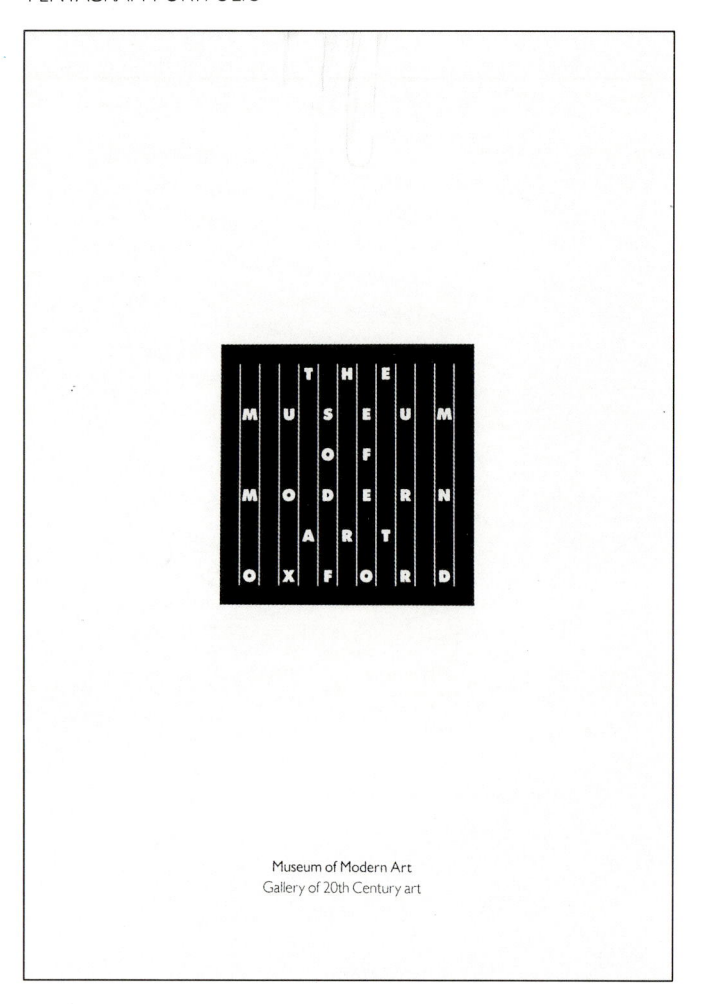

PENTAGRAM PORTFOLIO

Museum of Modern Art
Gallery of 20th Century art

BIBA
Fashion house

PENTAGRAM PORTFOLIO

PENTAGRAM PORTFOLIO

The Nature Company
Retailers

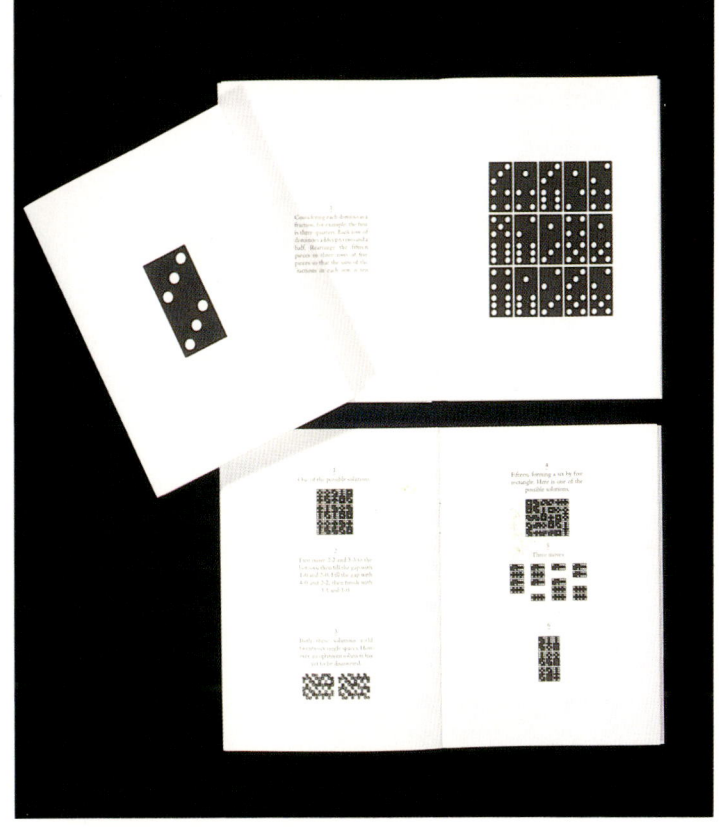

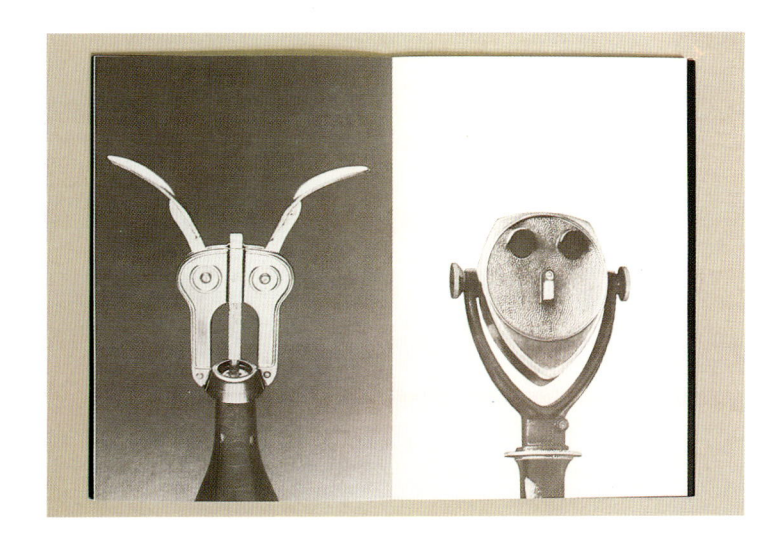

PENTAGRAM PORTFOLIO

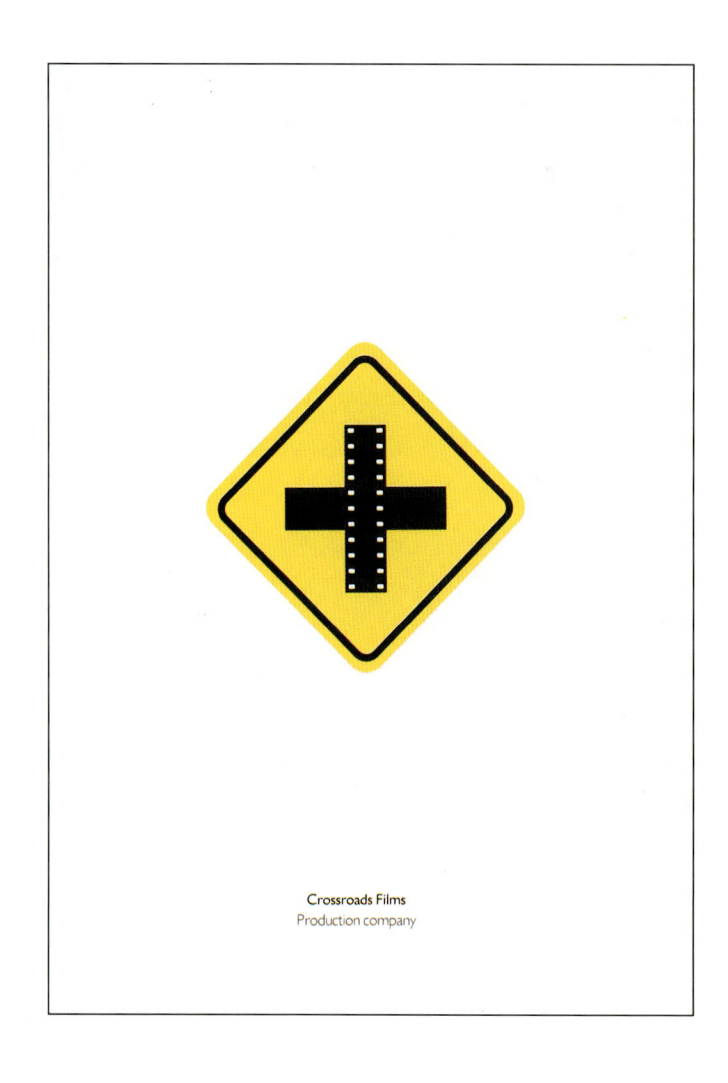

PENTAGRAM PORTFOLIO

Watney Mann Truman
Brewery

Crossroads Films
Production company

78

PENTAGRAM PORTFOLIO

Infoworks
Contact furniture market

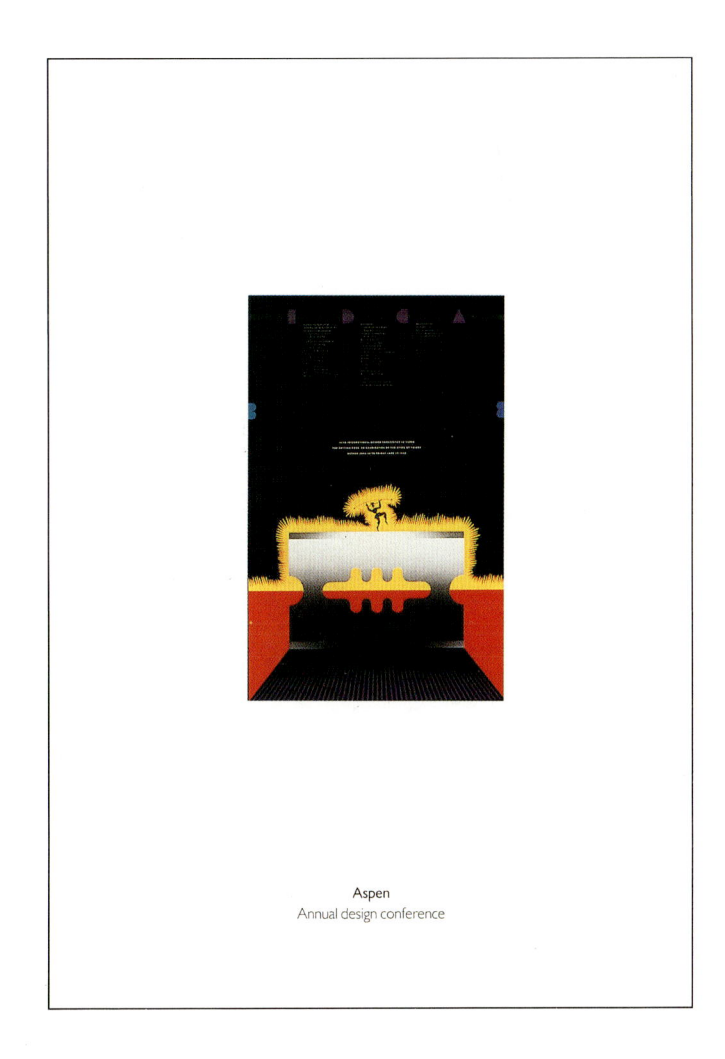

Aspen
Annual design conference

79

PENTAGRAM PORTFOLIO

Mandarin Oriental Hotels
De Luxe hotel group

Pentagram

PENTAGRAM PORTFOLIO

It is too witty to be a Bible,
too personal to be a reference book, too colourful
to be a tome, too intelligent to be a catalogue,
too useful to be missed.

Living by design: Pentagram
published by Lund Humphries Publishers.

Price £10

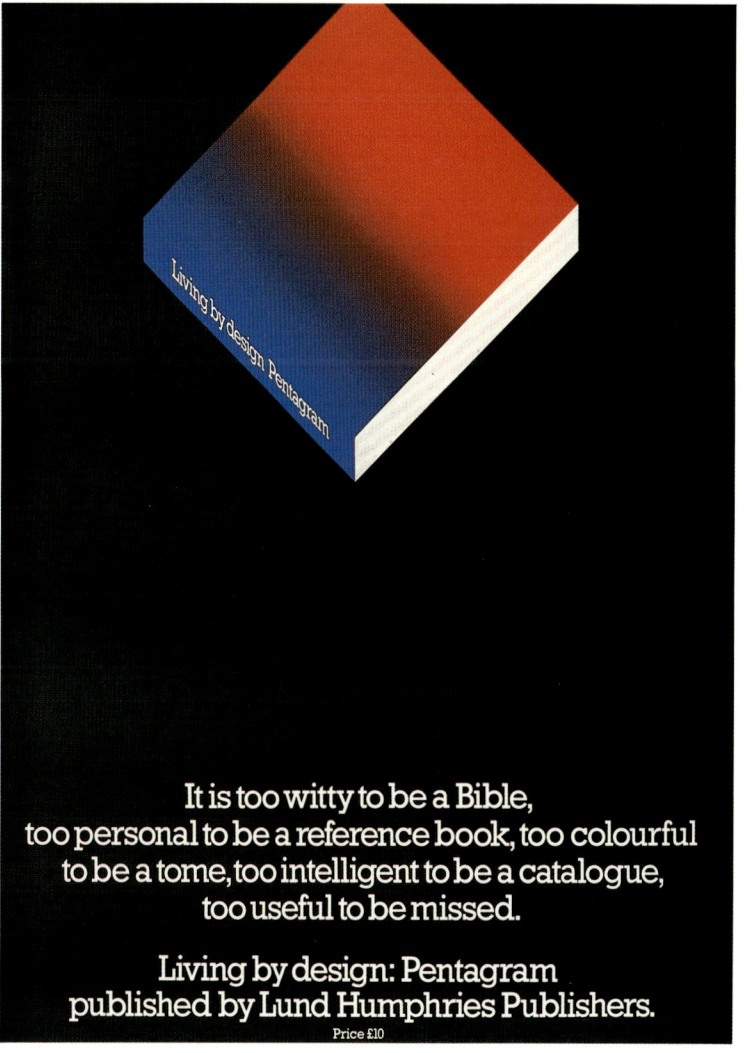

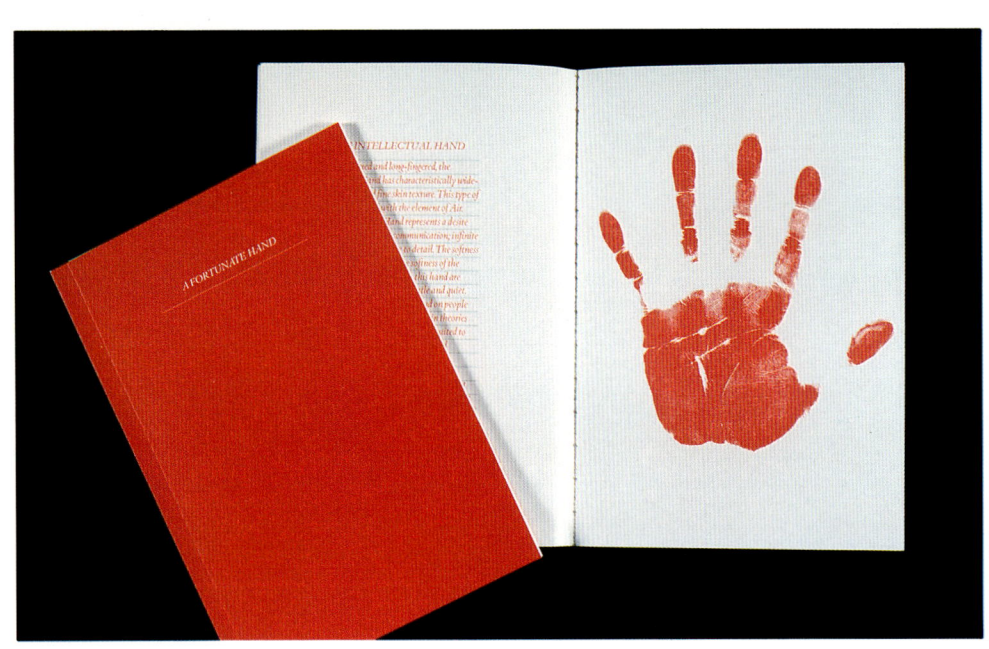

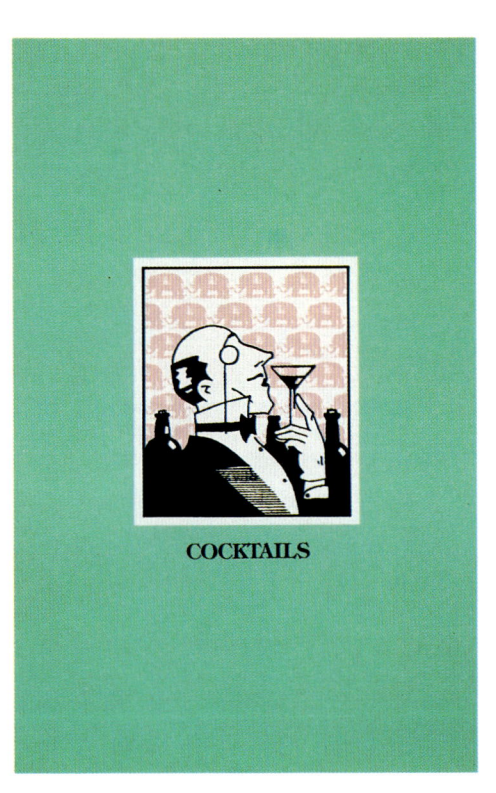

PENTAGRAM PORTFOLIO

EUROPE

PETER STONE
Graphic Designer, Typographer
Bromley, Kent, England

"I designed this letterhead in 1988, the commencement of a new phase in my working life. Getting the right feel was a major consideration. I chose recycled Speckletone Natural paper which feels good, takes typing or handwriting equally well, and is almost edible. The typing is light because I like it and it contrasts well with the soft paper. I chose red and blue because it's cheerful and positive and matches my studio bathroom. The rubber stamp is a late addition occasioned by new telephone codings for London and my new FAX machine."

A member of the Society of Typographic Designers and a Fellow of the Chartered Society of Designers, London-bred Stone has no formal design training. After concluding a prosperous design partnership in 1988, his solo practice has flourished with such projects as a series of books for Oxford University Press and publicity for typeface "Else."

LETTERHEAD COMMUNIQUES

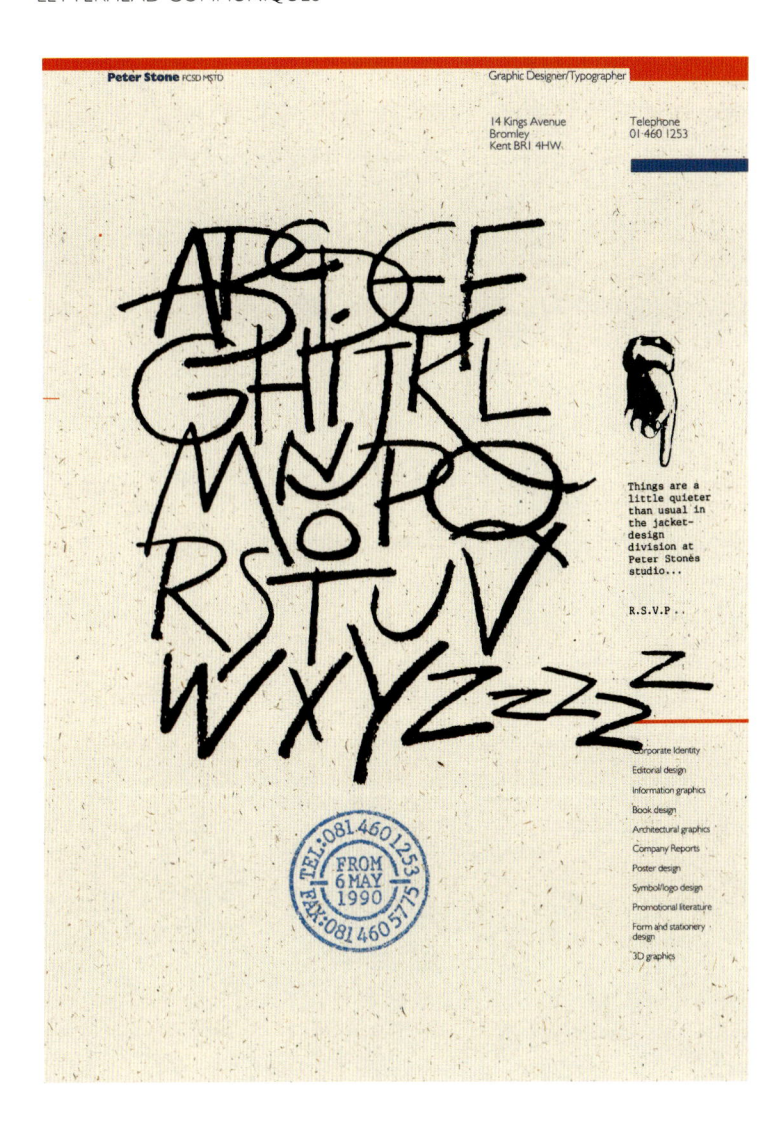

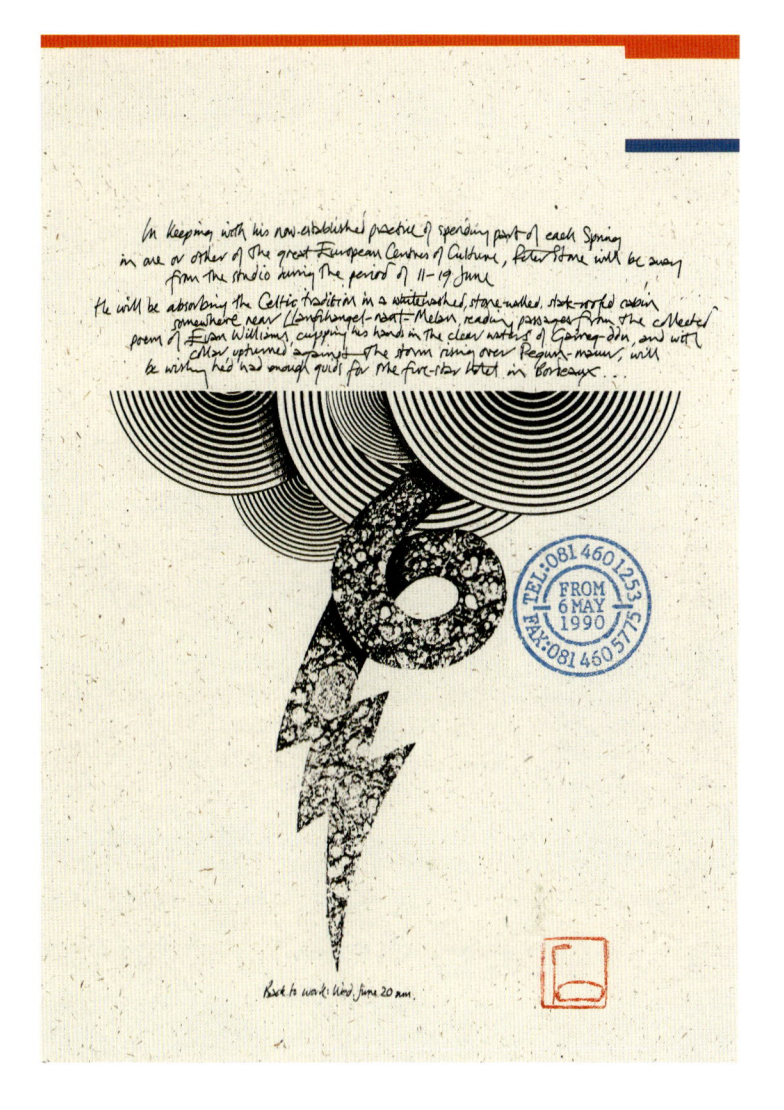

LOGOS

ESSEBLU
Susanna Vallebona, Owner
Milan, Italy

"In Italian ESSEBLU means S (the initial of my first name, Susanna) and *blue* (the color I prefer). The classic logotype close to the text in italic Helvetica, and the Conqueror paper in an unusual color express that the project is conceived to communicate rigor and cultural tradition mixed with the will of innovation and evolution."

Born in Milan, Susanna Vallebona began the Esseblu studio in 1981 when she was only 27. Esseblu specializes in image and graphic development for publications, corporations, products and exhibitions. A winner of the silver medal and Merit Award at the IGI Art competition in Vancouver, Canada, Vallebona has had her work published and exhibited throughout the world.

PROMOTIONAL BOOKLET

LOGOS

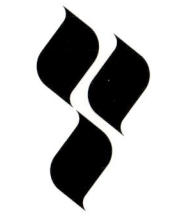

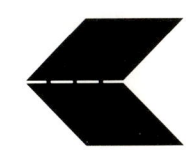

88

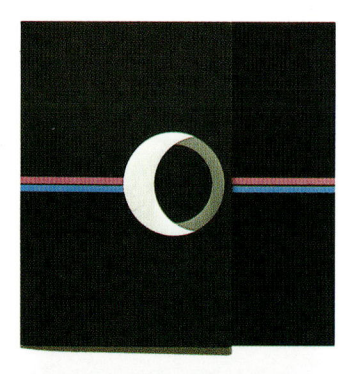

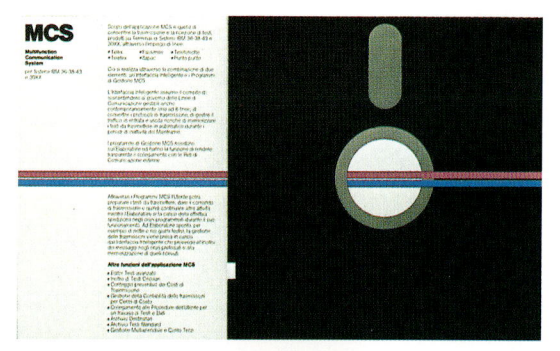

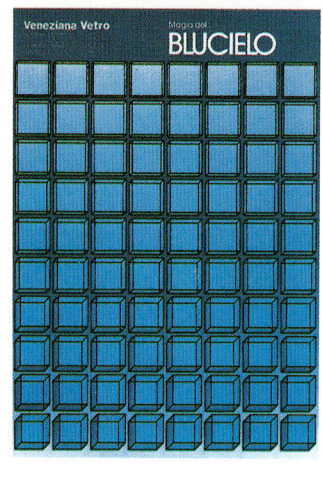

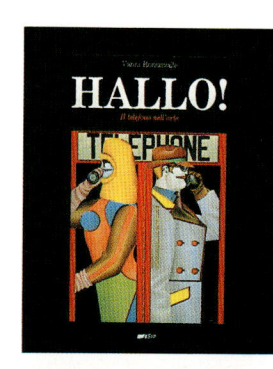

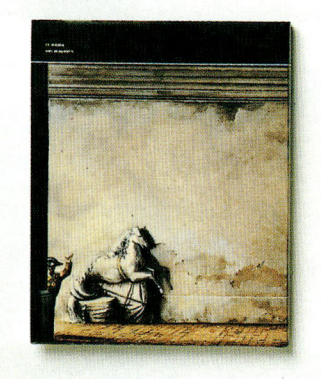

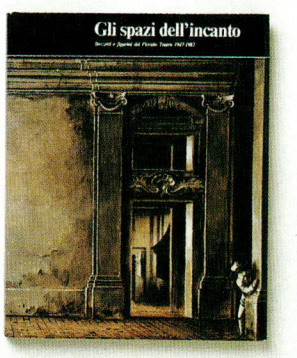

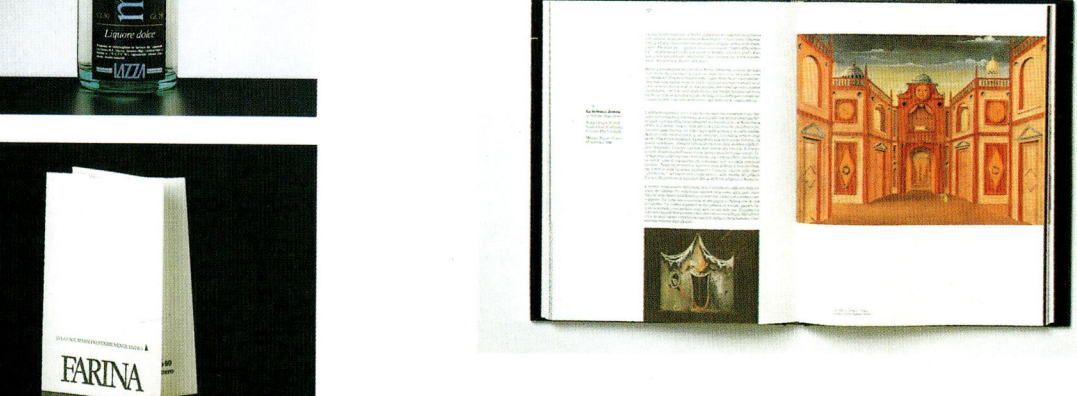

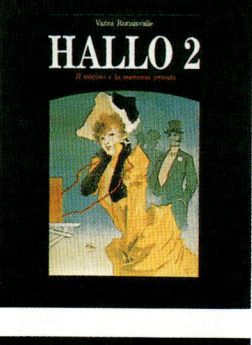

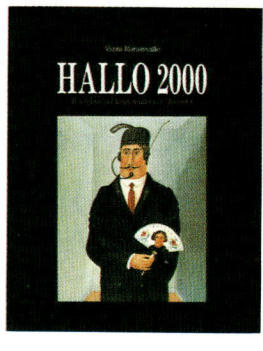

CONCEPTS DESIGN
Anne Stienstra, Floor Kamphorst, Robert Jan Hofhuis, *Partners*
Amsterdam, Netherlands

"**O**ur new identity has been called interesting, irritating and intriguing, funny, tricky and indulgent. For us, however, it remains functional, announcing the fact that Concepts has become Concept Design. Our logo maintains the simplicity and neutrality of our old identity, yet it enforces a feeling of strength through the dominance of the color red."

Located in Amsterdam, Concepts Design is managed by three partners and is made up of four design teams with an international complement. Emphasis is placed on an open structure. Experienced designers work together with young talent in a relaxed atmosphere on an equal basis. The design process is based on communication with, and involvement of the client, resulting in successful visual solutions. The outcome is a lasting relationship with both Dutch and International companies.

PROMOTIONAL BOOKLET

KAMEN POPOV

KAMEN POPOV POSTERS AND GRAPHIC DESIGN
Kamen Popov, *Proprietor*
Luxembourg

"The logo I am using is derived from an award-winning poster I entered in the 1976 Warsaw Biennial focusing on the theme, 'Habitat.' The poster is representative of what I think a poster should be: a laconic, clear message, understood by as many people as possible. It should resonate, and the 'Cry' of the image should remain in people's minds."

PROMOTIONAL BROCHURE

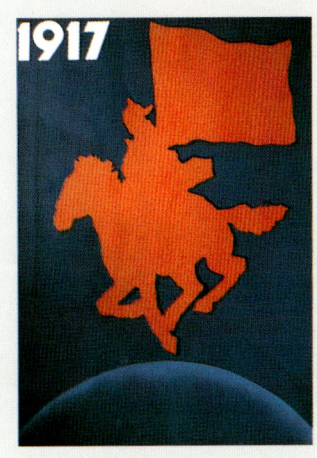

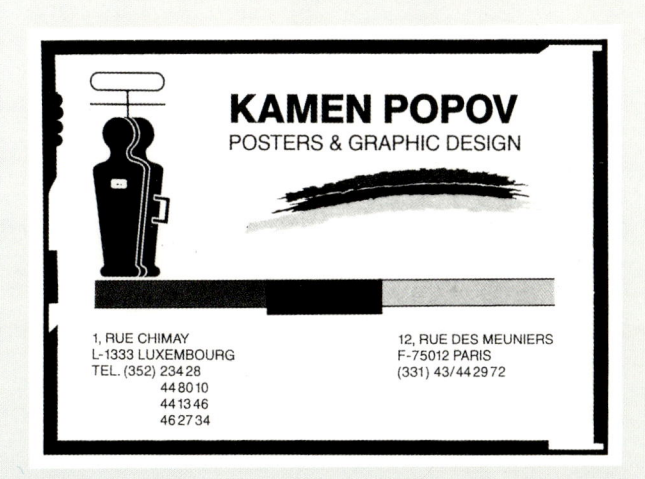

Kamen Popov's graphic designs appear in museums in New York, Israel and Paris. He resides in Luxembourg and Paris and has participated in exhibitions throughout the world.

STUDIO DE LISO
Giuseppi De Liso, *Director*
Bari, Italy

"**W**e recently decided to change Studio De Liso's image. Formerly our logo depicted hands that create Chinese shadows, exemplifying our work as 'creators of ephemeral works.' Our new image is less graphic and more typographical, simpler and more fashionable. It expresses the studio's transition over the last few years, from graphics to advertising and visual communication."

Opening his own Studio De Liso in 1969, Giuseppe De Liso has worked on graphic and typographical designs for publications and advertisements. His clients include the Apulian Regional Board, Bari Provincial Council, Firestone and other corporations.

LOGOS

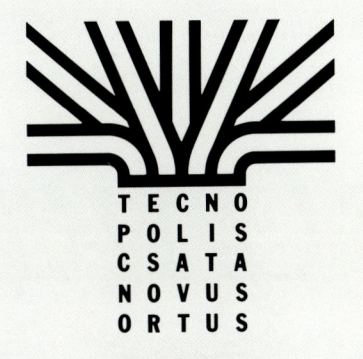

Studio De Liso
comunicazione visiva

design grafica pubblicità
via Turati, 14 - 70124 Bari
tel. 080/417901

associato AIAP
Associazione Italiana Comunicazione Visiva
associato TP
Associazione Italiana Tecnici Pubblicitari

Studio De Liso
pubblicità e comunicazione visiva

via F. Turati, 14 - 70124 Bari - tel. 080/417901 - c.f. DLS GPP41P28 A662K - C.C.I.A.A.r.d. 202463 - p.i. 01069990727
associato AIAP Associazione Italiana Creativi della Comunicazione Visiva
associato TP/AP Albo Nazionale dei Professionisti Pubblicitari

TECNOPOLIS
CSATA
NOVUS
ORTUS

L'ALTRO SOTTANO
CAFFÈ · BARI

POSTERS

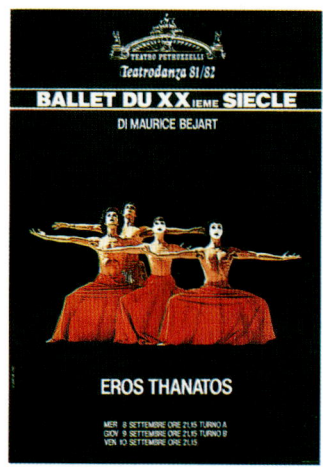

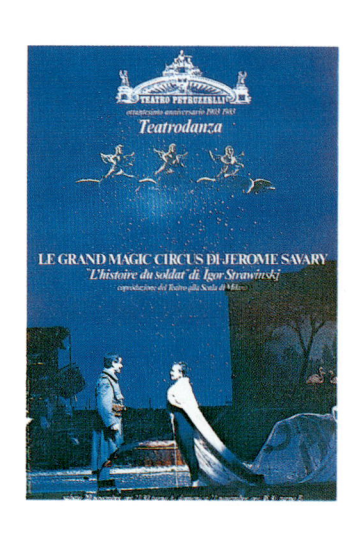

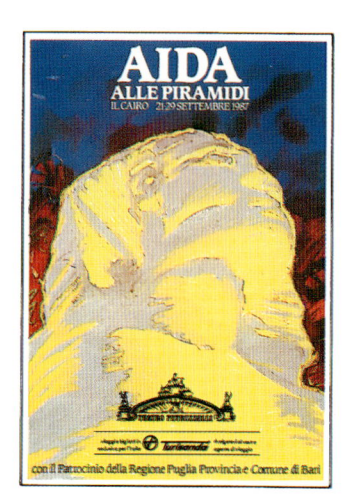

PROGRAM AND CATALOG

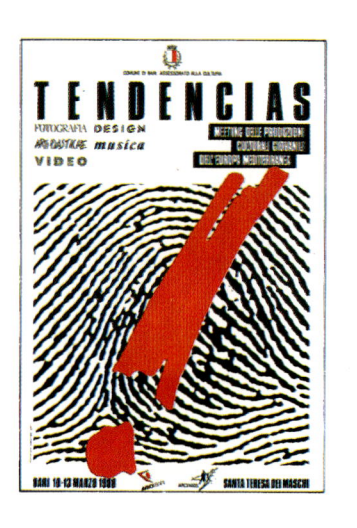

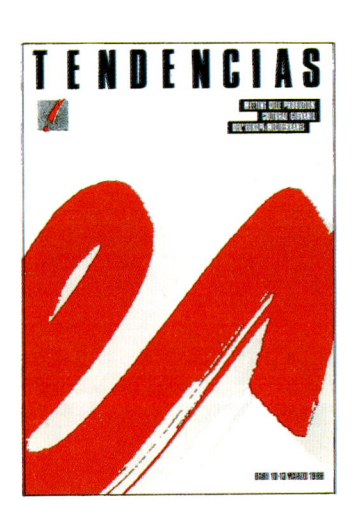

94

Junn Paasche-Aasen Design
Junn Paasche-Aasen, Owner
Oslo, Norway

"I designed my stationery so that it would relate to my work, which is primarily in book design. Since I write all of my letters by hand, I decided to use register lines from a book-spread as a functional decoration, thus making it easy to write on the straight lines. The envelope and visiting card are also cut out from the double spread."

Born in Oslo, Paasche-Aasen has had her own design studio in Norway since 1984, when she left the publishing house Aschehoug Fonag after seventeen years there. She is the recipient of various national and international awards for book designers.

Atelier Gérard Finel & Associés
Gérard Finel, *Manager*
Paris, France

"**O**ur visual identity is achieved without a logo: we are here to serve our clients, and we prefer to present ourselves with discretion. The square on our letterhead conveys organization, solidity and simplicity, while the golden yellow color adds dynamism and gaiety. The type selection, 'Goudy,' reflects our work in publishing. Our stationery is ruled to encourage hand-written letters which we advocate as an expression of humanistic philosophy and the art of living."

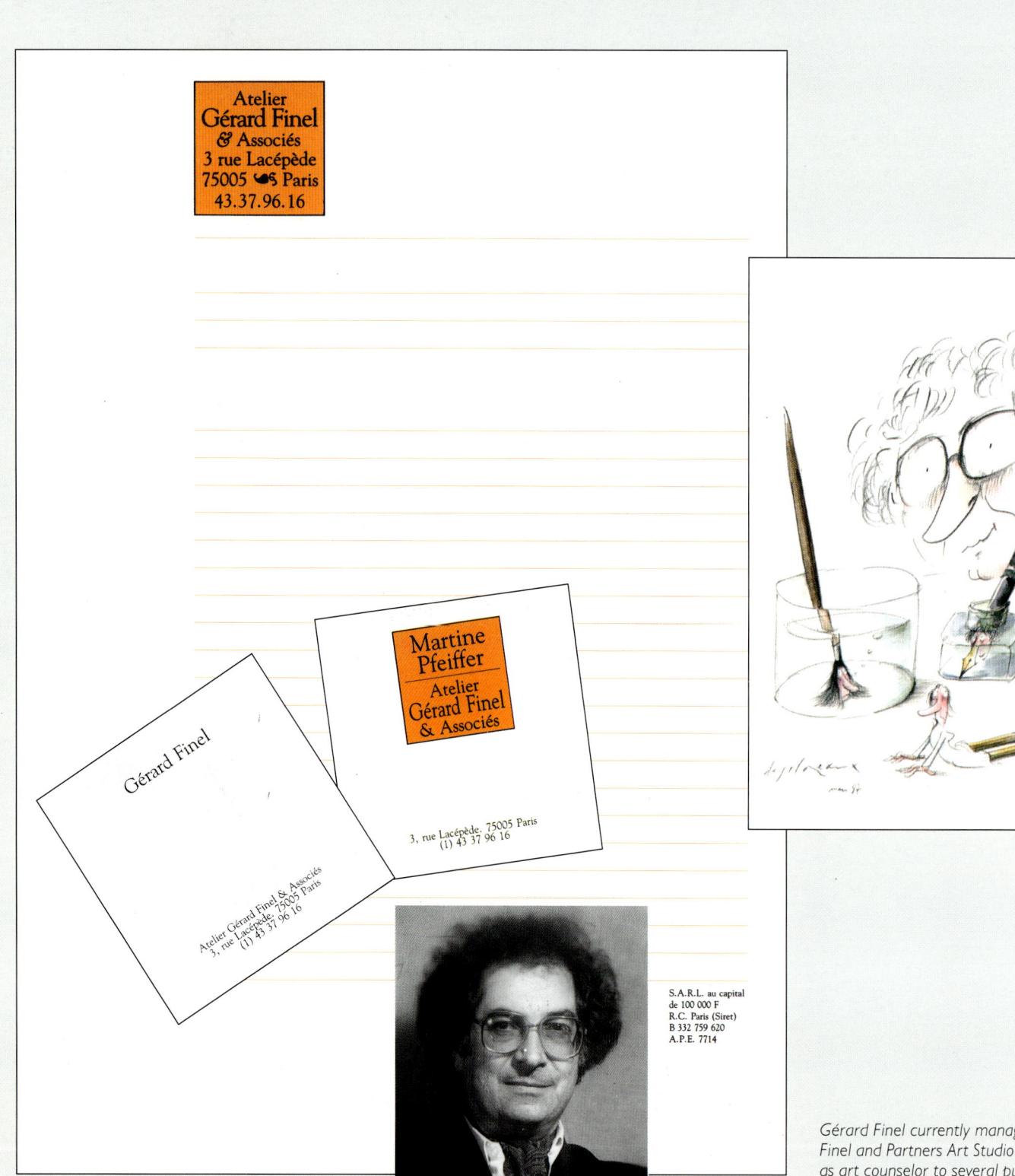

POSTCARD

Gérard Finel currently manages the Gérard Finel and Partners Art Studio as well as serving as art counselor to several publishing editors in Paris. He is vice president of the National Graphiste Union.

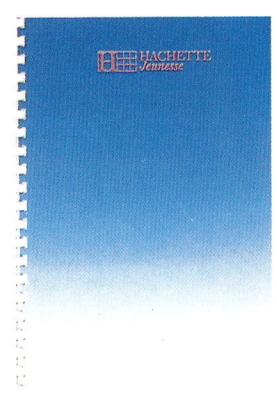

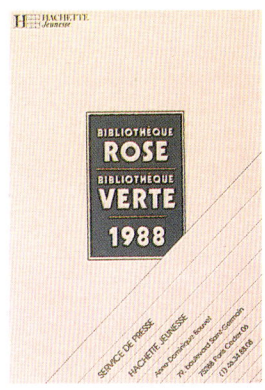

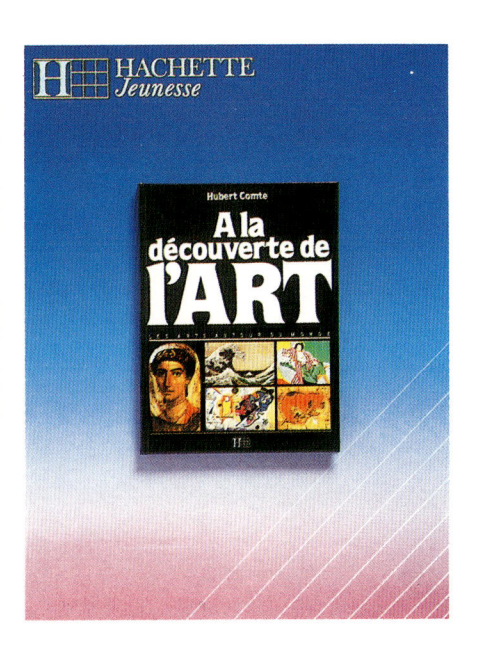

PROMOTIONAL BOOKLET

97

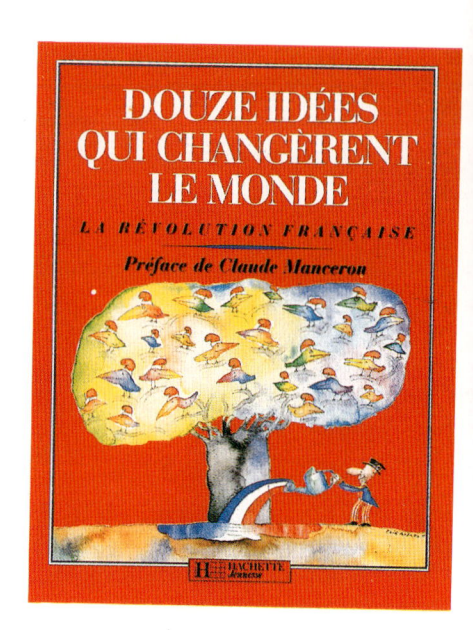

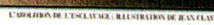

PROMOTIONAL BOOKLET

Per Arnoldi
Graphic Designer
Copenhagen, Denmark

"I designed a low-key, highly controlled letterhead to make up for lousy typing and an old typewriter. Since I am selling very strong colors, I also thought a discreet gray and red would be proper. Futura light ties in with the Bauhaus tradition which, in my opinion, is the only tradition able to carry messages through the postmodern chaos of fashionable nonsense noisily filling our surroundings."

PROMOTION PIECE

Arnoldi's work is best expressed as a light-hearted departure from the "seriousness" of the graphic arts. His use of color and subtle symbolic connections between a concept and its essence have distinguished his work.

POSTERS

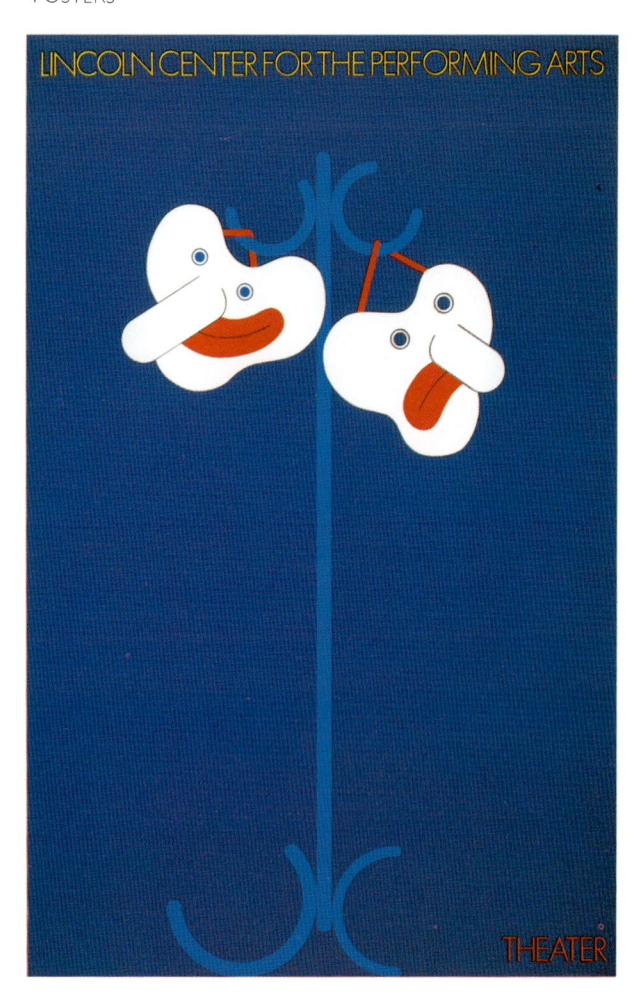

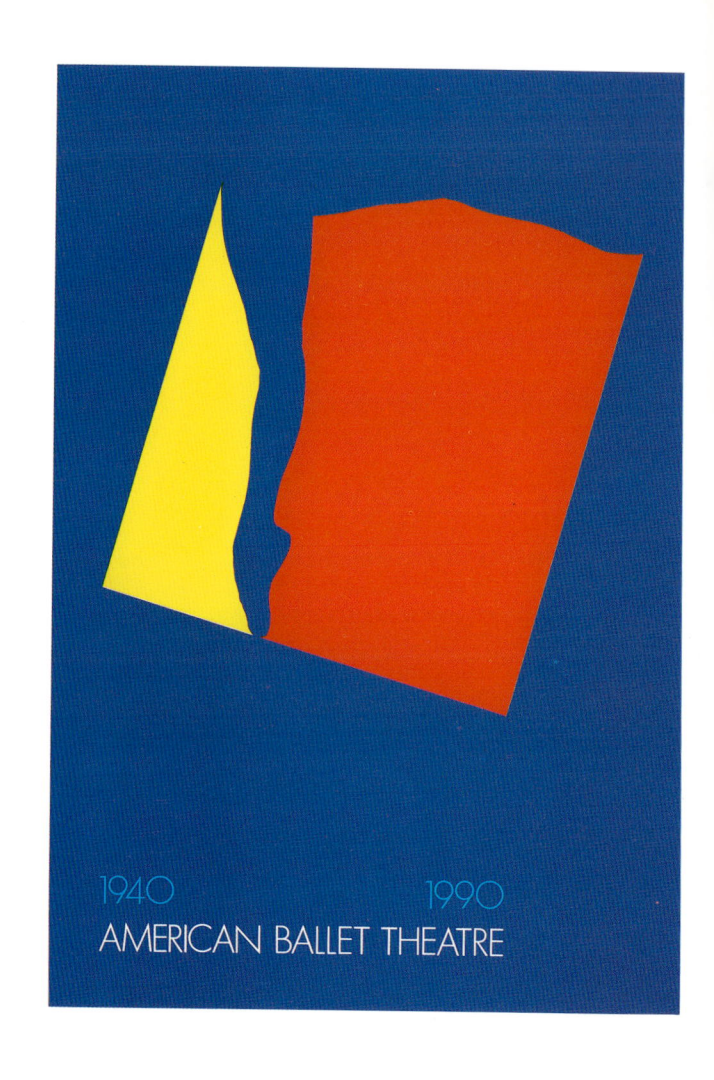

100

BUREAU D'ETUDES GARAMOND
Jacques N. Garamond, *Director*
Guainville, France

"**T**he graphic artist, in the broadest sense, is an 'inventor of images,' whose principle mission is *Communication* through an informative personal language. His vocabulary, drawn from sources in a constantly evolving environment, must submit to the imperatives posed by commercial as well as cultural problems. The designer's own graphic image must affirm a high visual level that will be expressed through his personal printed matter, exhibition and promotional materials."

Born in Paris, Garamond is one of those responsible for the evolution of modern graphic design. His clients include Air France, Shell and El Al, among others. From 1928 through 1931 he was graphic designer for the magazine l'Architecture d'aujord'hui, and in 1937 he was a participant in the House of Advertising at the Paris World Exhibition. In 1947, he organized the French Post-War Graphic Design Exhibition in the Bale and Zurich Museums. Garamond was also the founder of the Alliance Graphique Internationale (AGI) and former president of the Société des Artistes Décorateurs (SAD). In 1957, the American Society of Typographic Designers sponsored an exhibition of his work in San Francisco. Garamond is also a former teacher at the Ecole Nationale Supérieure des Arts Décoratifs and Ecole Supérieure d'Arts Graphiques. Still active in the design world today, Garamond is a regular contributor to international design publications.

POSTER

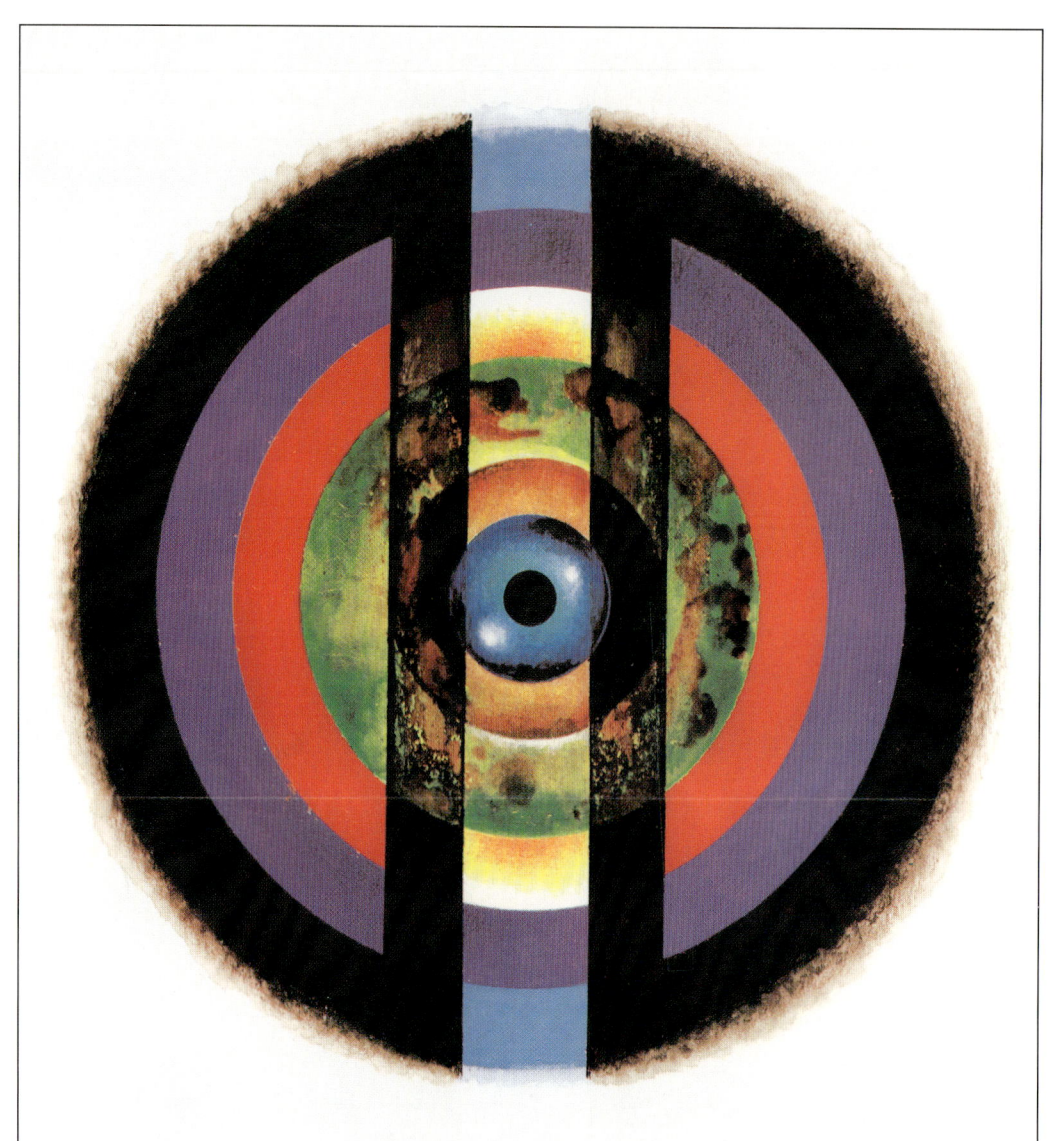

LOGOS

jacques n-garamond

AFFICHES

CENTRE MUNICIPAL DE L'AFFICHE - 58 AL. CHARLES DE FITTE - TOULOUSE

SEPTEMBRE - OCTOBRE - NOVEMBRE 1988

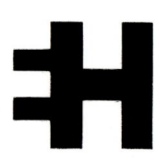

PROMOTIONAL BROCHURE

LOGOS

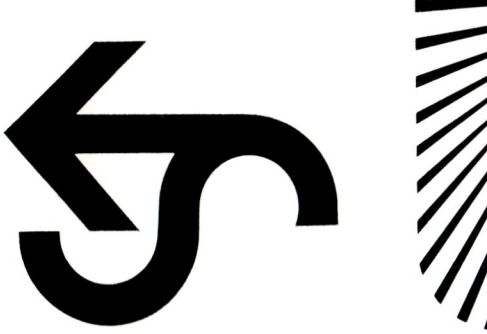

PROMOTIONAL BROCHURE

TANGRAM STRATEGIC DESIGN
Enrico Sempi, *Founder*
Novara, Italy

"**W**e decided not to use the tangram game in our logo because it was already used too many times in the world. We wanted our logo to communicate the expressive possibility of simple forms. The colors change in every application to suggest creativity and dynamism. We chose our letterhead paper for its typography qualities and to express our professional history and culture."

Born in Novara, Italy, Enrico Sempi has lectured, taught, and exhibited his work in Europe and America.

FRIEDRICH EISENMENGER
Identity Designer/Artist
Vienna, Austria

"In my profession as identity designer and consultant, every job begins with analysis and ends with visualization of corporate personalities. This is conveyed on my letterhead by my own face which connotes self-evaluation and self-portrait in different appearances on each sheet of stationery. The double-sided visiting card multiplies this idea of permanent metamorphosis without loss of personality."

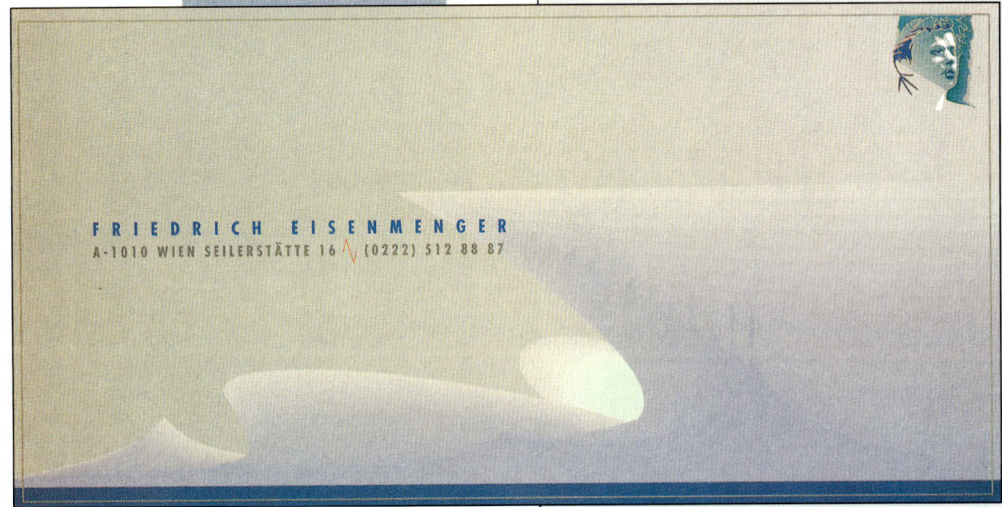

A graduate of the Academy of Applied Arts in Vienna, Friedrich Eisenmenger was one of the first Austrian designers to study corporate art. Since 1970, he has run his own graphic design studio, concentrating on corporate design. His most recent interests are in visionary artwork designed through the use of graphic computers.

MAG FRIEDRICH EISENMENGER A-1010 WIEN SEILERSTÄTTE 16 (0222) 512 88 87
MAG FRIEDRICH EISENMENGER A-1010 WIEN SEILERSTÄTTE 16 (0222) 512 88 87
FRIEDRICH EISENMENGER
A-1010 WIEN SEILERSTÄTTE 16 (0222) 512 88 87
FRIEDRICH EISENMENGER
IDENTITY
DESIGN
A-1010 WIEN SEILERSTÄTTE 16 (0222) 512 88 87
FRIEDRICH EISENMENGER
ARTIST
A-1010 WIEN SEILERSTÄTTE 16 (0222) 512 88 87

PRINZ-RABY DESIGN GRAPHIQUE
Noëlle Prinz, Michel Raby, *Owners*
Paris, France

"**W**e decided to change our image when we began to work on corporate graphic design for major companies. Using our first name initials, we designed our logo to look like two personalized flags on one mast. We kept our red and blue image colors, but we made them brighter."

POSTCARD

STICKER

Noëlle Prinze and Michel Raby joined forces in 1972 to form Prinz-Raby Design Graphique. Focusing on corporate identity and communication of cultural events, their firm has worked for such clients as General Maritime Company and France Telecom, the review of the French Ministry of Telecommunications. Their work has been exhibited in France, Czechoslovakia, Japan and Finland.

107

CALENDAR

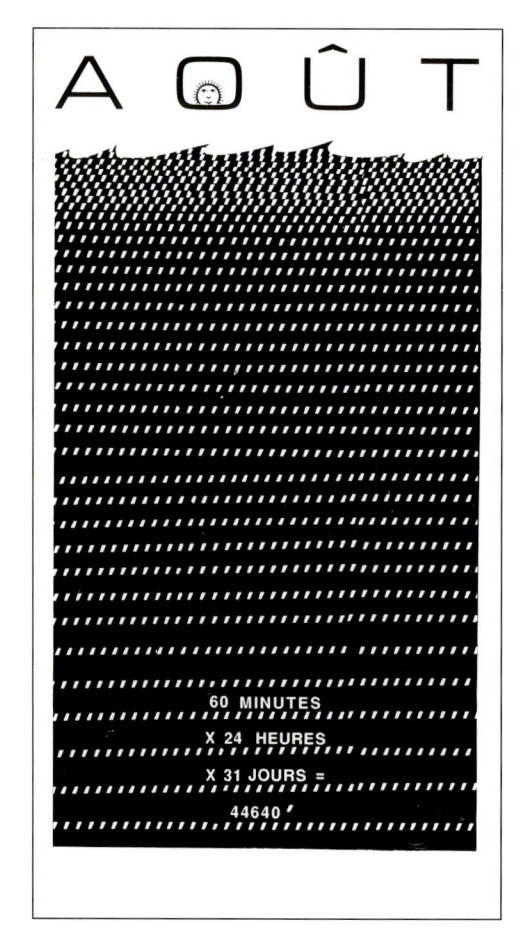

POSTCARDS

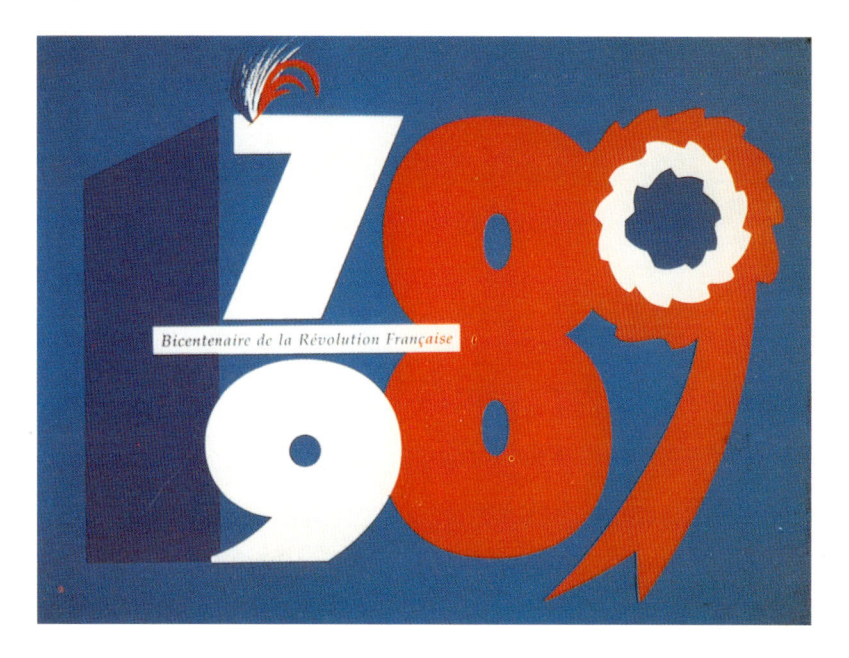

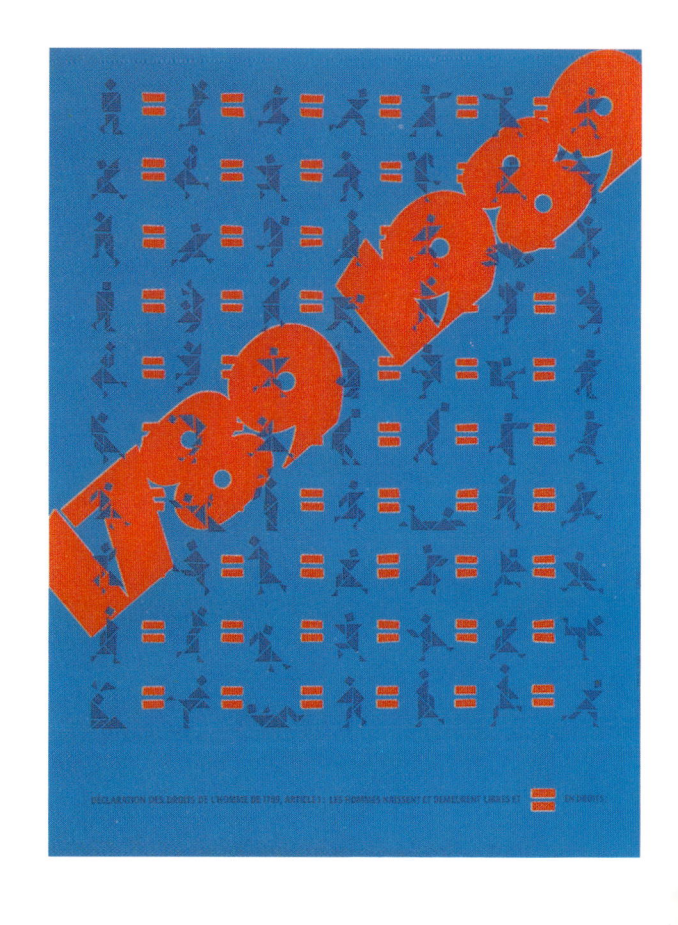

108

UWE LOESCH
Free-lance Graphic Designer
Düsseldorf, Germany

"My promotional materials include posters, which I publish from time to time under the headline 'Sign of Time.' The 'cow' was published after the Chernobyl disaster and is now in the collections of the Museum of Modern Art in New York. The dog, published with the headline 'Confidence Counts,' is a poster against the census in Germany in 1987. In the meantime it became quite up-to-date after the 'come-together-party' of East and West Germany."

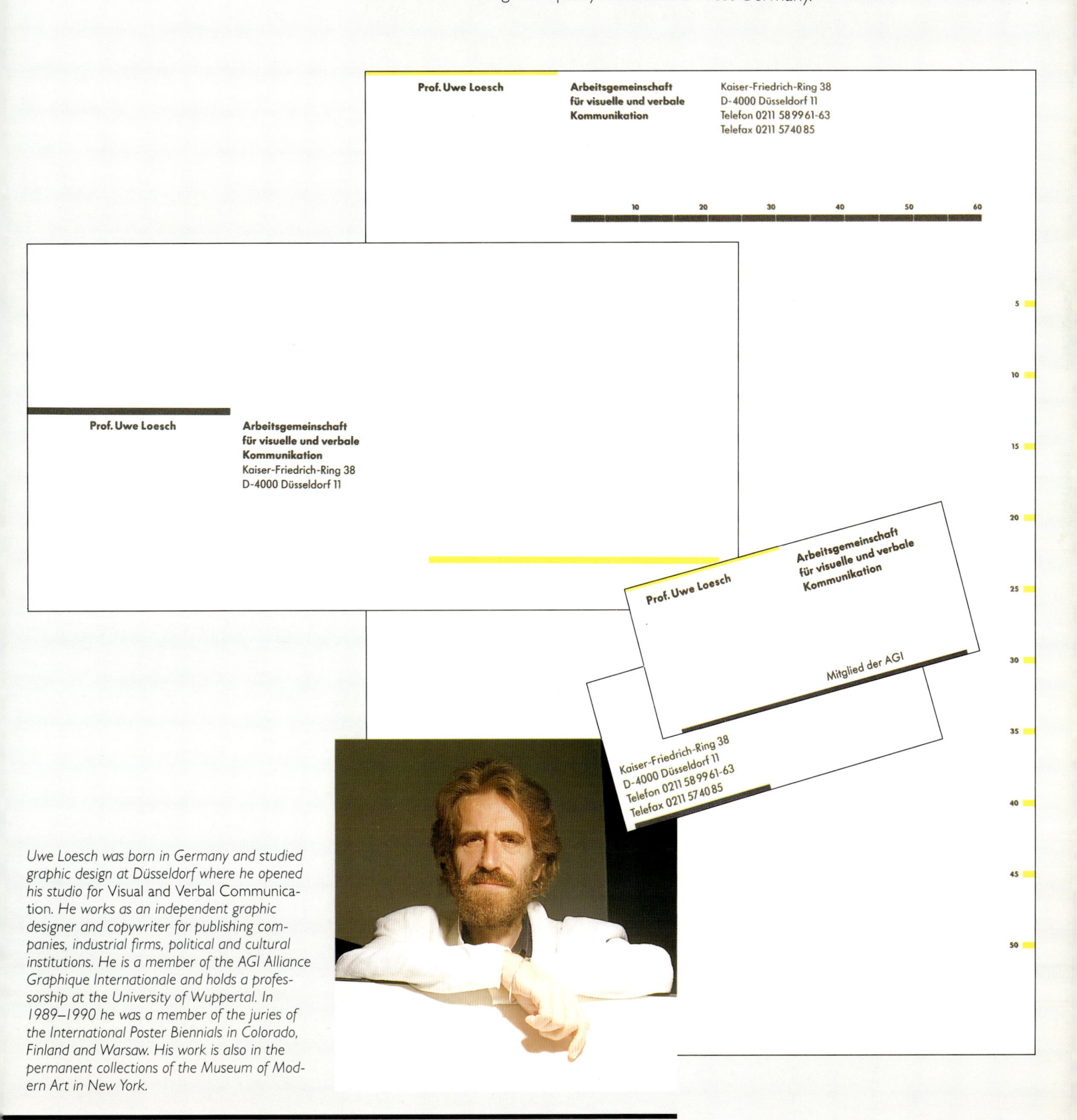

Uwe Loesch was born in Germany and studied graphic design at Düsseldorf where he opened his studio for Visual and Verbal Communication. He works as an independent graphic designer and copywriter for publishing companies, industrial firms, political and cultural institutions. He is a member of the AGI Alliance Graphique Internationale and holds a professorship at the University of Wuppertal. In 1989–1990 he was a member of the juries of the International Poster Biennials in Colorado, Finland and Warsaw. His work is also in the permanent collections of the Museum of Modern Art in New York.

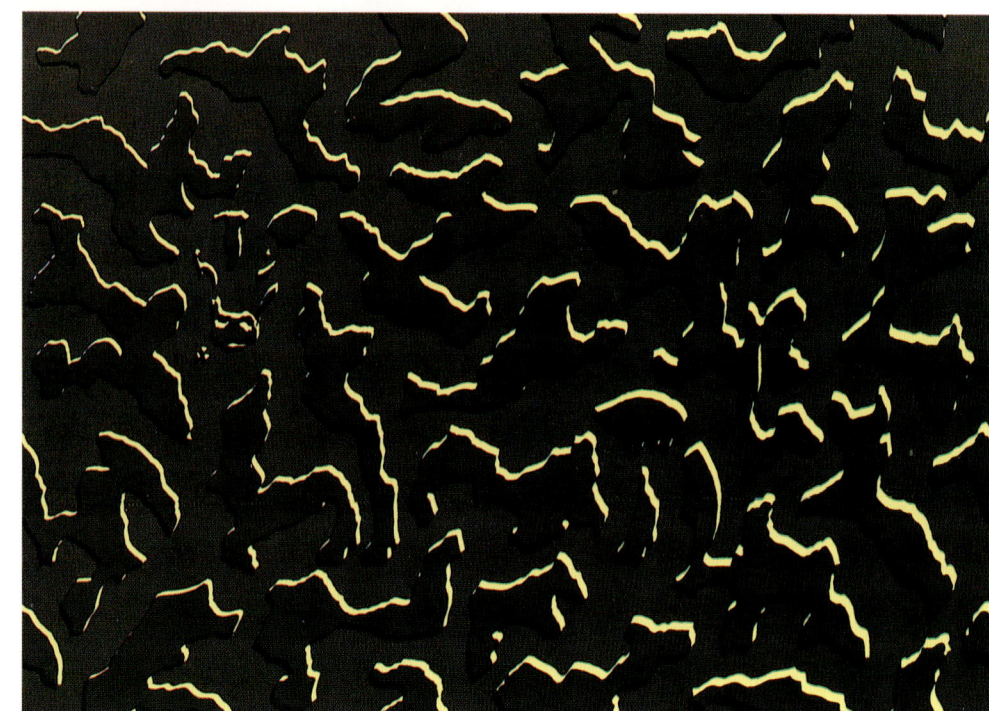

POSTERS

SAMENWERKENDE ONTWERPERS
André Toet, *Managing Director*
Amsterdam, Netherlands

"For our own stationery, we preferred a basic, businesslike look without any of the obligatory designer clichés. A low-profile stationery permits us a creative approach to the different projects we do for our clients—something which also more or less expresses itself in our SO Projectsheets—this is the 'Self Image' we send to our client or prospects once or twice a year."

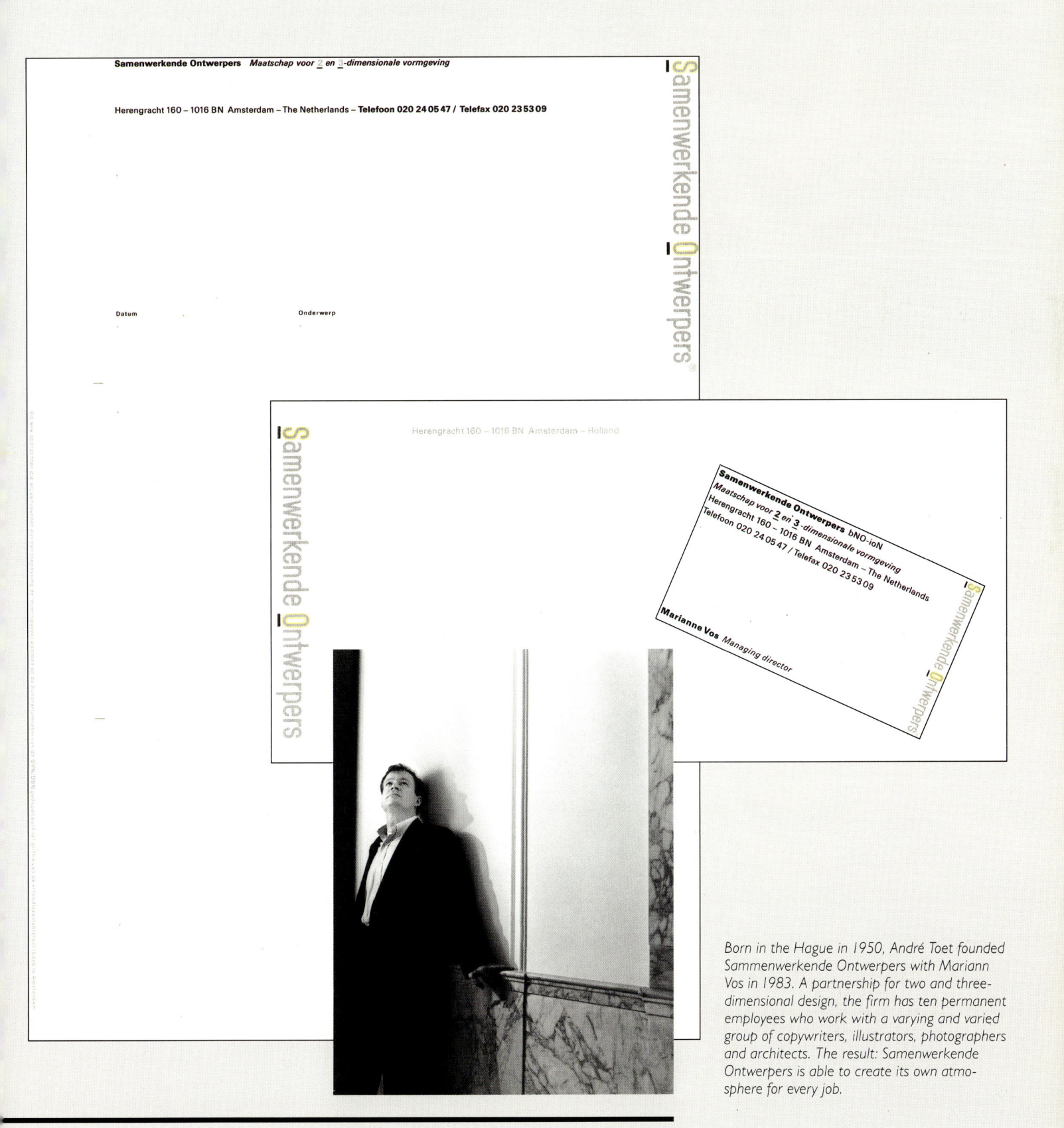

Born in the Hague in 1950, André Toet founded Sammenwerkende Ontwerpers with Mariann Vos in 1983. A partnership for two and three-dimensional design, the firm has ten permanent employees who work with a varying and varied group of copywriters, illustrators, photographers and architects. The result: Samenwerkende Ontwerpers is able to create its own atmosphere for every job.

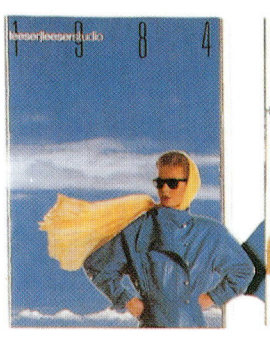

PROMOTIONAL BOOKLET

PTT/DEV

Federatie van
Kunstenaarsverenigingen/
Federation of Artist
Associations

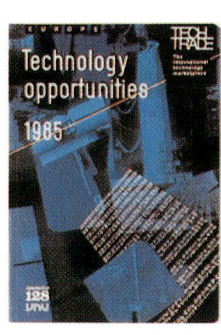

VNU Business Publications

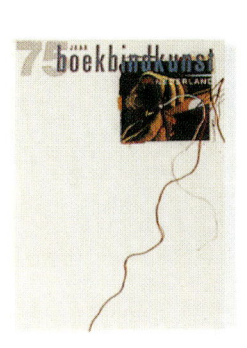

FGE/Dutch Manufacturers of
Graphic End products

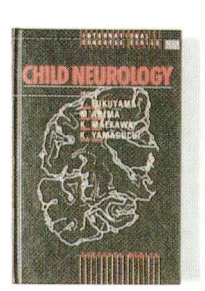

Elsevier NDU,
Excerpta Medica

Stichting
Burgerschapskunde/
Institute of Political
Education

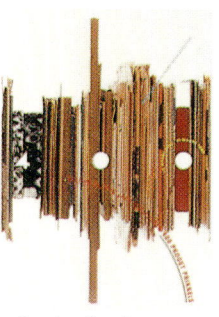

Proost en Brandt nv

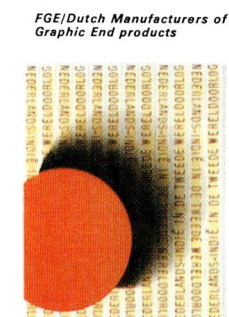

Rijksvoorlichtingsdienst/
Netherlands Information Service

Ministerie van Volkshuisvesting,
Ruimtelijke Ordening en
Milieubeheer
(Rijksgebouwendienst)/
Ministry of Housing, Physical ad
Environmental Planning
(Gouvernment Building Agency)

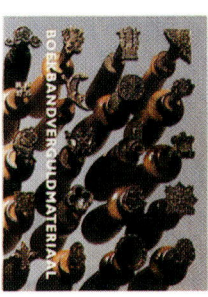

FGE/Dutch Manufacturers of
Graphic End products

Gemeente Amsterdam/
City of Amsterdam

112

SEGNO ASSOCIATI
Gelsomino D'Ambrosio, Pino Grimaldi, Owners
Salerno, Italy

"The mark of Segno Associati is an elaboration from the Apocalipsis cum solis of Albrecht Durer (Magonza, second half of fifteenth century). The sun, in a Mediterranean context, is seen as a source of infinite creative routes. A sweet irony can be caught in its particular, detached look towards the lighted things."

Gelsomino D'Ambrosio and Pino Grimaldi were both born in Salerno in 1948. In 1973 the two founded Segno Associati, a graphic design and communication firm where the contributions of both men have merged organically and inseparably. Segno Associati works in the field of image and identity research and design for Edizioni 10/17 and the magazine Grafica.

PROMOTIONAL CARDS

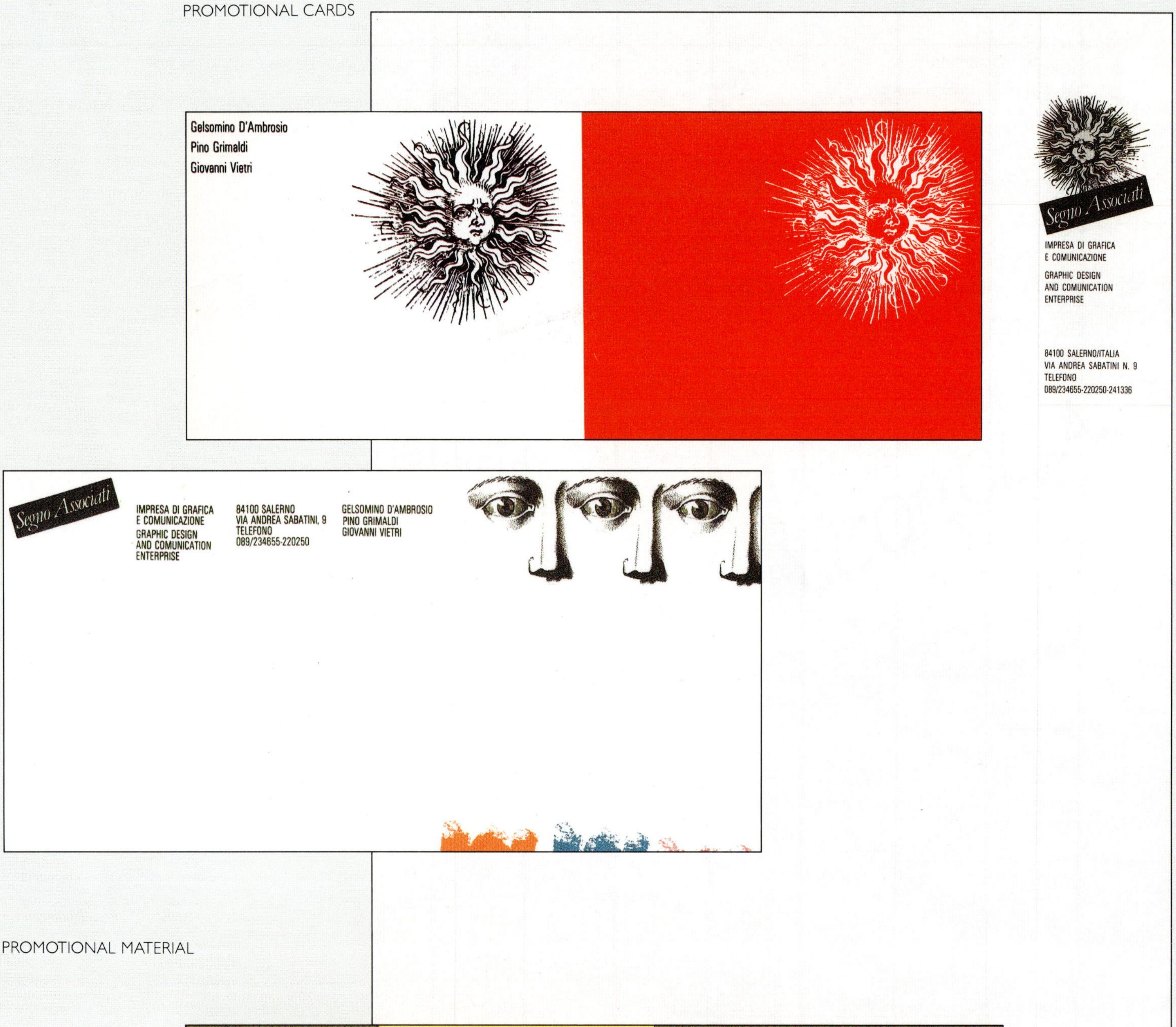

PROMOTIONAL MATERIAL

114

PROMOTIONAL CARDS

PROMOTION PIECE

Gelsomino D'Ambrosio
Pino Grimaldi

Basti Brothers
Boy Bastiaens, *Graphic Designer*
Maastricht, Netherlands

"I usually sign my illustrations with 'Basti.' For this stationery, however, I use the 'Basti Bros.' because some clients request lettering/typography work, while others specify illustration assignments (most of them prefer a combination of both). So, I decided to come up with the image of the lettering artist and the illustrator."

PROMOTIONAL MATERIAL

Since graduating in 1979 from the Municipal Academy in his hometown of Maastricht, Bastiaens has worked as a graphic designer and illustrator for various international clients such as Esprit, Lee, Wrangler, Playboy magazine, and Triton Press.

STUDIO TECNICO ASSOCIATO ARCHITETTI BOCCHIO & PALMIERI
Gabriella Bocchio, Giulio Palmieri, *Owners*
Torino, Italy

"We think that the best presentation of our activity is to be found in our ability to always give to our clients the best quality possible, either through development of the projects commissioned to us, or through the single choice of dealing with the exterior. For example, our usual New Year's gift for our clients is a pretext and vehicle for self promotion, in clear contrast to the 'pure graphic' that characterizes our stationery."

PROMOTIONAL CARD

Gabriella Bocchio and Giulio Palmieri founded their "atelier" design office in Turin, Italy, in 1984. Both graduated in architecture from the Politecnico of Turin and presently they are involved in corporate image and communication for public and private companies. In addition, they have consulted and curated graphic design in a broad range of publishing.

HOLIDAY CARD

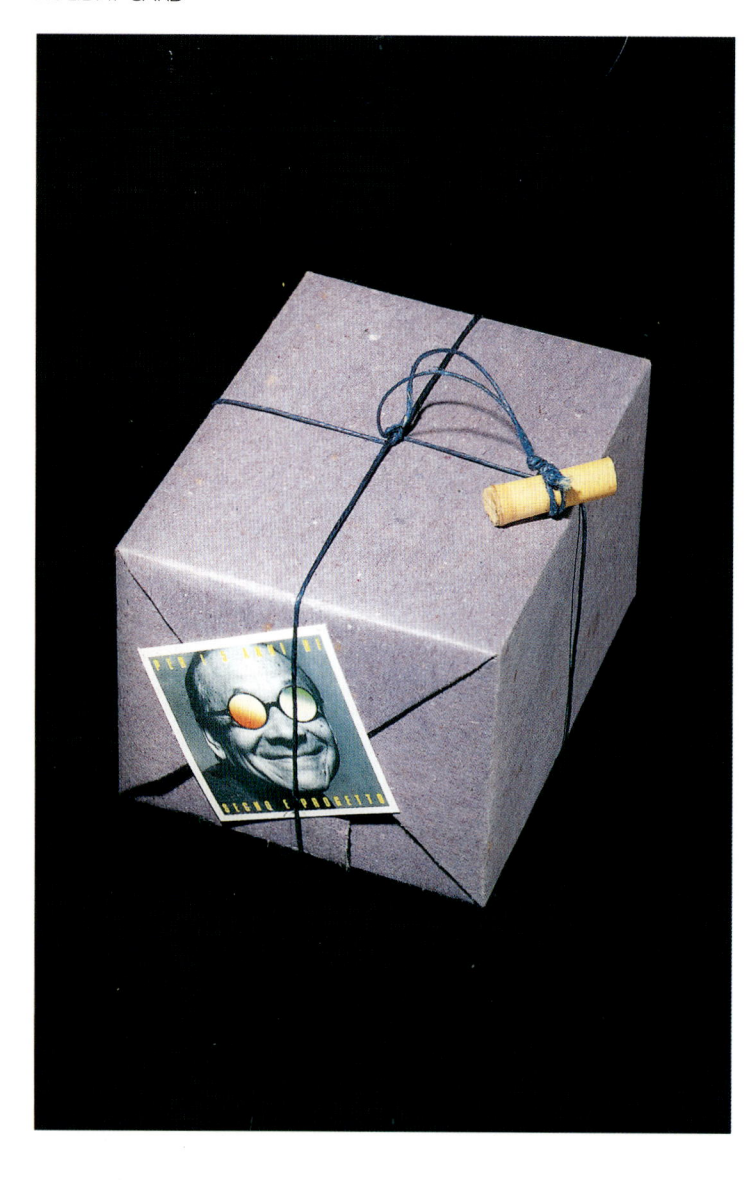

POSTER

LOGOS

RAN

Un film di
AKIRA KUROSAWA

118

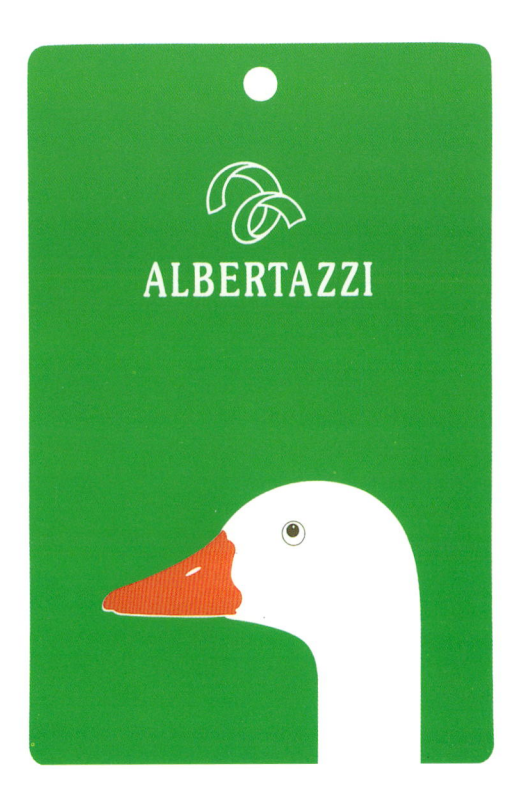

PROMOTIONAL BROCHURE

STASYS EIDRIGEVICIUS
Free-lance Artist/Illustrator
Warsaw, Poland

"I designed a series of stamps in Japan in 1980 which I use on my letters, drawings, name cards and autographs. Each stamp features my name, Stasy, which has three elements: a star, a book and a nest."

A master of small graphic forms, Stasys often fuses the animate with the inanimate in his work which abounds in surrealistic ideas.

POSTCARD

After attending Lithuania's School of Applied Arts and Fine Arts Institute, Eidrigevicius settled with his wife and three children in Warsaw, Poland where he has worked as a free-lance artist and illustrator since 1973. The recipient of numerous national and international honors, he was awarded both the Grand Prix at Triennale of Small Graphics Forms of the Baltic Countries in Latvia, and the IX Premio for Juvenile Literature in Italy in 1983. He received Communication Arts' Award of Excellence in 1985.

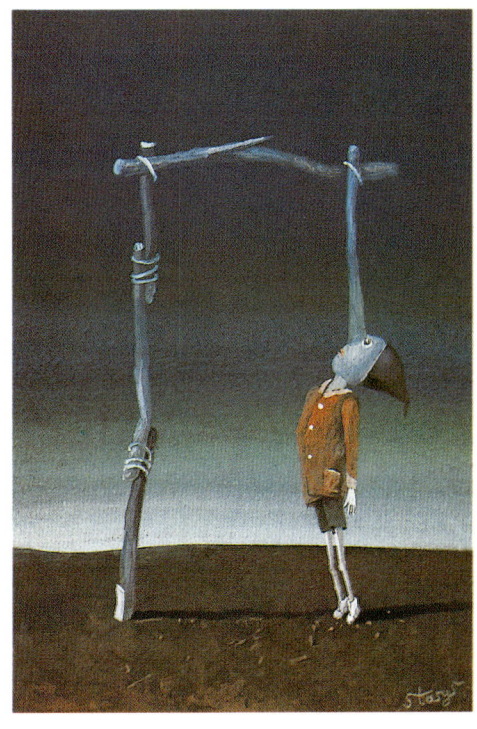

PROMOTIONAL CARDS AND PHOTOGRAPH

121

ANTERO FERREIRA DESIGN
Antero Ferreira, *Art Director*
Oporto, Portugal

"I created this first self visual image in 1989 for my first solo exhibition. The 'Eye' (my eye) represents, for me, the most important and the first step in my work—observation."

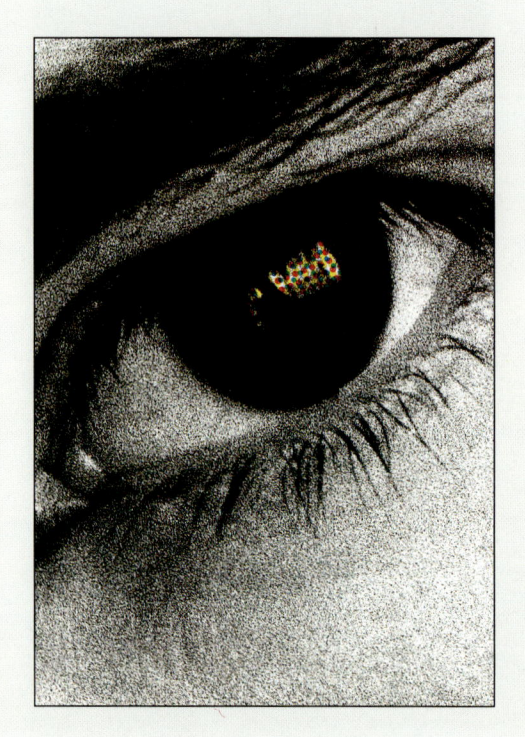

POSTCARD

CONVITE

A Escola Superior de Belas Artes do Porto tem o prazer de convidar V. Ex.ª para a inauguração da Exposição ANTERO FERREIRA DESIGN que se realiza no dia 10 de Julho de 1989 (Seg.-Feira), pelas 22h00 no Museu da ESBAP, Avenida Rodrigues de Freitas 265 4000 Porto.

Residing in Oporto, Portugal, Antero Ferreira runs his own studio and also teaches graphic design at two eminent learning institutions. In 1991 he was invited to act as visiting designer at the Nova Scotia College of Art and Design in Canada. His many awards include: the Salon International de l'Affiche (France, 1990), XIII International Poster Biennale (Warsaw, 1990), and the XIV Biennale of Graphic Design (Brno, Czechoslovakia, 1990).

PORTFOLIO

HELEN MUNRO

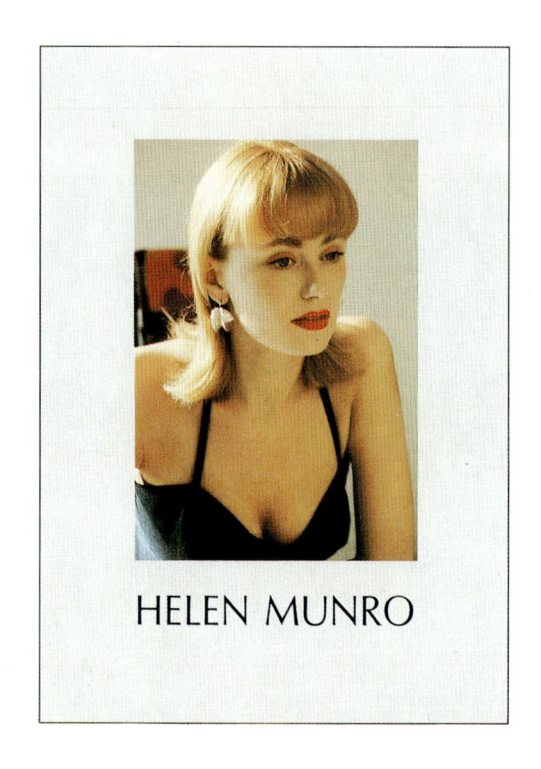

PORTFOLIO

PORTFOLIO

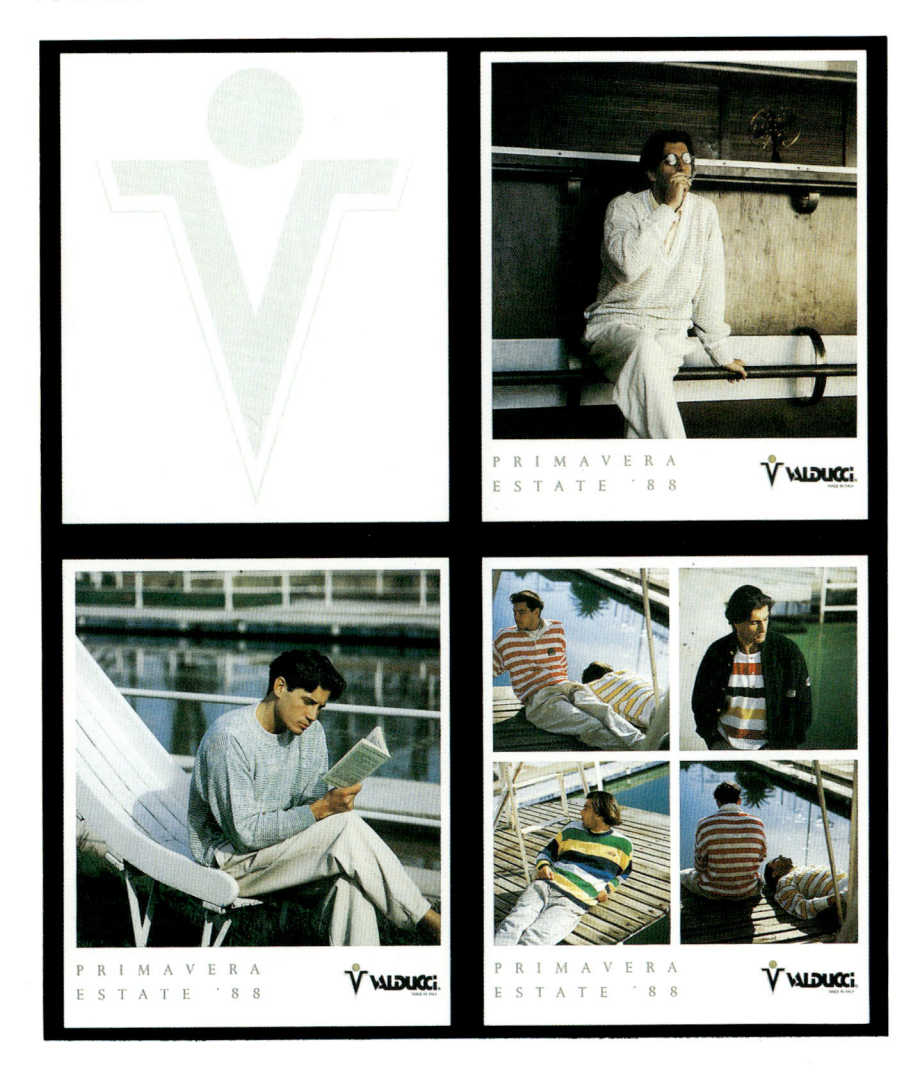

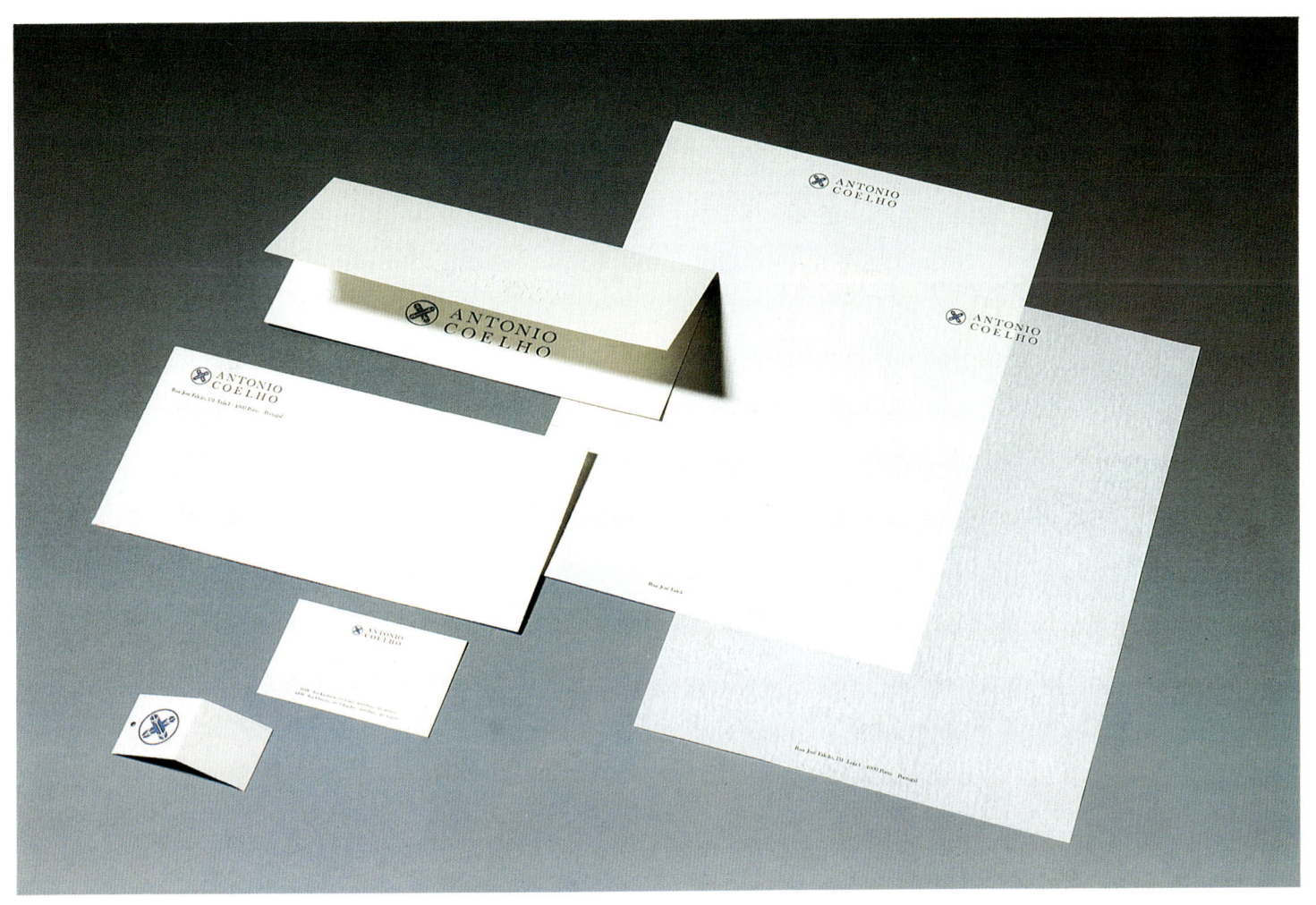

PORTFOLIO

FANTASPORTO '89 IX FESTIVAL INTERNACIONAL DE CINEMA DO PORTO

3/12 FEVEREIRO · AUDITÓRIO NACIONAL CARLOS ALBERTO E CINEMAS LUMIÉRE

VICTOR HUGO

126

PENCIL CORPORATE ART
Achim Kiel, *Art Director*
Brunswick, Germany

"Today the pencil is what the quill was in earlier times—the simplest and most common tool for the visualization of ideas and messages. The word 'PENCIL' is the pseudonym of the founder of the studio, his second name being Kiel, which is derived from the German word for QUILL."

"On our letterhead we use black exclusively, as it is the classic printing color for typography and it exudes the air of seriousness. The embossed inkblot is the creative counterpart, an indication of the lighthearted, sometimes playful component that is typical of our artistic work."

"A very important aspect of design for every business paper is the use of the typewriter. Although, from a typographic point of view, most typewriters employ almost unacceptable bastardized characters, we emphasize that as a first criterion a typeface family should be chosen that is represented on the letterhead already."

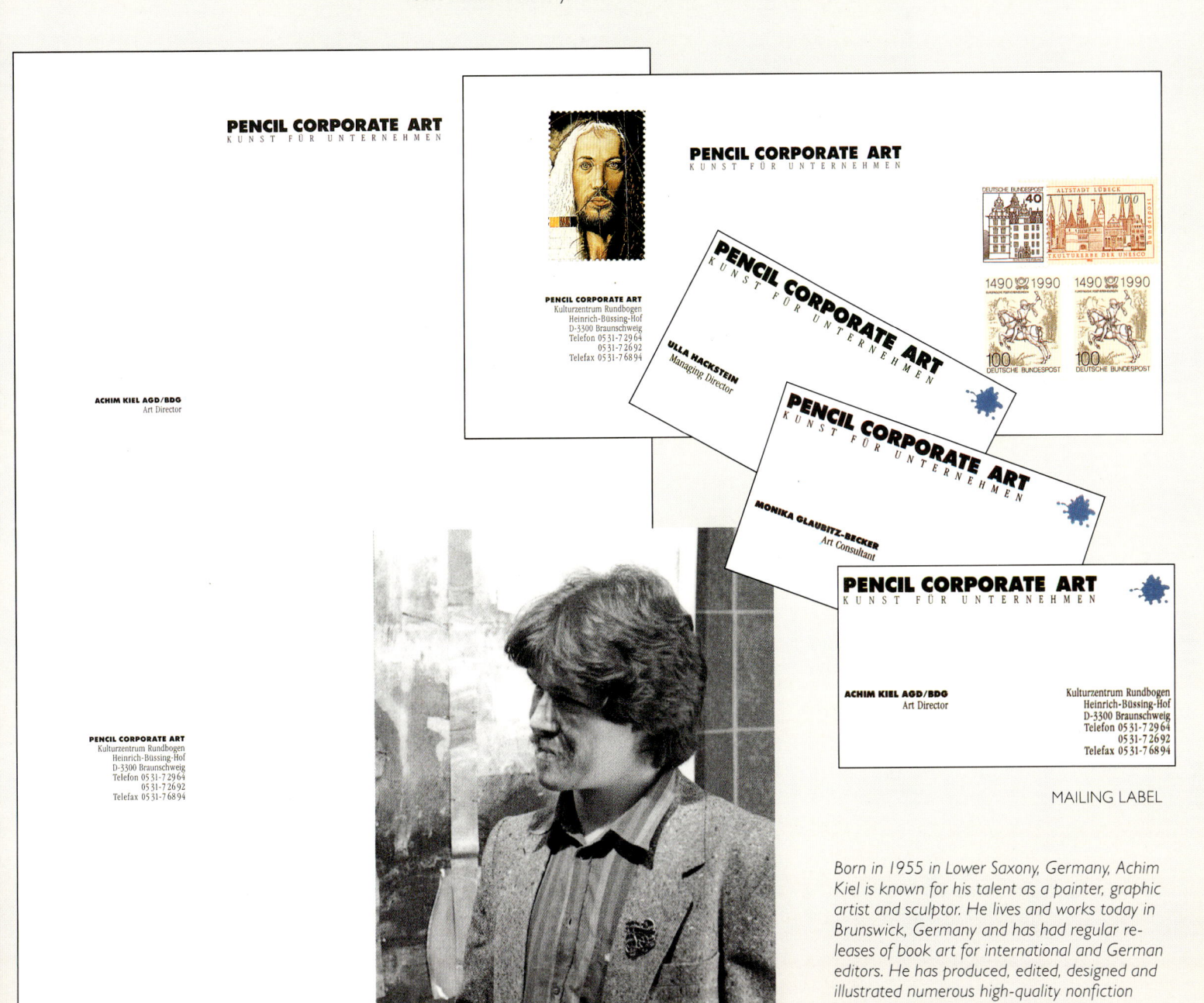

MAILING LABEL

Born in 1955 in Lower Saxony, Germany, Achim Kiel is known for his talent as a painter, graphic artist and sculptor. He lives and works today in Brunswick, Germany and has had regular releases of book art for international and German editors. He has produced, edited, designed and illustrated numerous high-quality nonfiction books. Kiel has received fifteen awards and medals at international competitions for his fine art and design.

PORTFOLIO

ROCK POP JAZZ KLASSIK UNERHÖRT

Detlev Kutscher auf der Spur von Grenzgängern im musikalischen Niemandsland

Herbert von Karajan dirigiert Werke von den Sex Pistols: Der Skandalhit der englischen Krawall-Punkband „God shave the Queen", eingespielt von den Berliner Symphonikern und dem spätpubertierenden Sängerknaben Peter Hofmann als Leadsänger. Ein raffiniertes Horrorszenario?

Mit Sicherheit nicht. Solche peinlichen Ausflüge sind Legion in der an Attraktionen gewiß nicht armen Geschichte von den Wanderern zwischen den Musikwelten.

Aber nicht nur Aufnahmen von Grenzgängern, die das hehre Reich der E-Musik fliehen und in die niederen Sphären der sogenannten U-Musik steigen, liegen in den Auslagen der Plattengeschäfte. Jazzer versuchen sich in der Klassik, Rockmusiker blasen ihre eher ärmlichen Kompositionen mit schwülstigen Streicherarrangements auf, und schließlich versuchen sich jene im Musikgeschäft, die fern aller Dogmen neue Klangwelten erforschen. Finden solche Grenzgänger überhaupt Platz in einem Musikbetrieb, der, sklavisch abhängig von den Hitparadenplazierungen, jedes Experiment scheut? Sicher ist, daß die ungewöhnlichen Grenzgänger nur ein Nischenpublikum finden, wenn sie überhaupt je auf der Bühne stehen, sicher ist auch, daß gerade solche Grenzgänge à la „Klassik meets Rock" durchaus die Hitparaden anführen können. Es sei hier nur an die ärgerlichen Aufnahmen „Rock meets Klassik" der Londoner Symphoniker erinnert. Von Peter Hofmanns verlorengeglaubter Jugend atemlos hinterhergehechelten „Rockklassics"-LPs einmal ganz abgesehen. Hofmann, mit Sicherheit einer der besten Wagner-Tenöre des Kontinents, begibt sich auf einen Boden, auf dessen von ihm angelegter Schleimspur sich jeder Rocksong die musikalischen Gräten bricht. Und bitte, es rede doch niemand von Richard Clydermann. Der blonde Elsässer soll ja angeblich klassische Klavierkonzerte zum besten geben, wobei sich Klassik ja wohl eher auf den klassisch geschmacklosen roten Frack bezieht, den er zu tragen pflegt. Dann schon lieber Liberace, den größten musikalischen Weichspüler aller Zeiten. Der kürzlich an AIDS verstorbene, aus Ungarn stammende amerikanische Superstar hatte wenigstens die Chuzpe, absolut jeden Schönton zu horrenden Preisen zu verkaufen und damit eher sein Publikum als sich selbst lächerlich zu machen.

Aber bei aller Arroganz, selbst diese monetaristisch orientierten Musiker dürfen sich durchaus das Signum des musikalischen Grenzgängers ans Revers heften - freilich dürfte ihnen ein Platz in der „Hall of Fame" von den strengen Türstehern auf immer ver-

wehrt werden. Schließlich reicht der Raum ja kaum für jene, die sogenannte große Kunst auf ihre Fahnen schreiben. Und dann bewirbt sich noch eine Spezies um ehrenvolle Aufnahme, deren musikalischer Output sich jeglicher Schönfärberei entzieht. Zugang zu den anderen, den Lauten, Mutigen, Schrillen und Unbequemen findet aber nur, wer den aufregend gefahrvollen Weg ins Unbekannte wagt. Friedrich Gulda, einer der wohl besten Mozart-Interpreten unserer Tage, spricht vom „Land des Unerhörten". Einer Musiklandschaft, die den Hörer „plötzlich aus gewohnter Umgebung wie von wunderbarer Hand auf eine schöne Blumenwiese versetzt".

Gulda, dieser genialische Clown der Klassik, dieser innovative Witzbold, hat sich genug in jenes Land fern aller bekannten Dogmen begeben. Seine Einspielungen „Liberation" und „Concerto für Ursula", eröffnen neue Klangräume, regen auf, stoßen ab und erheitern, aber hinterlassen niemals Leere und Gleichgültigkeit.

Zugegeben, gerade „Liberation" gebärdet sich besonders sperrig, und das „Konzert für Violoncello und Blasorchester" erinnert fatal an die halbherzigen Experimente der englischen Hardrock-Band Deep Purple mit den Londoner Symphonikern. Doch dann: Ein „Concerto für Ursula", das auch atemberaubenden Slalomläufen durch alle Musikstile schließlich in einem orgiastischen Jodler endet - wer da nicht lauthals auflacht, sollte seine musikalische Heimat bei Clydermann und Konsorten suchen.

Und auf keinen Fall in den Klangwelten des amerikanischen Streichquartetts Kronos. Diese Musiker, laut New York Times die „bemerkenswerteste Live-Gruppe" der Vereinigten Staaten, scheut keine Risiken. Sie entführt den Zuhörer in die wunderbar schräge Welt der Dissonanzen in einer Art und Weise, wie sie bislang von keiner Kapelle zu hören war. Selbst in den wildesten Kaskaden sich überschlagender Kakophonien, selbst in der Interpretation des Jimi Hendrix-Klassiker Purple Haze, verliert das Quartett nie den Überblick. Innerhalb kürzester Zeit reichen sie dem Zuhörer wieder die Hand, verführen ihn mit sanften, wunderschönen Melodiebögen, um ihn blitzschnell danach mit dem lauten und asthmatischen Krächzen eines verstimmten Cellos wieder am Boden festzunageln.

Dieses musikalische Experiment, Zucker, Brot und Peitsche-Philosophen musikalisch einzukleiden, ist mit Sicherheit gelungen, wenn auch manchmal schwer verdaulich.

Ebenso wie Gulda und die Kronos-Streicher durchlebt auch die griechische Sopranistin

26 27

UNERHÖRT Doppelseitige Aufmacher-Illustration in einem deutschen Kultur-Magazin zum Thema GRENZGÄNGER IN DER MUSIK: Klassik-Interpreten, die zum Saxophon greifen und Jazzer mit Frack und Violine. Paradebeispiel: FRIEDRICH GULDA. Die bewußt dissonanten, *farbigen Querschläger* im unteren Bildrand orientieren sich dennoch an den Achsen der Körper und Instrumente. U.a. fand die vorliegende Arbeit Eingang in ein mehrsprachiges Jahrbuch der redaktionellen Grafik.

UNHEARD OF A double page illustration for a german cultural magazine taking the theme FRONTIER BREAKERS IN MUSIC. The picture plays with the contrasts between classical and jazz musicians juxtaposing their integrating in both forms of music. Intentional dissonance is introduced by the *coloured splashes* at the bottom of the picture. These never-the-less are orientated according to the axes formed by the musicians bodies and instruments. Amongst other things this work has found a place in a multilingual editorial art annual.

■ 20 LAGEBERICHT BILANZSUMME MRD DM

IM GESCHÄFTSJAHR 1987 KONNTE DIE DG HYP IM DARLEHENSNEUGESCHÄFT NICHT AN DAS AUSSERORDENTLICH HOHE VORJAHRESVOLUMEN ANKNÜPFEN. TROTZ DER GÜNSTIGEN ZINSENTWICKLUNG.

Die gesamten Darlehenszusagen von 4,4 Mrd DM blieben um 1,0 Mrd DM unter dem Vorjahreswert. Infolge stark gestiegener Darlehenstilgung nahm die Bilanzsumme nur noch um 1,6% auf 33,2 Mrd DM zu. Andererseits konnte die Bank ihre Ertragslage deutlich verbessern und die Ertragskraft früherer Jahre zurückgewinnen. Der Jahresüberschuß wird mit 70 Mio DM nach 50 Mio DM im Vorjahr ausgewiesen. Das geringere Neugeschäft betraf allein die Hypothekendarlehen. Mit 15.300 (V.J. 22.000) Zusagen in Höhe von 1,8 Mrd DM lagen die Neuausleihungen um 1,0 DM oder 36 % unter den Vorjahreszahlen. Hierzu trug vor allem die hohe Liquiditätsausstattung der Volksbanken und Raiffeisenbanken bei, die wegen ihres allgemein rückläufigen Kreditgeschäftes in erheblichem Umfange die langfristigen Finanzierungen selbst übernahmen.

1979 ■ 16,3 1981 ■ 21,8 1983 ■ 26,4 1985 ■ 30,5 1987 ■ 33,2

BUSINESS REPORT An eyecatching double page spread from a business report for a bank society. The complete design consists of three dimensional *tableaus* within which can be found differing topographic planes allowing for a relevant but stimulating text layout. As an alternative to conventional graphic display of economic data *building type* structures are used - a metaphor for the *companys' business*. The chronological order of the accounts is represented by the equivalence of their growth from the picture's backround into the present.

GESCHÄFTSBERICHT Aufmacher-Doppelseite aus dem Geschäftsbericht einer Hypothekenbank. Der gesamte Seitenaufbau besteht aus dreidimensionalen *Tableaus*, deren verschiedene topografische Ebenen eine sachliche, aber dennoch aufmerksamkeitsfördernde Textgestaltung ermöglichen. Anstelle der konventionellen grafischen Darstellung der wirtschaftlichen Daten erscheinen hier plastische *Baukörper* - eine Metapher für den *Gegenstand des Unternehmens*. Der zeitlichen Reihenfolge der Bilanzsummen entspricht das phasenweise Herauswachsen dieser Quader aus dem Bild-Hintergrund in die Gegenwart.

128

PORTFOLIO

GRAN TURISMO A lithograph especially designed for a collector of classic two-seater sports cars and oldtimers. In the brightly lit almost museum-like atmosphere of an empty workshop the worth of this Lotus Elite is enhanced through it's powerful colour and daring design transforming this production line car into a work of art. This 6-colour lithograph has become a much sought after collectors item, especially in Great Britain and the United States through automobile clubs and special interest magazines.

GRAN TURISMO Druckgrafik-Edition eines Sammlers klassischer zweisitziger Sportwagen und Oldtimer. In der hellen, fast musealen Atmosphäre des leeren Werkstattraumes erfährt dieser Lotus Elite gerade wegen seiner kräftigen Farbe und des mutigen Ausschnittes eine Aufwertung, die das Serienprodukt Automobil mit einem Kunstobjekt gleichsetzt. Die 6farbige Lithografie wurde vor allem in England und den USA durch Automobilclubs und Special Interest Magazine zum begehrten Sammelobjekt.

FACTORY ARCHITECTURE The Hofbrauhaus Wolters is part of an original print edition entitled Securing the Evidence, a lavish work on the theme of *19th century industrial culture* in Braunschweig. The six multicolour etchings were designed following extensive archival research and on site observation. They not only document the architectural remains of the *industrial era* in Germany, but offer over and above this, through sketches and quotations, insights into the architectural concept and former function of these buildings. Several museums and national archives have included this print edition in their collections. The pictures also hang in the executive suites of prominent companies and are presented as gifts at official occasions by the city of Braunschweig.

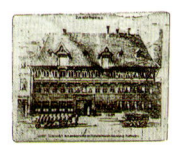

FABRIK-ARCHITEKTUR Das Hofbrauhaus Wolters aus der Druckgrafik-Edition Spurensicherung, einem aufwendigen Mappenwerk zur *Industriekultur des 19. Jhd.* in Braunschweig. Die 6 mehrfarbigen Radierungen entstanden nach intensiven Recherchen in Archiven und vor Ort. Sie dokumentieren nicht nur einen baulichen Restbestand der *industriellen Gründerzeit* in Deutschland, sondern bieten darüberhinaus durch Skizzen und Zitate Einblicke in das architektonische Konzept und die ehemalige Funktion der Anlagen. Mehrere Museen und Staatsarchive haben diese Edition in ihre Sammlungen aufgenommen, sie hängt in den Vorstandsetagen bedeutender Unternehmen und wird von der Stadt Braunschweig als Präsent bei offiziellen Anlässen eingesetzt.

TRIPTYCHON Tafelbild 1989. Tischtuch, Glas und Bestecke Mitte 19. Jhd. Tintenfaß und Fayence-Fragment 18. Jhd., Sand und Steine noch älter. Federn, Krebs, Wein und Brot sind neuzeitlich; auf Holz. 100 x 200 x 15 cm

TRIPTYCHON Panelpicture 1989. Table cloth, glass and cutlery from middle 19th C. Inkwell and Fayence fragment 18th C., even older sand and stones. Feathers, crab, wine and bread – modern; on wood. 100 x 200 x 15 cms

131

PORTFOLIO

SCHOLEM ALEJCHEM ist einer der erfolgreichsten Schriftsteller jiddischer Literatur. Weltberühmt wurde er durch das Broadway-Musical ANATEVKA, einer amerikanischen Fassung seines Romans TEWJE DER MILCHMANN. Das Titelbild oben stammt aus einer homogenen Reihe von Buchillustrationen zu Klassikern der jüdischen Weltliteratur, denen es gelingt, durch Farben und Ductus die mystisch-skurile Atmosphäre der jiddischen Erzählungen authentisch einzufangen. Zusammen mit diesem Portrait gingen über 100 weitere Buchkunst-Arbeiten zu Texten von POE, HEMINGWAY, TRAVEN, DE MAURIER u.v.a. auf eine dreijährige Ausstellungstournee durch Europa.

SCHOLEM ALEJCHEM is one of the most successful writers in Jewish literature. He became world famous through the Broadway musical ANATEVKA, an american version of his novel TEWJE THE MILKMAN. To create the authenticity the cover above, one from a series of book illustrations for the classics of Jewish world literature, through colour and form enshrines the mystical yet rather droll qualities to be found in Jewish stories. This portrait was one of over 100 book illustrations for works by POE, HEMINGWAY, TRAVEN, DE MAURIER and other well known authors, that went on a three year exhibition tour of Europe.

PORTFOLIO

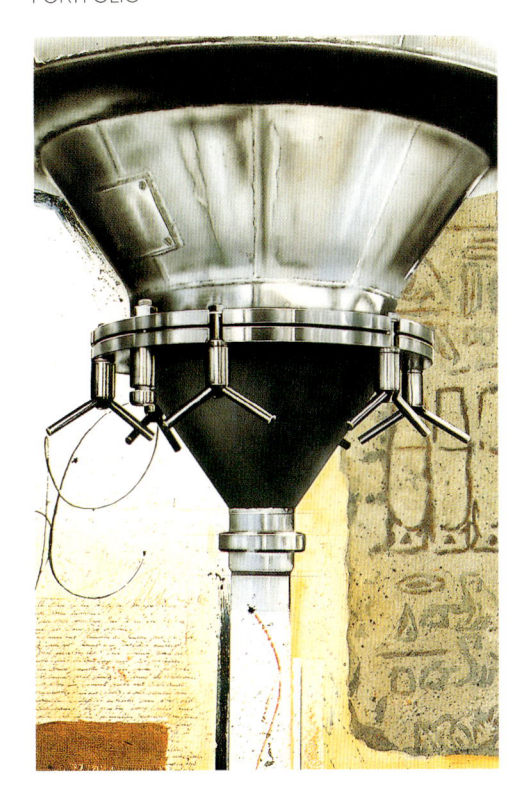

UdSSR-KAI Titel-Illustration für eine Projekt-Studie der Hansestadt Lübeck. Im Wettbewerb mit anderen Ostseestädten plant die Stadt Lübeck den Bau umfangreicher Hafen- und Bahnanlagen, um Anlaufpunkt für Eisenbahnfähren aus der UDSSR zu werden. Die bautechnischen Datenblätter und Pläne der Studie sind durch attraktive Fotoseiten und Essays mit Informations- und Unterhaltungswert ergänzt. Empfänger der in kleiner Auflage produzierten Entscheidungshilfe ist die wirtschaftliche und politische Führung der Sowjetunion, inbesondere Michail Gorbatschow.

USSR QUAY A cover illustration for a study of the Hanseatic town of Lübeck. In competition with other Baltic seaports, the city of Lübeck has extensive plans for a port and rail terminal designed as part of a mayor rail/ferry link with the USSR. The construction plans and technical data used in this study are enhanced by the inclusion of attractive photographs along with informative and interesting articles. This limited publication is being received by the industrial and political elite of the Soviet Union, notably Mikhail Gorbachev.

PORTFOLIO

THE PREMINGER ART COLLECTION

Die Bilder Skulpturen und Objekte von ACHIM KIEL in der Galerie des Hauses PREMINGER in Hannover

The pictures sculptures and objects by ACHIM KIEL at the gallery of the house of PREMINGER in Hannover

134

DER KREIS Anzeige und Karte zur Jahreswende für einen internationalen Apothekeneinrichter. Glänzende Stahlkugeln umkreisen als Planeten ihr astrologisches Zentrum, die Erde – hier: ein flacher Kieselstein, umstellt von einer Art STONEHENGE aus schweren, *bleiernen* Tierkreiszeichen. Ein dynamisches Netz von Drähten und Fäden überzieht das Ordnungsprinzip des Kreises in den verschiedensten Richtungen, knüpft an alte Verbindungen wieder an, weist neue Wege und bildet dabei die künftigen Konstellationen.

THE ZODIAC A promotional Christmas and New Years greetings card for an international pharmacy outfitters. Gleaming steel balls circle like planets around their terrestrial center the earth, symbolized here by a flat pebble, surrounded in turn by the signs of the Zodiac set in *leaden stones* reminiscent of STONEHENGE. A dynamic network of wires and threads laid in various directions overrides the fundamental order of the circle, re-establishing old ties, indicating new destinations and so forming the future constellations.

STUDIO KROG
Edi Berk, *President*
Ljubljana, Yugoslavia

"**S**tationery, especially a business card, is your first direct contact with your client. The design, color and type all convey information that can tell a lot about the bearer. Our logo is a lost pencil that found its home in a circle (KROG means circle). He was very happy to find us and we like him."

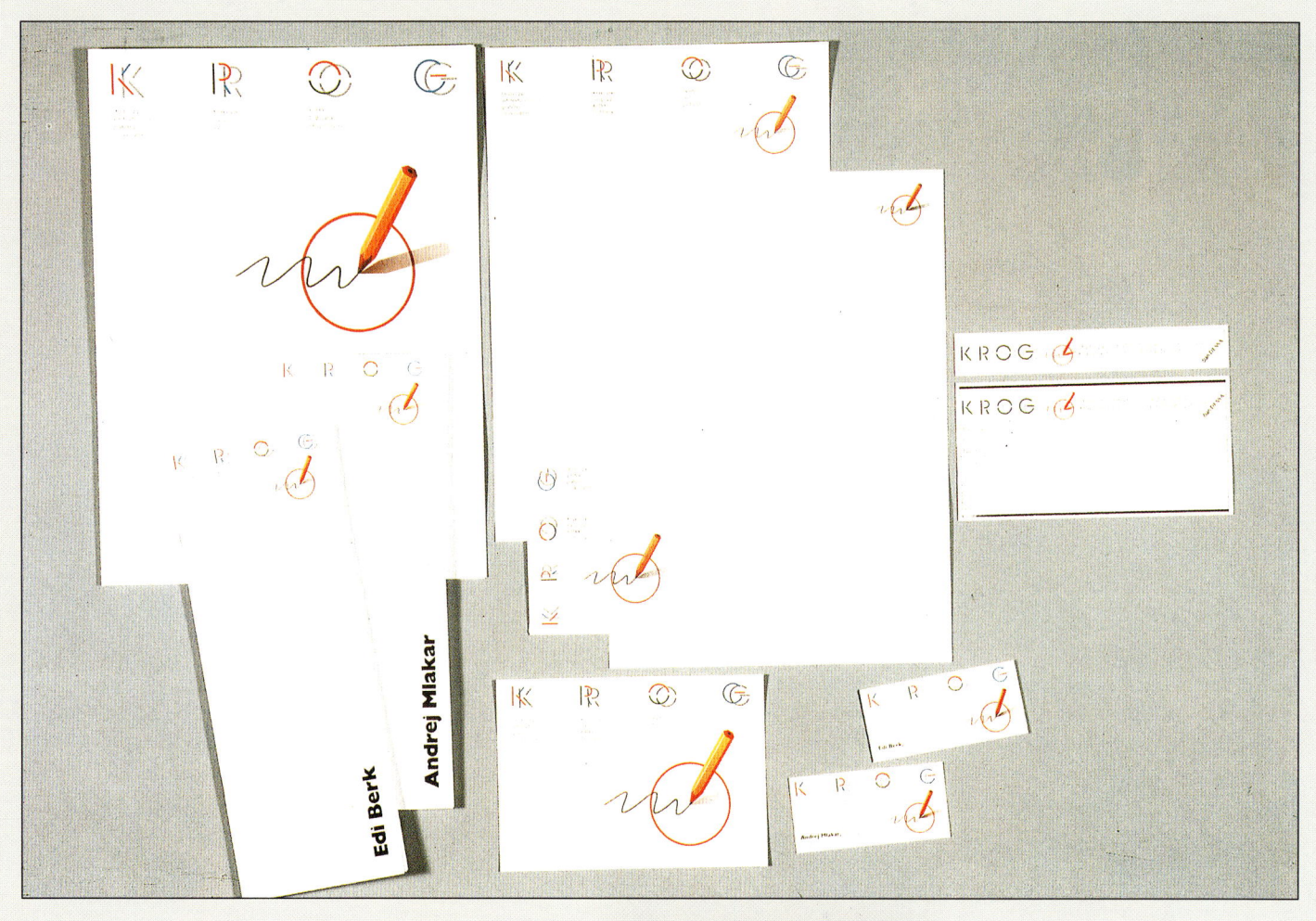

A graduate of the Faculty of Architecture in Ljubljana, Yugoslavia, Edi Berk founded Studio KROG in 1982. Andrej Mlakar joined the firm in 1984. Studio KROG develops architectural and graphic design solutions for corporate clients.

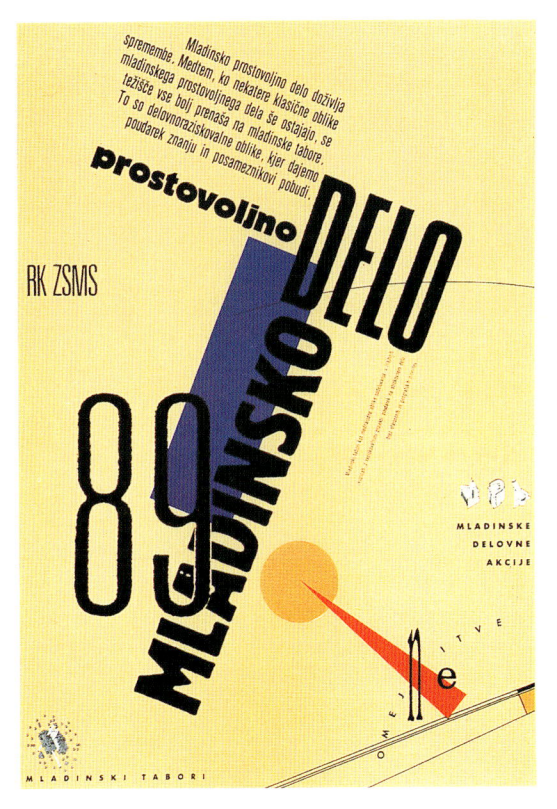

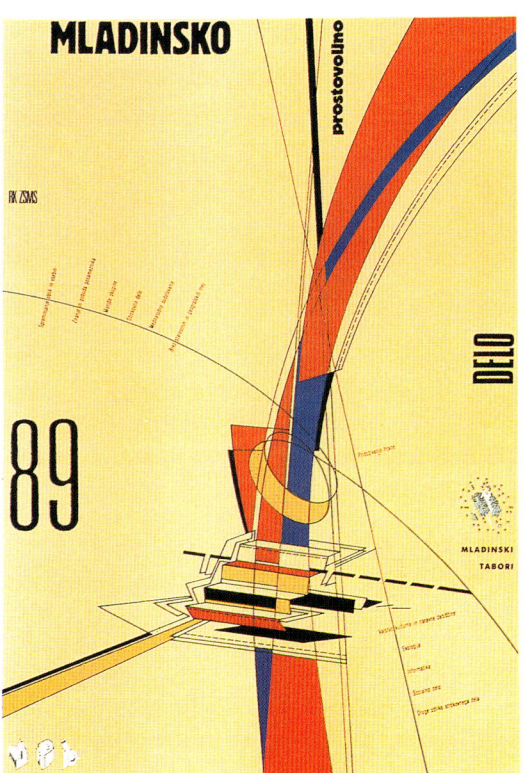

KROG PORTFOLIO

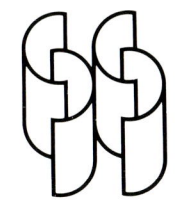

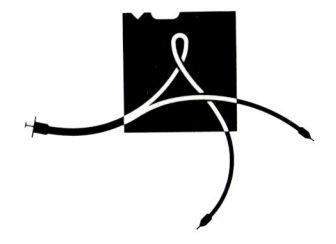

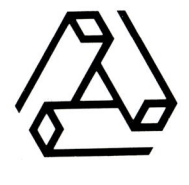

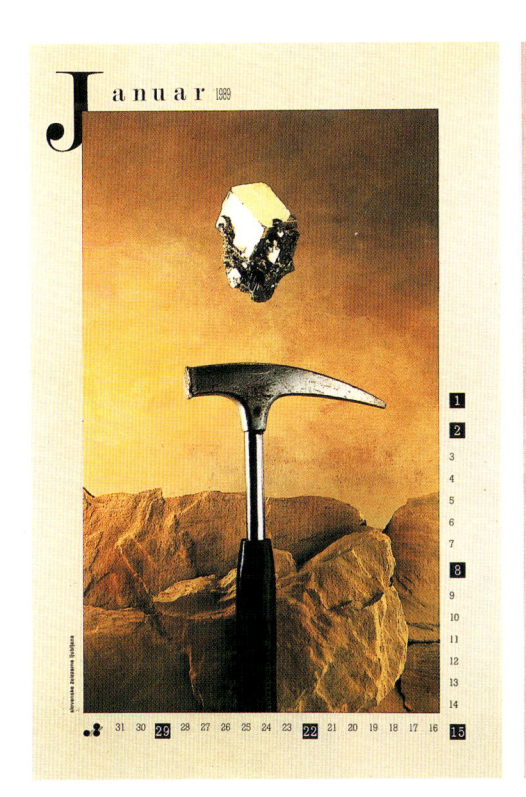

T.A. LEWANDOWSKI

Designer
Paris, France

"I have never designed my own letterhead; however, I have had many opportunities to design posters for my own exhibitions. For the past ten years I have been playing with letters, adding arms and legs…so they look like dancing cossacks. I named the alphabet, 'Dancing Kosak's [sic] Alphabet.'"

"At last, in 1989 I had the opportunity to design a typographic image and all its applications (logo, letterhead, calling cards, posters, etc.) for the project '17 Articles for '89' celebrating the Bicentennial of the French Revolution. The work received a Silver Medal at the Brno Biennale in Czechoslovakia in 1990."

T-SHIRT

PROMOTIONAL CARD

PHOTO: © M. QUENNEVILLE

Born in Poland, Lewandowski has lived and worked in Paris since 1967. He teaches at the National School of Art, Clergy-Pontoise and has won many distinctions including New York Art Directors Club awards and a Silver Medal at the last Brno Biennale in Czechoslovakia.

POSTCARDS: ALPHAFEET

| Above | Baby | Cool! | Dance | E.T. | Free | Go! | Help! | Idea | Jogging |

ABCDEFGHIJ

| Aïe! | Baba | Chiche | Dada | E.T. | Faux | Gaieté | Hourra! | Idem | Judo |

| O.K.! | Punch | Quick | Rock'n'roll | K.O. | Love | Mickey | Nothing |

OPQR KLMN

| Oh! | Passion! | Quoi? | Rage | Kif-kif | Lapsus | Machin | Non |

| Sorry! | Twist | Ugly | Vodka | Western | X-rays | Yes! | Zigzag |

STUV WXYZ

| Sexe | Terrible | Ubu | Vice | Wroom! | Xénophilie | Yoga | Zut! |

João Machado
Graphic Designer
Oporto, Portugal

"I prefer a well-defined, simple and clear design that explores the essence of the subject. My stationery personifies me and reveals my intention to be myself."

POSTERS

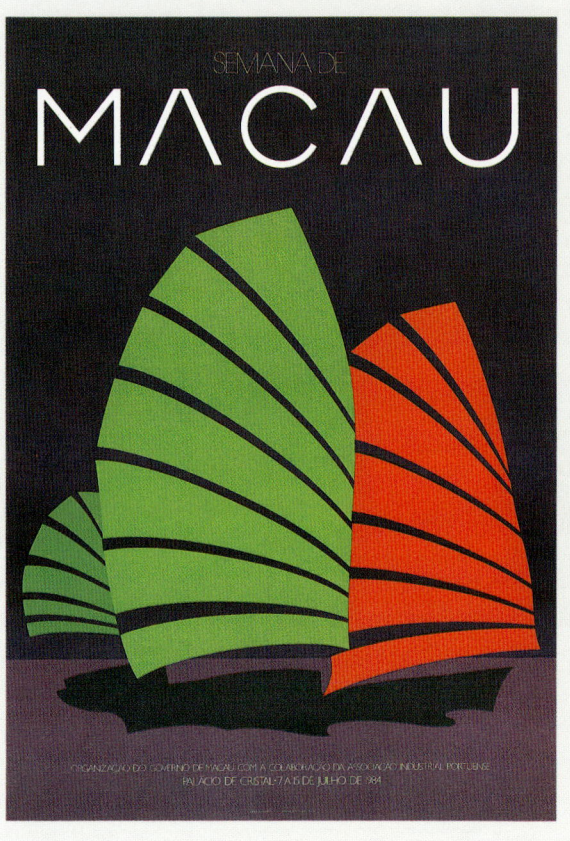

Born in Coimbra and educated in sculpture at the Fine Arts School of Porto, Machado has exhibited his works collectively and privately since 1967. Besides being well represented in museums throughout the world, his work has been published in a variety of prominent specialized design publications. He is the recipient of The National Prize of Gulbenkian for the best illustration for children's books, the Prize Grafiporto, and the First National Prize of Design.

FESTIVAL DE MÚSICA
LUSO-AMERICANA
Sexteto de
MARIA JOÃO
AUDITÓRIO NACIONAL CARLOS ALBERTO
13 DE MAIO/88
21.30H
COLABORAÇÃO: SECRETARIA DE ESTADO DA CULTURA
AMERICAN CULTURAL COUNCIL - JOMAR
AMERICAN LIFE INSURANCE COMPANY

CICLO DE CULTURA
Americana
AMERICAN
LANGUAGE INSTITUTE
AMERICAN
CULTURAL COUNCIL
PORTO 21/5 A 5/6 DE 1985

POSTER PORTFOLIO

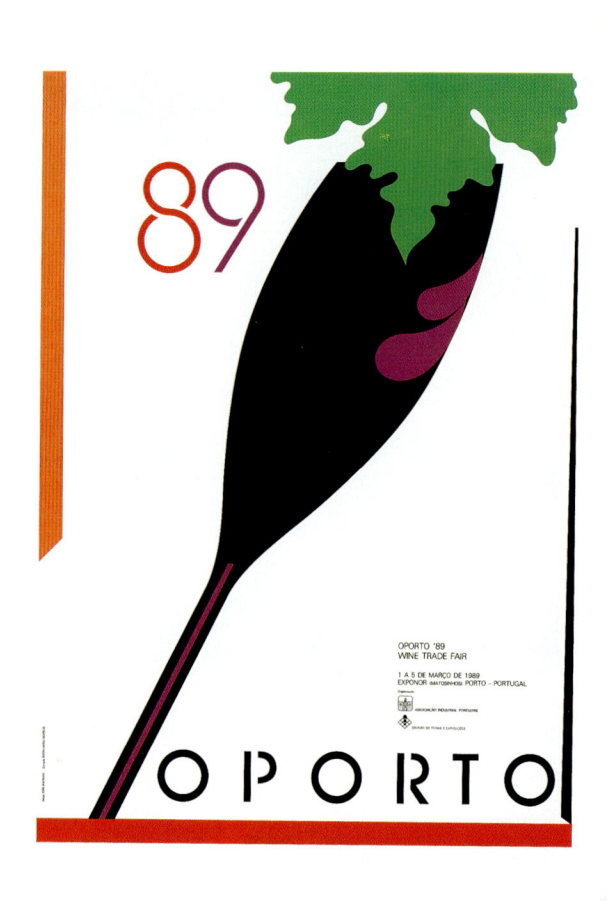

SONSOLES LLORENS
Free-lance Graphic Designer
Barcelona, Spain

"The symbol of my graphic identity, a plural number of suns, is based on my name, 'Sonsoles,' which means 'they are suns.' I wanted a serious professional image, but I didn't want to lose my uniqueness as a small and independent studio, so I decided to handwrite all of my correspondence. The contrast between the printed, stamped paper and my calligraphy gives a special personality to my letters."

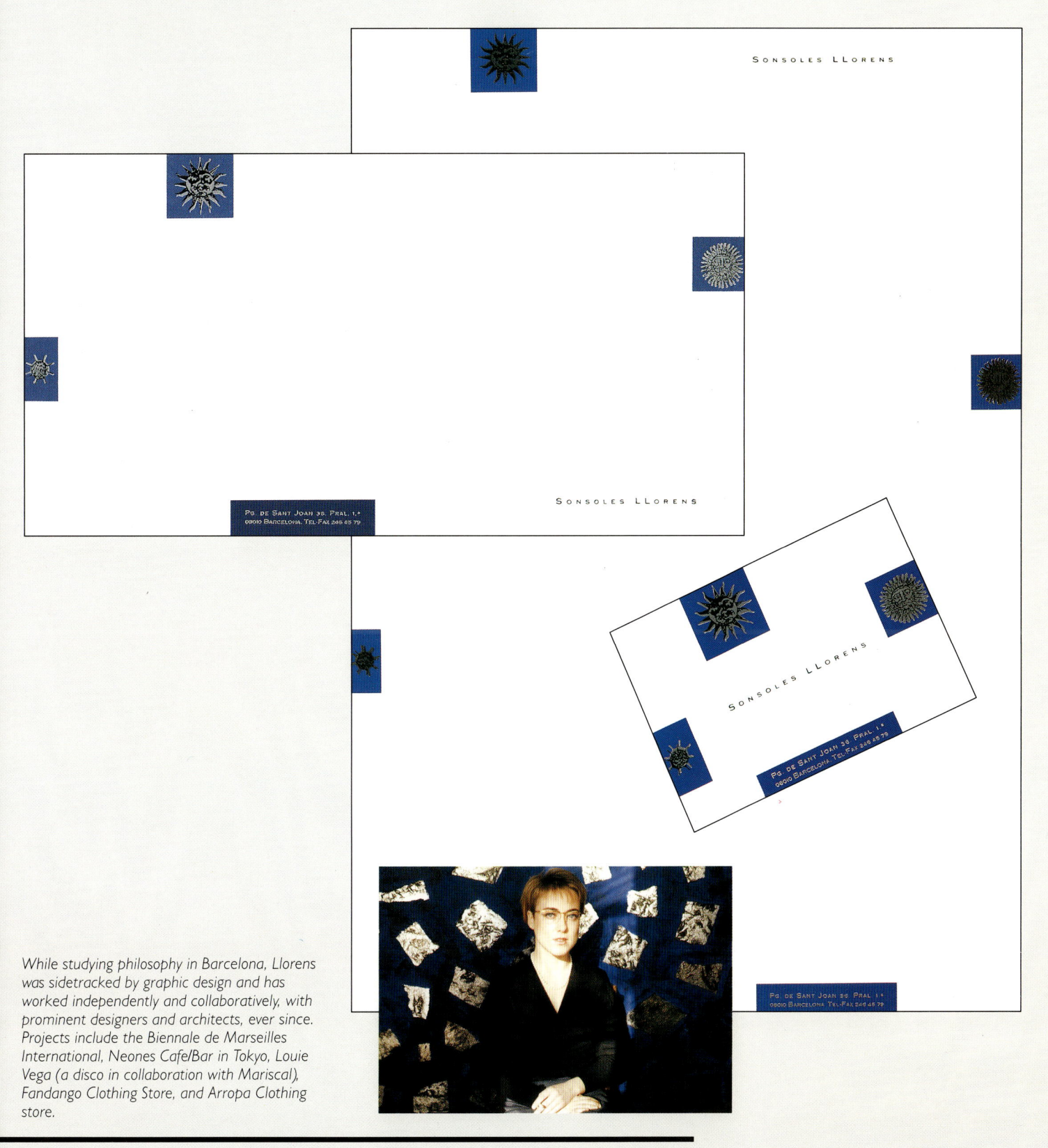

While studying philosophy in Barcelona, Llorens was sidetracked by graphic design and has worked independently and collaboratively, with prominent designers and architects, ever since. Projects include the Biennale de Marseilles International, Neones Cafe/Bar in Tokyo, Louie Vega (a disco in collaboration with Mariscal), Fandango Clothing Store, and Arropa Clothing store.

SONSOLES
llorens

aribau
21 bis
1º 2ª
08011
barcelona
t. 254 92 29
N.I.F. 35019558-B

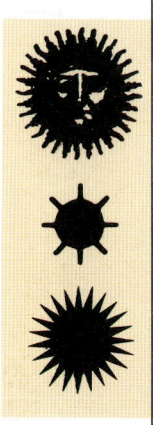

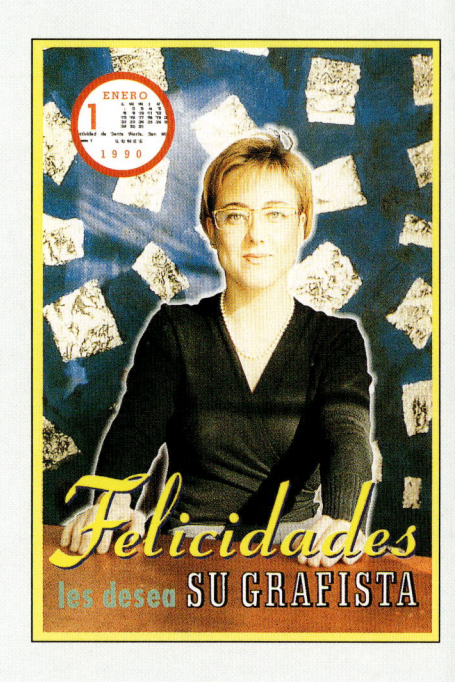

Felicidades les desea SU GRAFISTA

PROMOTIONAL CARD

SONSOLES
llorens

aribau
21 bis
1º 2ª
08011
barcelona
t. 254 92 29

144

DESIGN CORNU MALCOURANT
Jean-Michel Cornu, Véronique Malcourant, *Owners*
Paris, France

"**O**ur firm believes that origins are more important to good design than self-conscious originality. Ethnic groups that are widely separated geographically, culturally and historically often share the same aesthetic images and symbols. We are interested in using these archetypes because, for us, they represent a fundamental element of communication between different cultures. We are planetary designers who seek the essence and the archetypical significance in every object. Our battle cry is: 'Symbolic Design!'"

Véronique Malcourant studied plastic arts at the Met de Penninghen studio in Paris and then went on to acquire practical experience in the furniture industry. Jean-Michel Cornu studied at the Paris School of Fine Arts. In 1984 he was the first French designer to be awarded an "Hors les Murs" Medicis Scholarship. Through their design agency they practice graphic and industrial design based on their belief that origins are more important to good design than self-conscious originality.

PROMOTION PIECE

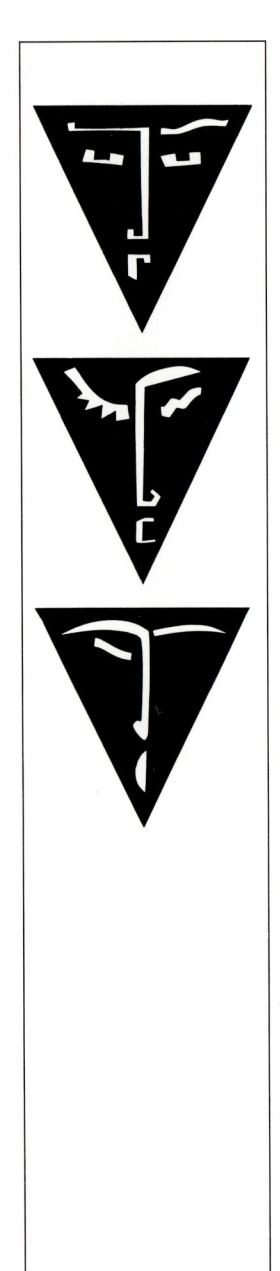

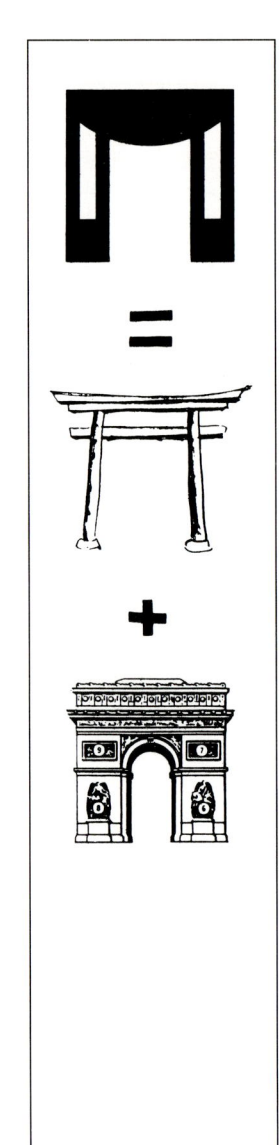

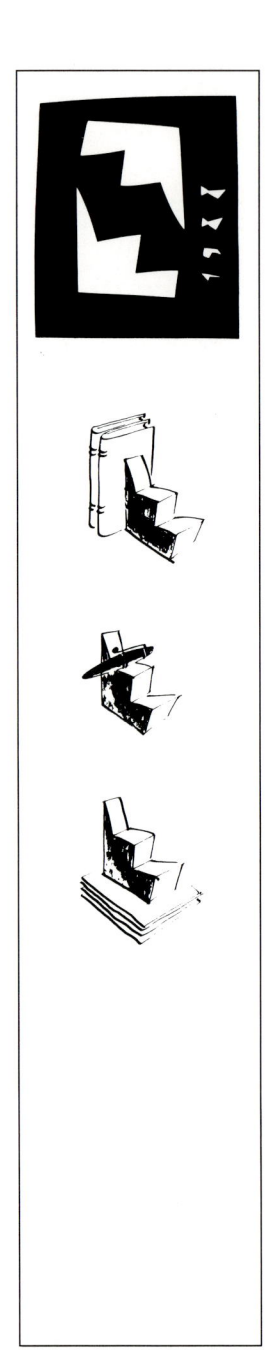

POSTCARD

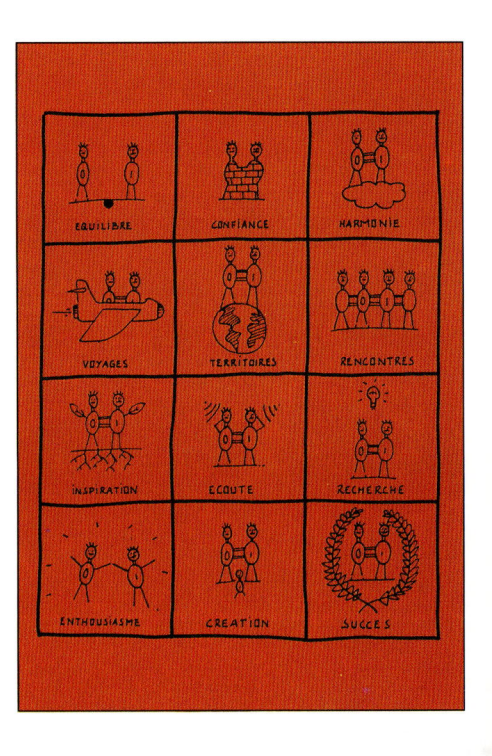

FUORISCHEMA DESIGN STUDIO, M&M COMMUNICATIONS AGENCY

Massimo Dolcini, Art Director, Fuorischema
Pesaro, Italy

"Fuorischema's logo uses a sign that has always been in use—the cross from basic design. It has various meanings: in nomadic culture it stands for the stars; in western culture it means denial and prohibition; in the industrial world it means poison and danger. It is a strong and aggressive sign. The most frequently used colors in our field are yellow and black, two colors that give maximum legibility."

"M&M adopted the initials of Media and Messages as its logo, using the colors red, green and blue."

MAILING LABEL

FUORISCHEMA DESIGN GROUP

MAILING LABEL

M&M
Comunicazione e pubblicità
61100 Pesaro/v.le Verdi 51
T. 0721/68462-34391 Telefax 0721/68257

M&M

M&M s.r.l. 61100 Pesaro/v.le Verdi 51 T. 0721/68462-34391 Part. IVA 00268760410

M&M

Cap. soc. 40.000.000 i.v.
Iscr. Trib. PS n. 2389 reg. soc.
Cod. fisc. e Part. IVA 0026876 041 0
C.C.I.A.A. PS n. 70044

M&M s.r.l.
Comunicazione e pubblicità

M&M

61100 Pesaro/v.le Verdi 51
T. 0721/68462-34391 Telefax 0721/68257
Part. IVA 00268760410

Born in 1945, Massimo Dolcini graduated from the Superiore Course of Graphic Arts in Urbino in 1969, where he studied with Albe Steiner and Michele Provinciali. He taught graphic design at the Superiore Course of Graphic Arts and photography at the Academy of Fine Arts in Urbino. Residing in Pesaro, Dolcini opened the graphic design firm, Fuorischema, and the communications agency, M&M, in 1973.

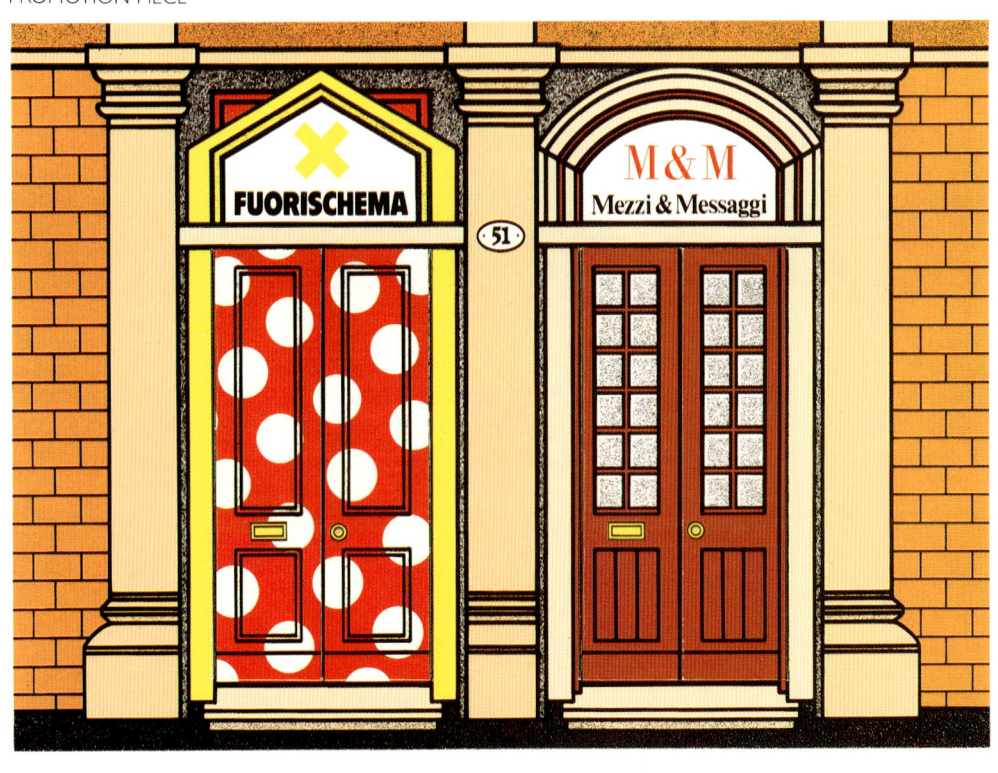

PROMOTION PIECE

STICKER

149

PORTFOLIO

PORTFOLIO

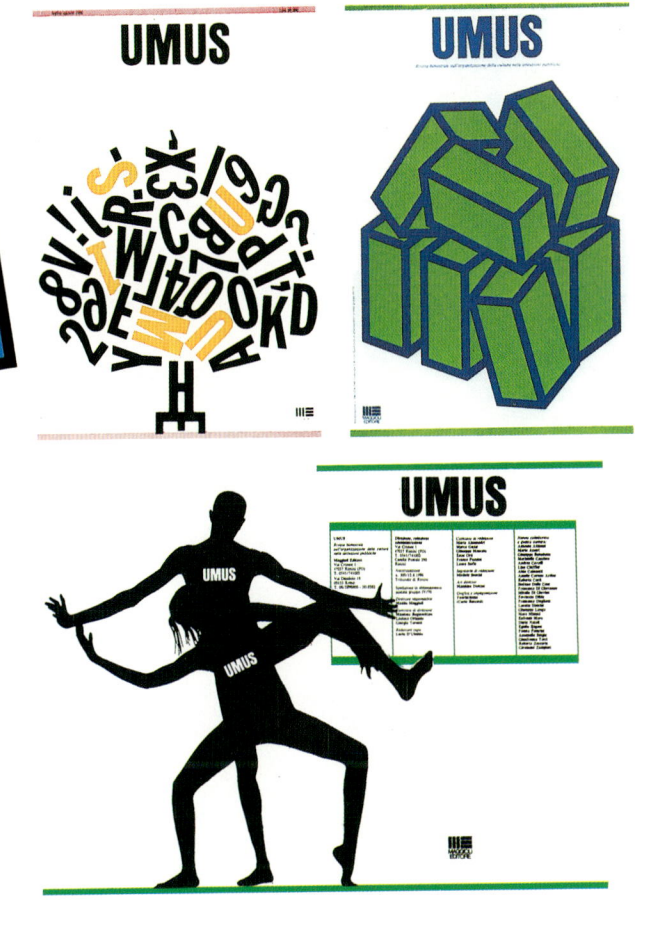

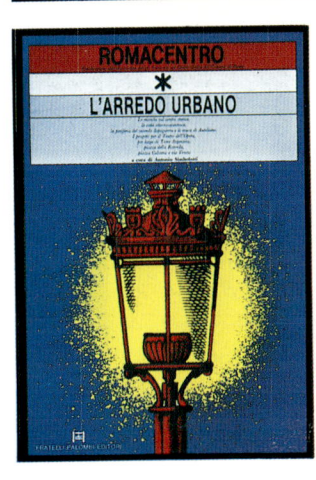

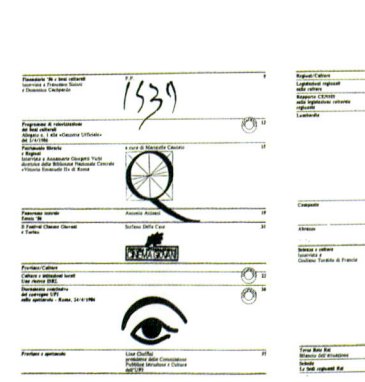

PORTFOLIO

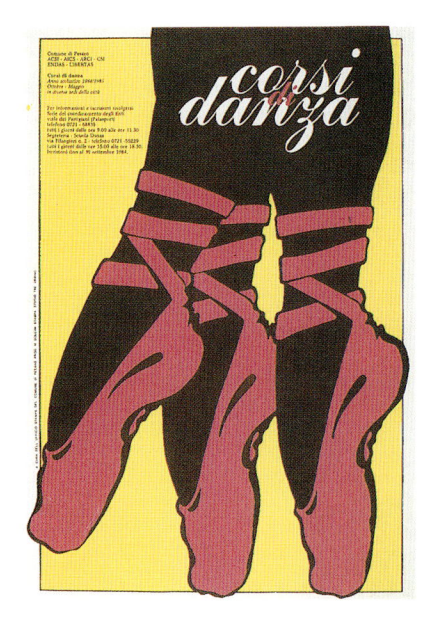

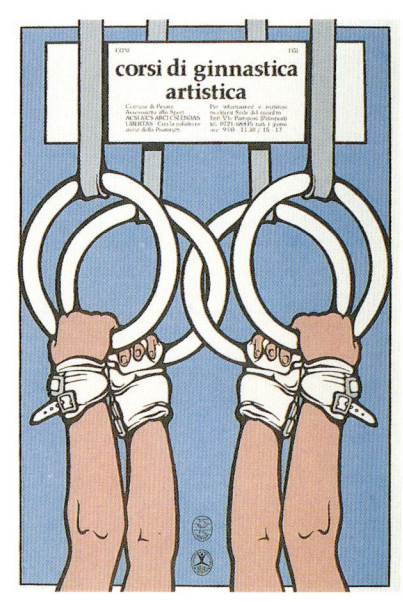

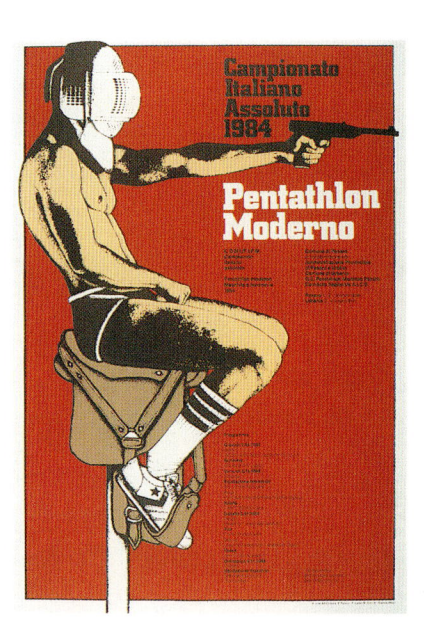

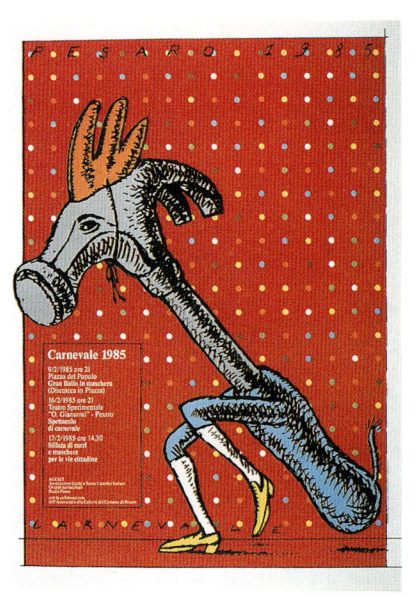

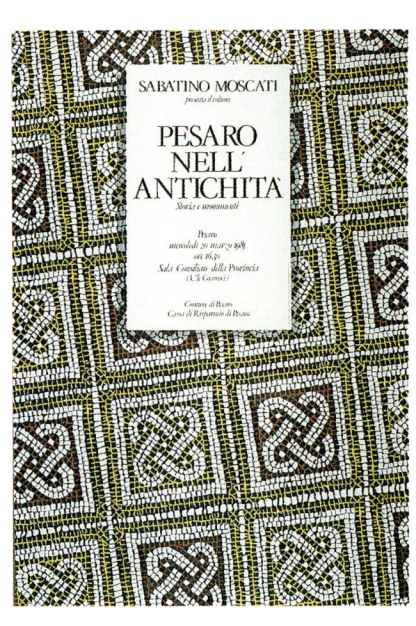

PORTFOLIO

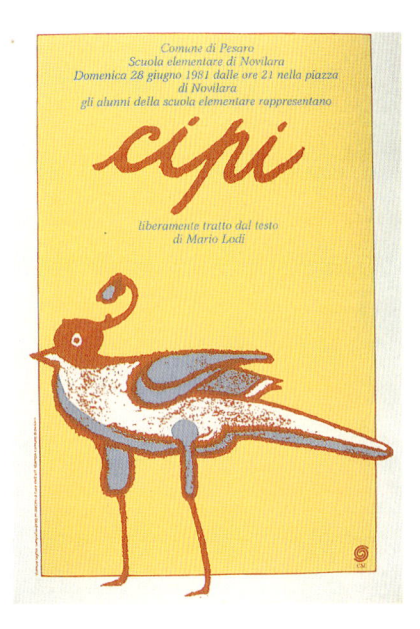

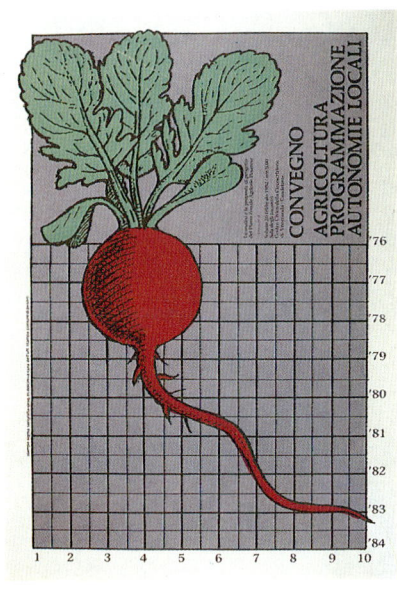

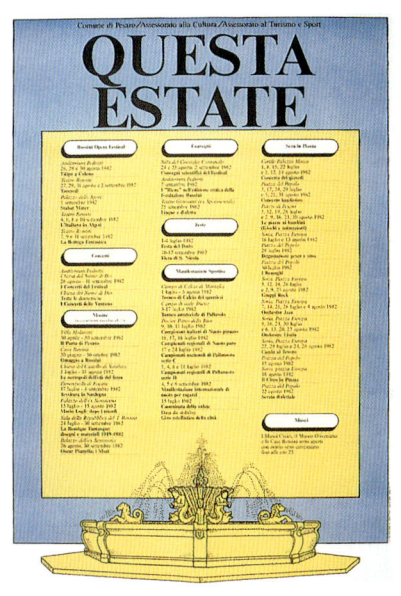

PORTFOLIO

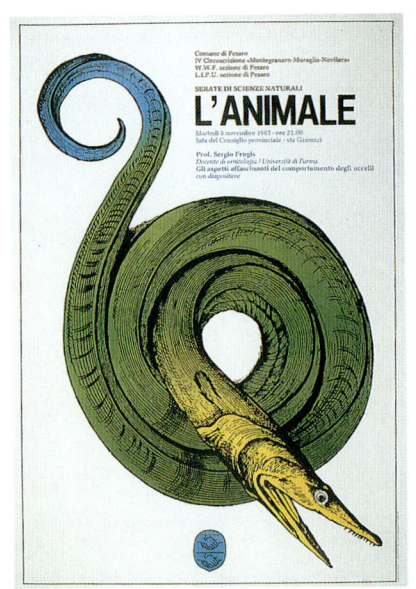

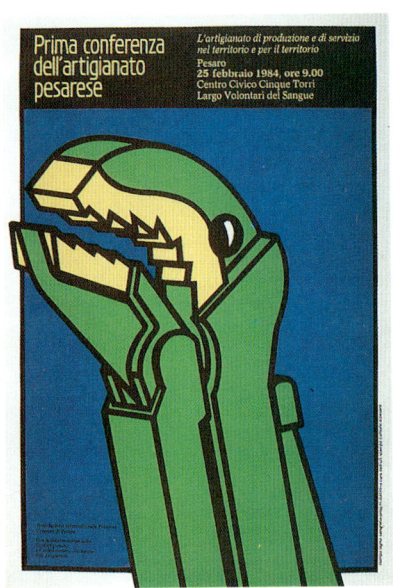

154

PORTFOLIO

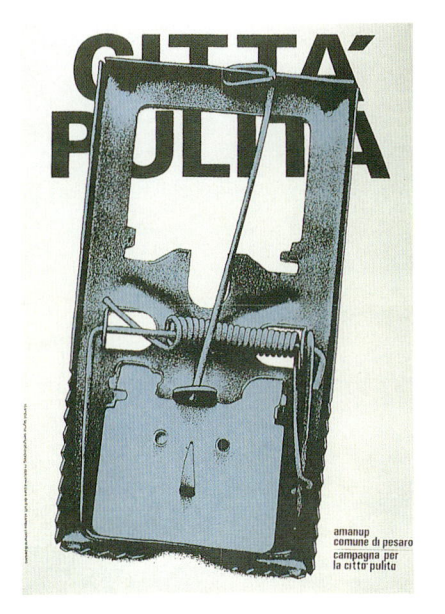

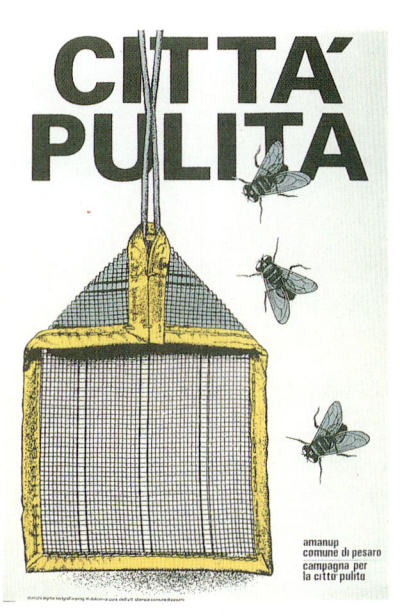

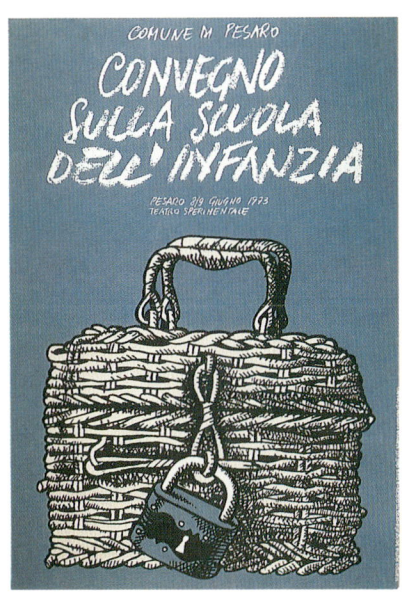

REA NIKONOVA
Artist
Eysk, USSR

"According to Soviet standards, I am a marginal person. As a founder and member of a small group of Neo-Futurists, I've carried on and developed the Russian avant-garde tradition of 1910–1920, the influence of which has been thoroughly assimilated. I began designing stationery and promotional materials in 1978, and since 1987 I've carried on a regular correspondence with mail-artists and visual poets throughout the world."

Born in the Soviet Union, Rea Nikonova has been involved in literature since 1959 and in painting since 1962. Together with Serge Segay, she was editor of the manifold script journal Nomer in 1965, and Transponans from 1979 through 1986. A founder and member of the transfuturists artists and poets group which has had joint poetry shows in Leningrad and Moscow, Nikonova has also participated in Soviet underground and international exhibitions.

INTERDESIGN
Marc Piel, *Project Director*
Paris, France

"**A**t InterDesign visual identity has three sets of criteria: our commercial and corporate approach is serious, high quality and not ostentatious or expensive; our practical approach is conceived as an unlimited number of 'bricks' that can be added to easily to get a personalized message across while, at the same time, ensuring a uniform total identity from one message to another; for our presentation material we backpedal the InterDesign name in order to flatter the work conceived and the client's product and name."

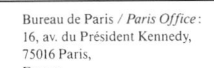

PROMOTIONAL CARD

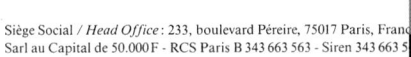

French-born designer Marc Robert Piel taught at the Parsons School of Design American College in Paris from 1985 to 1989 and co-founded the Paris-based product and graphic design office InterDesign in 1987. The French expert for Afnor (French Standards) for public information symbols, and the European correspondent for Design World for the past six years, Piel has been widely published in Cree, Novum Gebrauchsgraphic, Icographic, Design Magazine, Domus, Industrial Design *and* Idea.

PROMOTIONAL CARDS

Best & Gee est un fabricant de boissons alcoolisées par distillation.

© InterDesign®

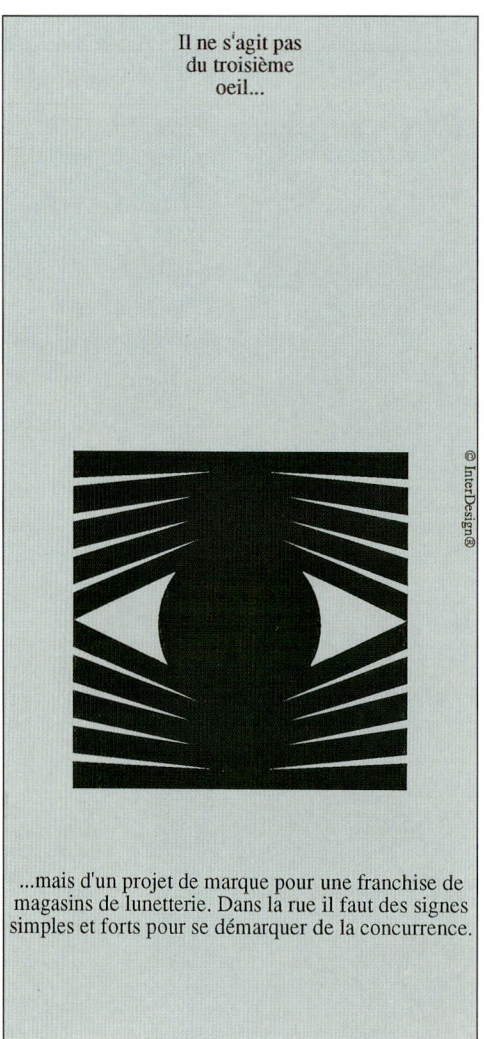

Il ne s'agit pas du troisième oeil...

© InterDesign®

...mais d'un projet de marque pour une franchise de magasins de lunetterie. Dans la rue il faut des signes simples et forts pour se démarquer de la concurrence.

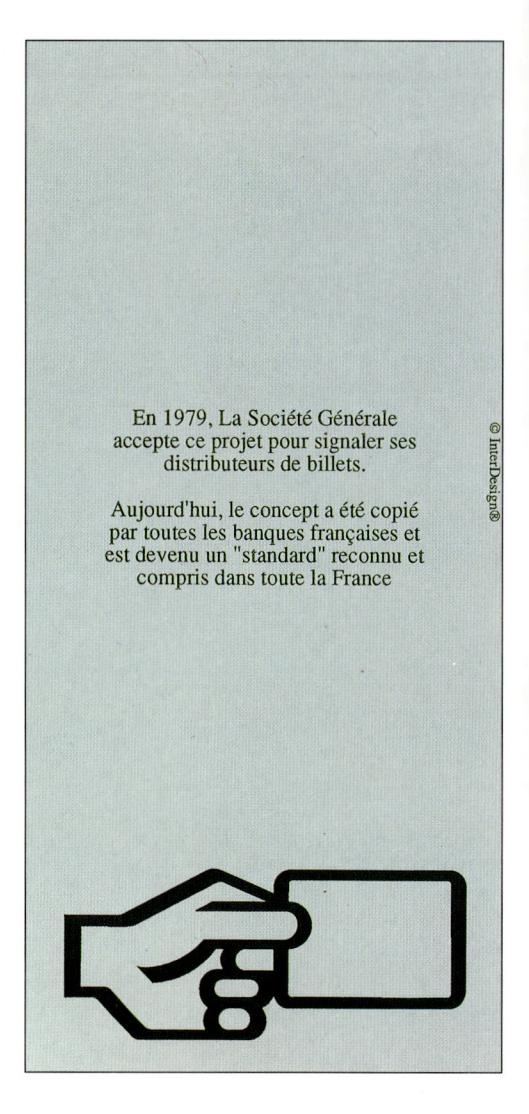

En 1979, La Société Générale accepte ce projet pour signaler ses distributeurs de billets.

Aujourd'hui, le concept a été copié par toutes les banques françaises et est devenu un "standard" reconnu et compris dans toute la France

© InterDesign®

InterDesign®

WALTER TAFELMAIER
Graphic Designer
Munich, Germany

"**T** is the first letter of my name, and for many years I collected *T* letter forms. Between 1975–1989 the *T* became central to my work. I used it on my letterhead and on a bookplate which shows the *T* as a ruler indicating the measurements of my body."

STICKER

PROMOTIONAL CARD

Walter Tafelmaier is a graphic designer, painter and teacher in Munich, Germany. His exhibitions have appeared in Warsaw, Krakow, Brunn, Bradford, Brussels and Stockholm. Among the many publications featuring his work are: Important Grafik Design Issues, Gebrauchsgrafik, Novum, *and* Graphis.

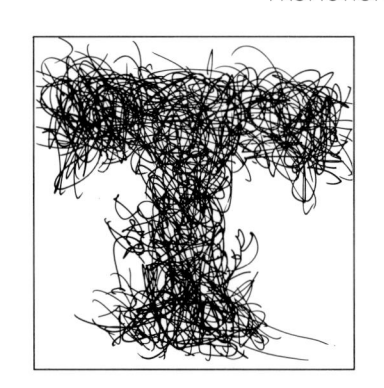

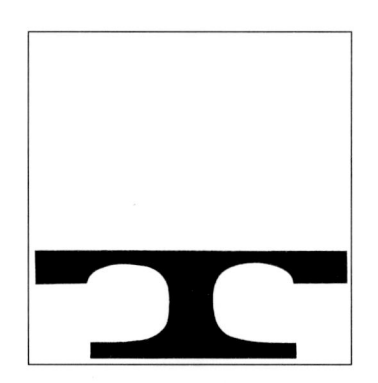

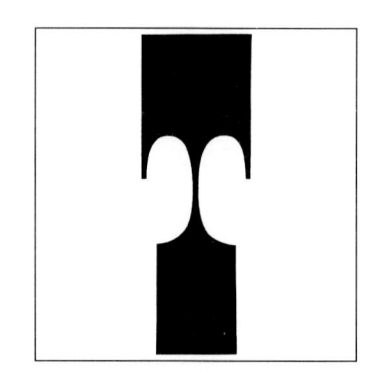

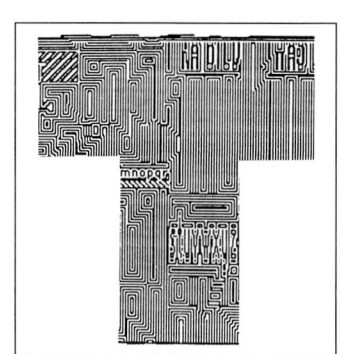

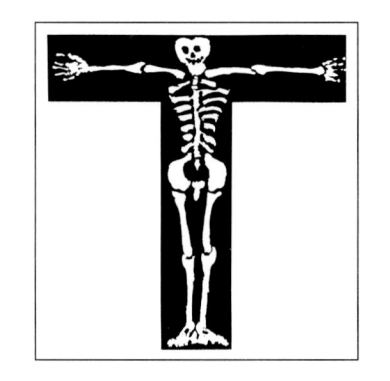

PROMOTIONAL BOOKLET

ILLUSTRATORENE
Sarah Rosenbaum, *Free-lance Illustrator/Designer*
Oslo, Norway

"Illustratorene is a group of eight illustrators, all working in very different styles. We wanted to design a letterhead that would not tie us down to a specific illustrative style. The solution, inspired by the work of El Lizitsky, was a picture made of type, using all the letters needed to spell our group name. The simple red and black colors against cream-colored paper were in line with the Russian style. The figure, standing up and drawing, always remains the same, but the legs change positions from item to item. For a moving announcement, the figure was moved on a fotostat machine."

PROMOTIONAL MAILER

A U.S. citizen, Rosenbaum obtained her degree and currently resides in Oslo, Norway, where she has worked as a free-lance illustrator and designer since 1987. In both 1985 and 1990, she was the recipient of the Illustratorfond Scholarship; and she won Norwegian Form/Gullbyanten awards from 1985 through 1989. In 1988 and 1989, she received the silver award from The Society of Newspaper Design's Annual Competition and diplomas from the Arets Vakreste Boker (Annual Book Design Awards), respectively.

MICHAEL LEVIN COMMUNICATION VISUELLE
Michael Levin, Owner
Paris, France

"This identity combines the issues of quality with self-conscious design to reflect a new professional position while referring to and sustaining its previous priorities of humor and human touch. The image confers a juxtaposition of interpretations—reassuring the more staid clients as well as giving a professional wink."

PROMOTIONAL CARD

Born in Tel-Aviv and educated at the Bezalel Academy of Arts and Design in Jerusalem, Levin lives and free-lances in Paris following a four-year stint as art director for Ariely Publicity. His clients now include Perrier, Café Aux Deux Magots, La Villette, and Ministre pour les Grands Travaux. Levin's work has been exhibited in Israel and France, and he was the recipient of the Grand Prix "Object 2000" in 1989.

162

Serge Segay
Visual Poet
Eysk, USSR

"I began creating experimental poetry in 1962, and since the 1970s my poems have become increasingly visual. When I began participating in the mail-art network in 1986, my poems were published in various magazines in countries outside the USSR (I have no publications in my country). At that time, I created my letterhead using colorful frottages combined with rubber stamps. The stationery conveys my poetical intentions."

From 1979 through 1986, Serge Segay, along with his colleague Rea Nikonova, published the samzidat magazine Transponans where many of the Soviet unofficial avant-garde poets participated. Since 1986 his visual poems have appeared in various magazines in the U.S., Italy, Australia, France and Canada, but never in the Soviet Union. Segay's first book of visual poems Poèmes pour Ballerines du Grand Théatre was published in Canada in 1990 by ASFI Editions.

MARIE STERTE
Free-lance Illustrator and Graphic Designer
Surte, Sweden

"I designed my stationery when I started to work as a free-lancer, and I didn't have too much money at the time. So, I decided to print it on my own Xerox machine on plain Xerox paper and to make the red dot on the card by hand. The card is printed on a Canson Inguss Paper. The fish is a 'car-belly-fish' that I used to have in my aquarium and was very fond of. The red dot is just something that has followed me."

Marie Sterte
Skårdalsvägen 85
445 00 Surte
tel. 031-98 37 31

grafisk form & illustration

Currently, Sterte works as a free-lance book designer in Gothenburg, Sweden. Educated in Stockholm and Salt Lake City, Utah, she received the Swedish Book Art Award in 1988.

MIDDLE EAST

Gad Almaliah
Free-lance Graphic Designer
Tel Aviv, Israel

"**A**leph is the first letter of my name, Almaliah. It is also, of course, the first letter of the Hebrew alphabet, so I thought it would work well as my logo. The typeface I selected is a classic one. It has a very interesting look that can be appreciated by anyone, whether or not they are familiar with Hebrew."

Gad Almaliah's numerous first-place awards in poster, stamp and medallion graphic design, as well as his work with the high tech and kibbutz industries, have earned him a well-deserved reputation. In 1980 he was appointed president of the Graphic Designers Association in Israel. He also compiled and produced the Israel Graphic Design Book.

PROMOTIONAL MATERIALS

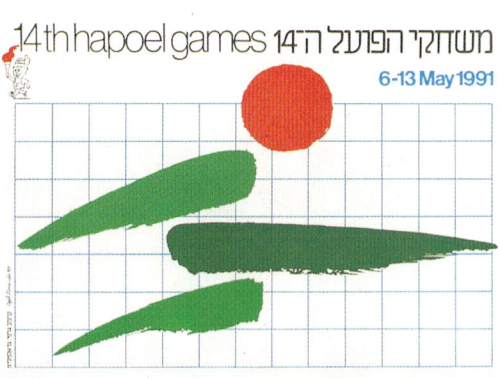

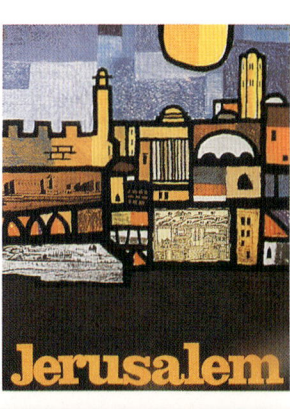

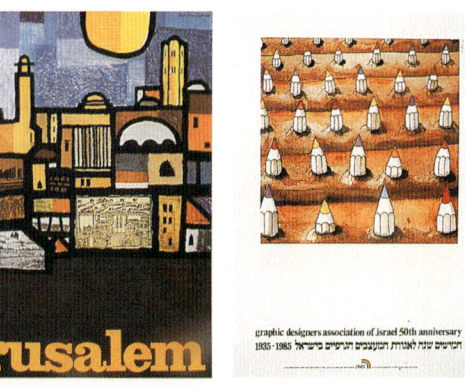

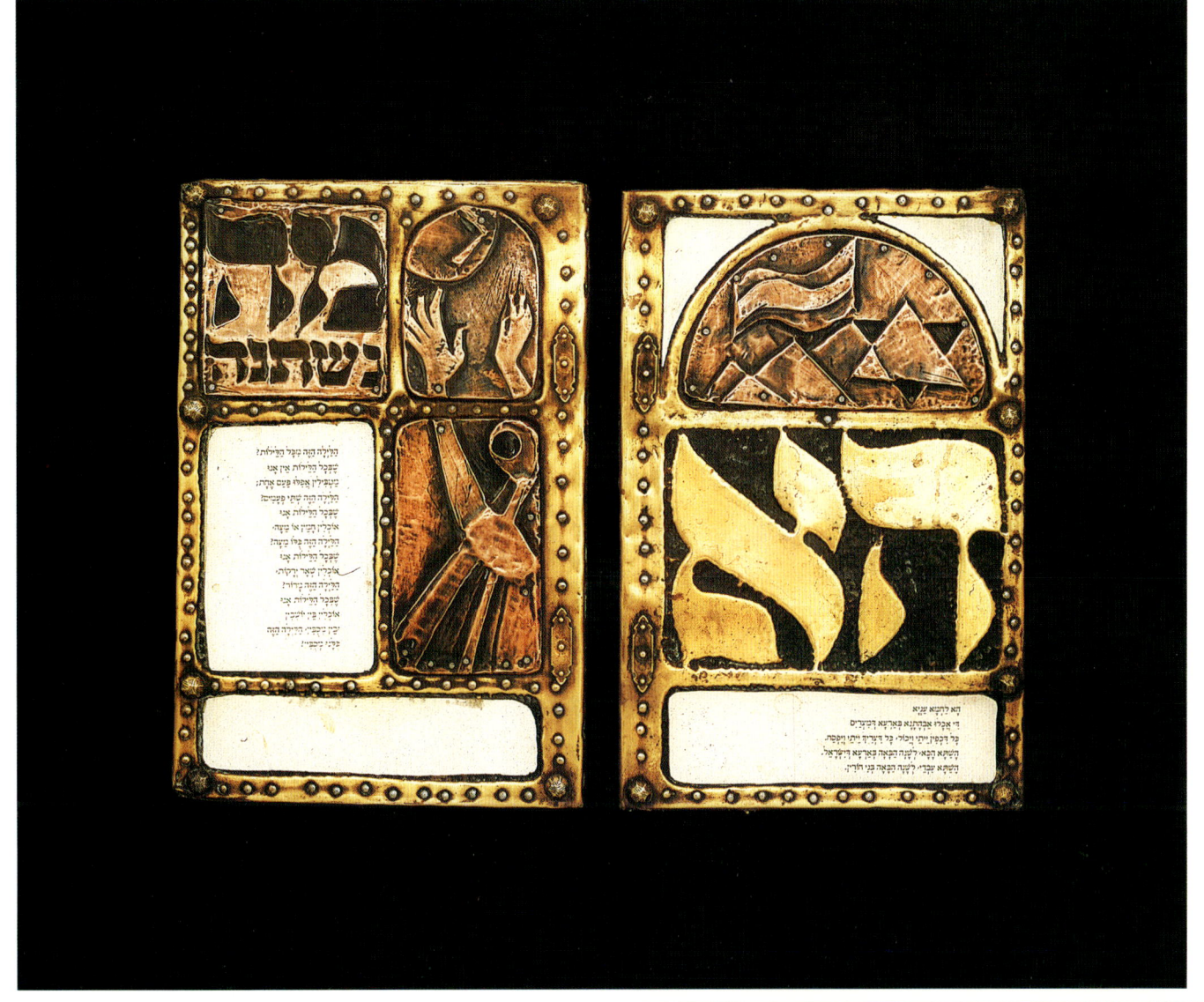

PROMOTIONAL MATERIALS

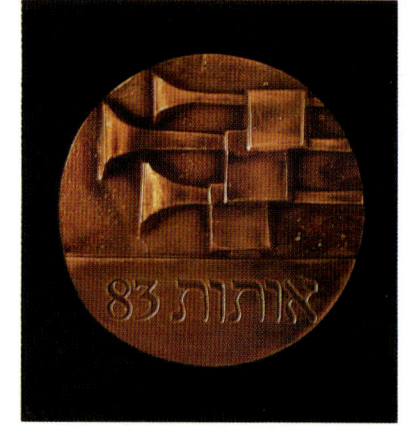

LOGOS

168

REISINGER GRAPHIC COMMUNICATION
Dan Reisinger, *Designer/Painter*
Tel Aviv, Israel

"**A**s the fourth generation in a family dynasty of artists, I see myself as carrying on a tradition that began when my great-grandfather decorated ceilings and walls throughout the Austro-Hungarian Empire. Assuming that the Reisingers (my sons included) will continue to work in design-related fields, I have emphasized the family name on the letterhead, using a particular shade of red that has always symbolized the Reisinger family identity."

Dan Reisinger formed his own design studio in 1967 and has expanded his artistic achievements from poster design and painting to corporate identity, packaging, sign systems, and environmental design. He has received many awards for design excellence, and his works have been on display in museums throughout the world.

NATAN KARP STUDIO
Natan Karp, Owner
Tel Aviv, Israel

"My logo attempts to represent three dimensions molded into two on paper. I designed two squares into which I cut my initials, N.K. The color is added by hand to express my mood and to create a personal and informal way of relating to the addressee, making him or her part of my art."

Natan Karp is best recognized for his continuous medal and commemorative coin designs, many of which have been incorporated into the currency of Israel. He has also won awards for his work in logo and poster design. He is a member of several national and international design associations.

PROMOTIONAL MATERIAL

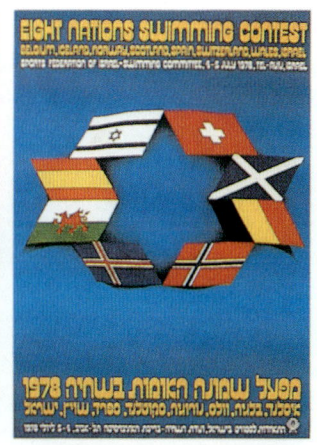

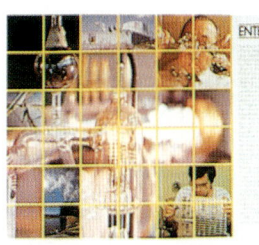

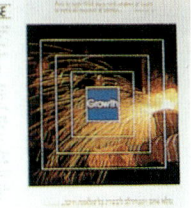

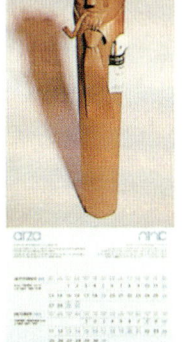

STICKER

MICHEL KICHKA
Proprietor
Jerusalem, Israel

"My letterhead is in French because it is my mother tongue and is more natural for me, even though I live in Israel and am fluent in Hebrew. The colors Turkish Blue and Hot Yellow are a contrast to my native country's Belgian Gray. When I emigrated, I chose the colors of Israel's blue sky and sea, and yellow sun and sand. The smile is simply mine, in life and in work."

Michel Kichka is among the most widely-known graphic design and poster cartoonist artists outside of the art industry itself. Many of his award-winning designs are promotional advertisements for large media events. His critical, yet humorous illustrations have earned him a well-deserved international reputation.

POSTCARDS

PROMOTION PIECE

173

PROMOTION PIECE

AVI EISENSTEIN
Director
Graphic Design Department, Bezalel Academy
Jerusalem, Israel

"My stationery utilizes my family name as a typographical element creating an image and identity for my design studio. My business cards utilize the same design, but they change colors every year."

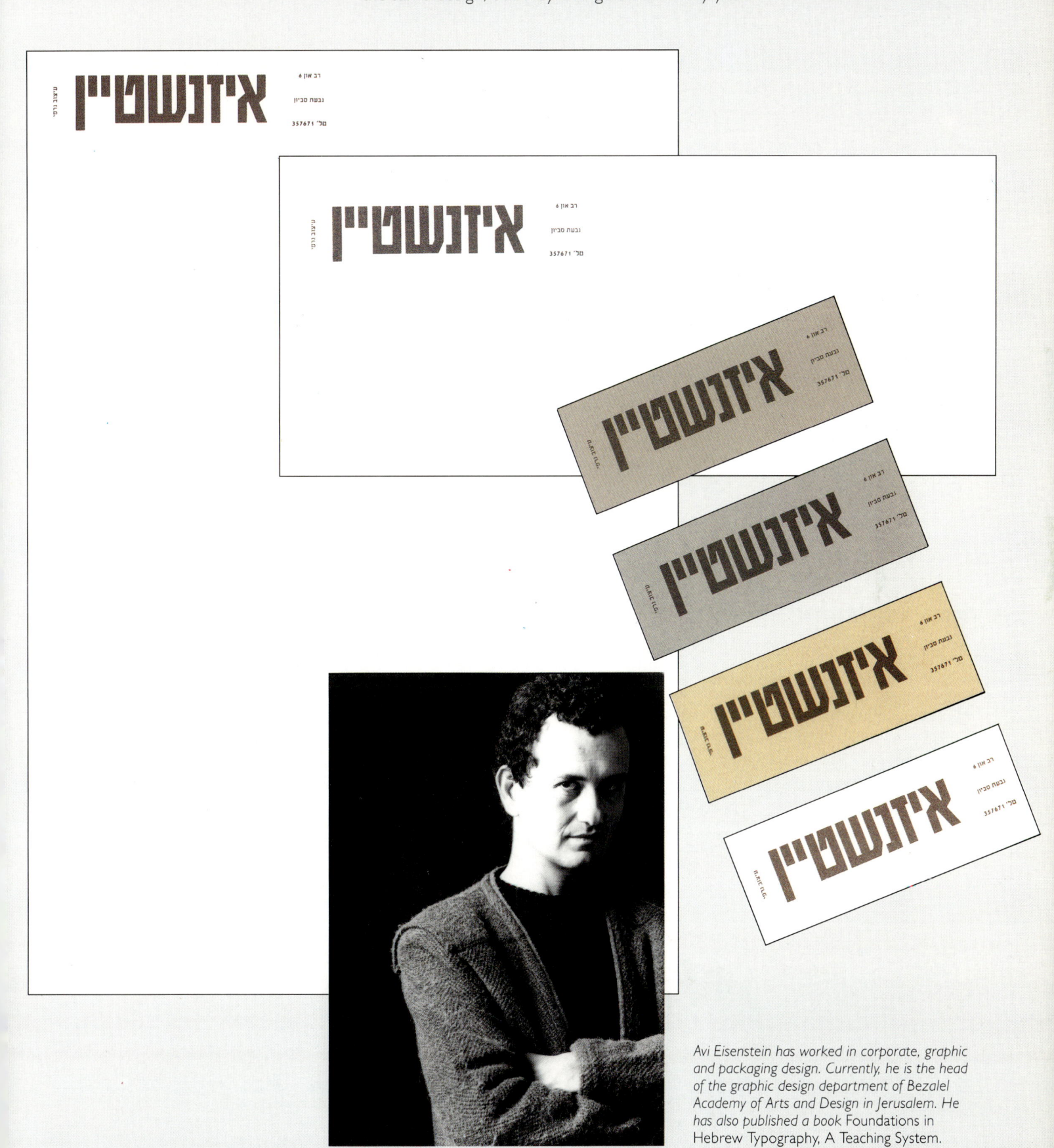

Avi Eisenstein has worked in corporate, graphic and packaging design. Currently, he is the head of the graphic design department of Bezalel Academy of Arts and Design in Jerusalem. He has also published a book Foundations in Hebrew Typography, A Teaching System.

DAVID HAREL

Graphic Artist/Painter
Jerusalem, Israel

"I debated how I should appear on my stationery. Since I have so many different aspects, and I try to work in various techniques, I feel divided by my need to design and my need to express myself as an artist. Therefore, I decided to represent myself as a silhouetted head which includes a number of the techniques I work in. Drawing is my strong point: softened geometric and colorful shapes represent the Macintosh computer in my studio, and the photography symbolizes a technique which often helps me."

"However, all this did not satisfy my artistic side and the painter in me. So, I decided to add my painting shoes, which symbolize the fact that I do paint. I change shoes when I paint in oils, since the paint drips from my hand to my shoes. My stationery's symbols close a circle between the head, thinking of techniques and computers about design solutions, through the body, until it reaches the foot's end—shoes."

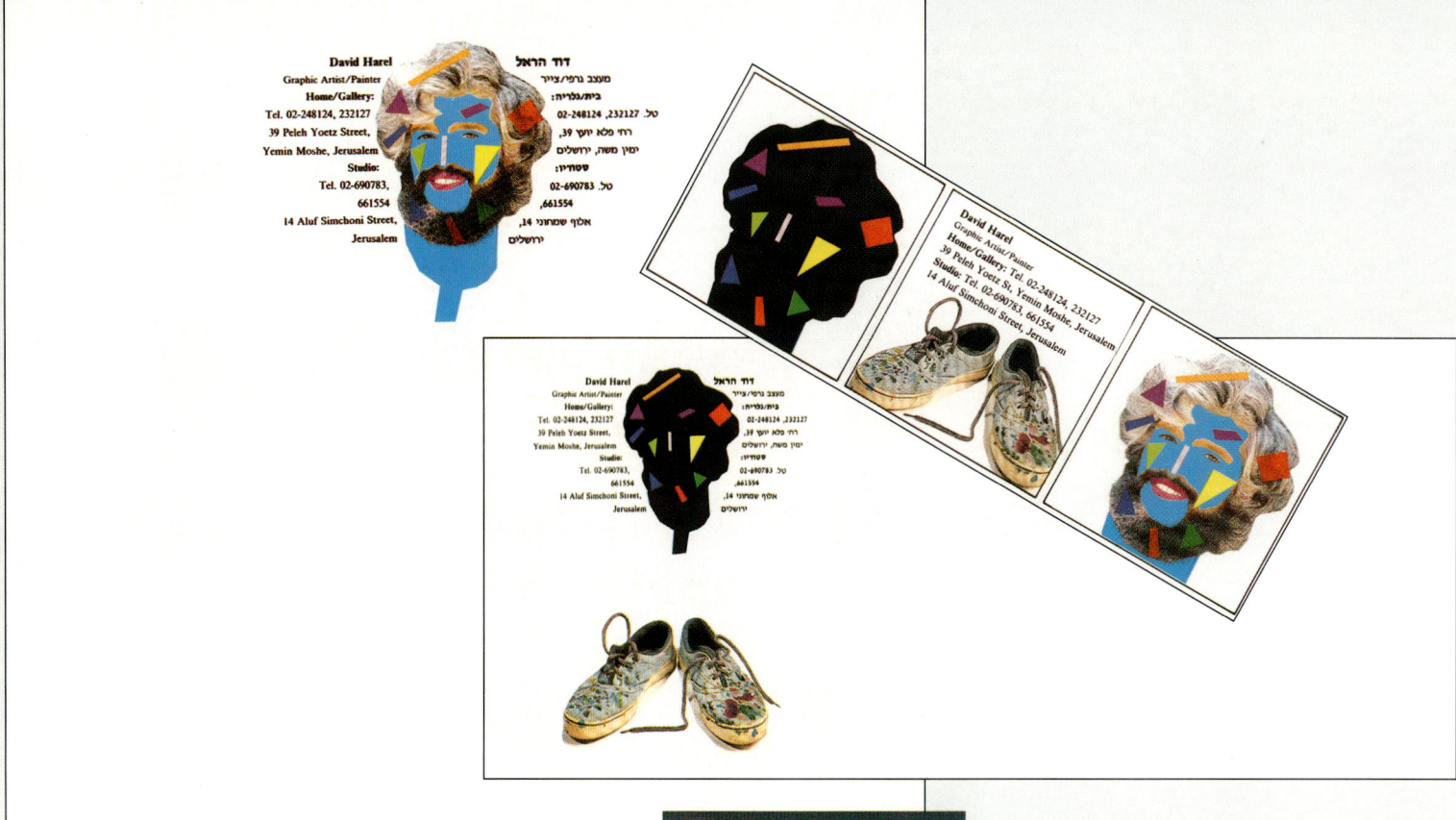

A professional graphic designer specializing in mass communications and animation, David Harel has run an independent studio in Jerusalem since 1972. His portfolio includes: a poster for the renovation of an ancient city (1987); publicity for the campaign to Save Water (1986); and animated films about municipal taxes for the municipality of Jerusalem.

FAR EAST

GRAPHIC COMMUNICATION LTD.
Henry Steiner, *Managing Director*
Hong Kong

"The Chinese lunar calendar is based on a twelve-year cycle named after the dozen animals of the Chinese Zodiac. In 1974, the year of the Tiger, I designed a set of stationery based on a specially-drawn blue tiger, and for each of the next eleven years we changed our stationery according to the relevant animal. We created each set to be as different as possible from the last, and this variable corporate identity created great interest. By 1985, we had completed the set of twelve. At that time, I decided to settle on the design based on the Ox, and I have been using it ever since."

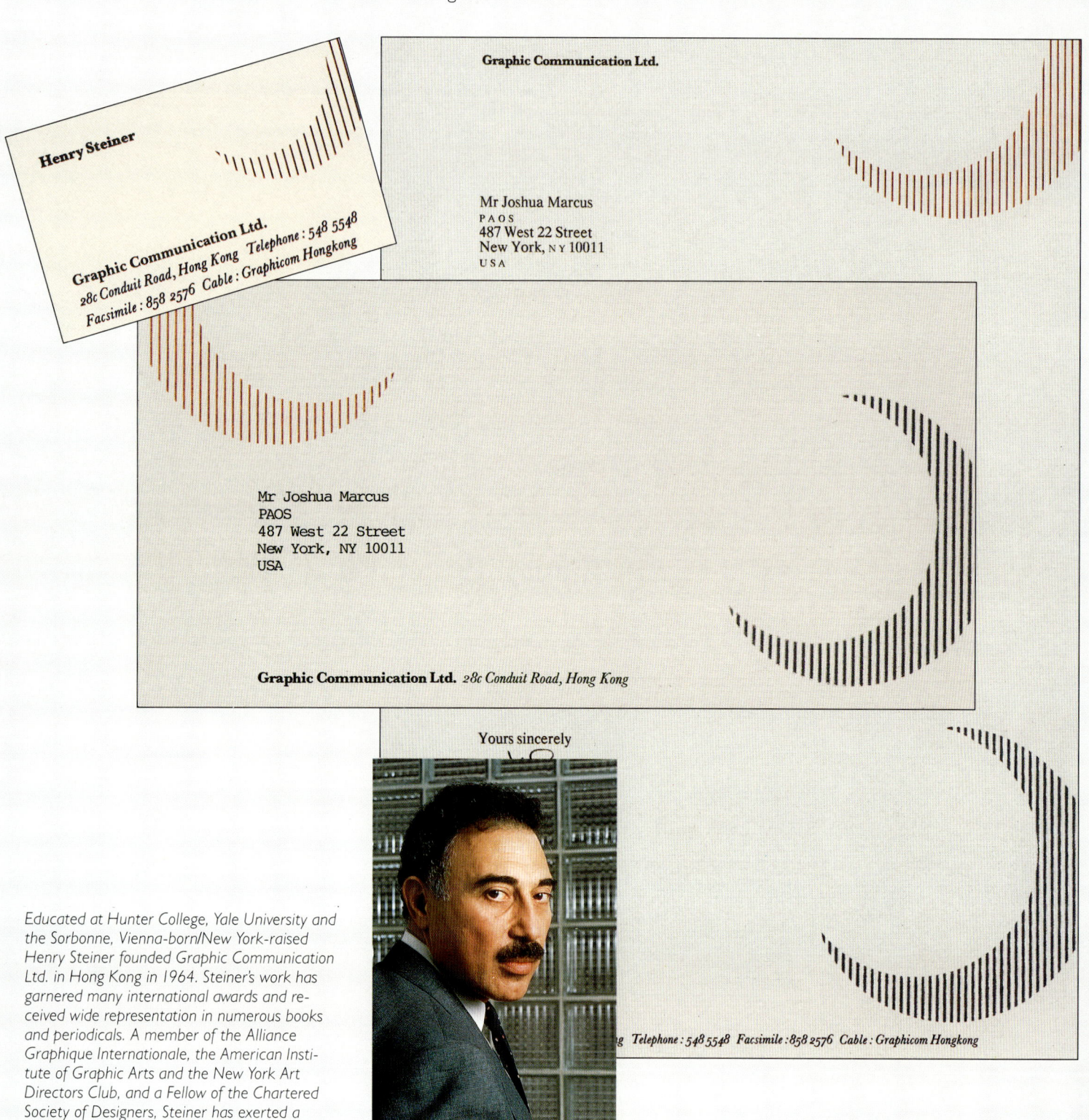

Educated at Hunter College, Yale University and the Sorbonne, Vienna-born/New York-raised Henry Steiner founded Graphic Communication Ltd. in Hong Kong in 1964. Steiner's work has garnered many international awards and received wide representation in numerous books and periodicals. A member of the Alliance Graphique Internationale, the American Institute of Graphic Arts and the New York Art Directors Club, and a Fellow of the Chartered Society of Designers, Steiner has exerted a marked influence on design in Asia.

LETTERHEAD LOGOS

Graphic Communication Ltd.

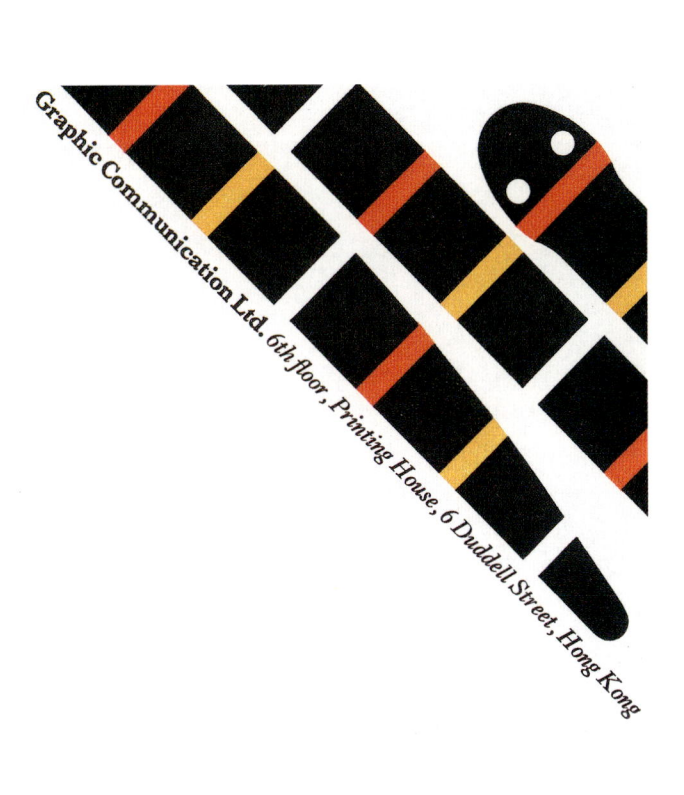

6th floor, Printing House, 6 Duddell Street, Hong Kong
phone:5-230101 cable:Graphicom Hongkong

TO COMMEMORATE
THE YEAR OF THE CANINE PERSON
25 January 1982 – 12 February 1983

IGARASHI STUDIO
Takenobu Igarashi, President
Tokyo, Japan

"I chose the brush stroke as our studio logo because I am a Japanese designer. I always design conceptually. However, I deliberately selected this brush stroke, in itself having no significant meaning, because I wanted it to evolve into defining Igarashi Studio."

Educated in Japan and America, Igarashi maintains offices in both countries. His works have been selected as part of the permanent collections for the Museum of Modern Art in New York as well as many other museums and universities throughout the world. His wide span of international activities includes projects related to graphic design, industrial design and environmental form creation. Among Igarashi's main achievements are shopping bags and calendars for the Museum of Modern Art in New York, and corporate identity projects for Mitsui Bank, Meiji Milk Products and Suntory Limited.

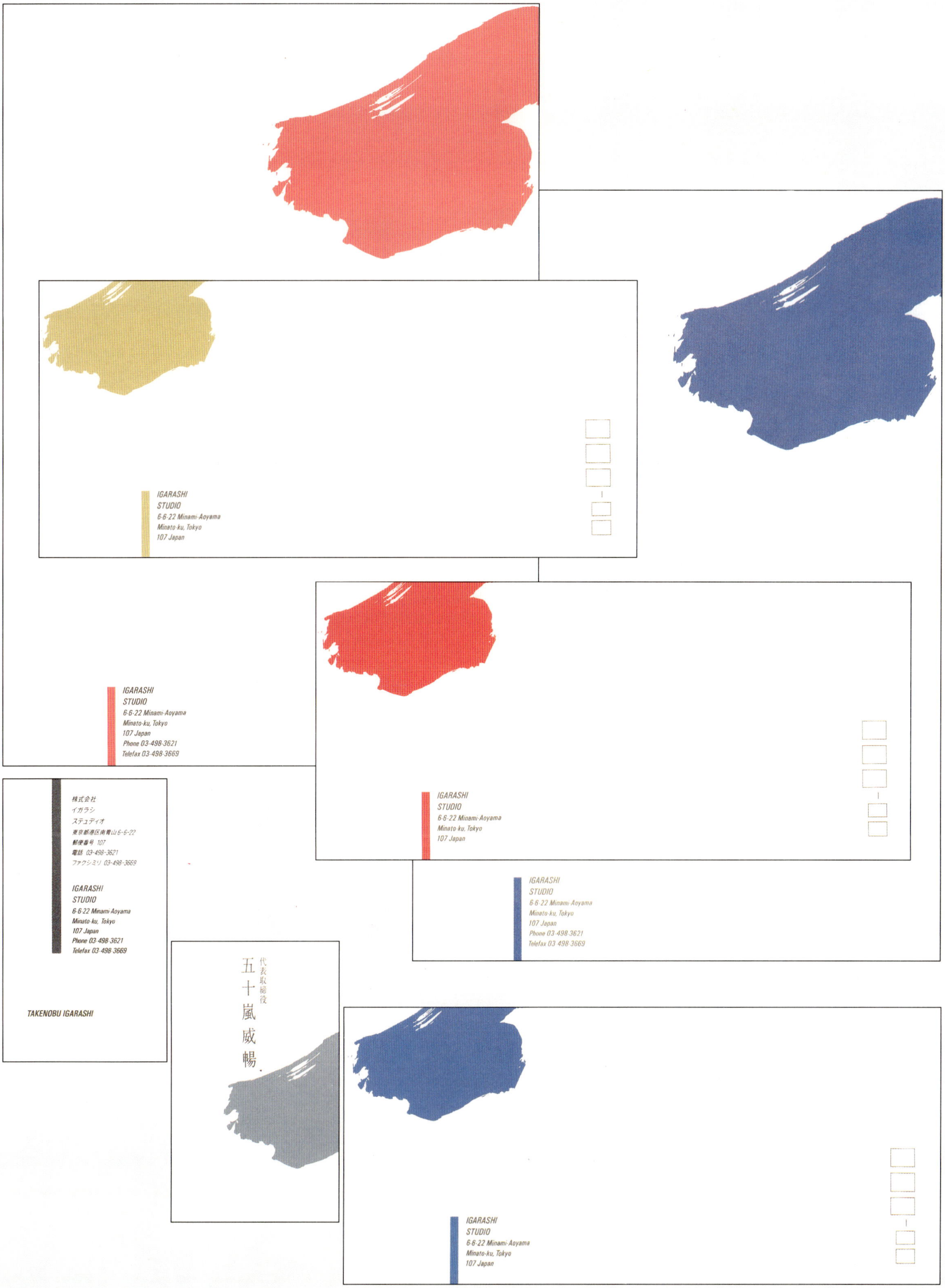
IGARASHI
STUDIO
6-6-22 Minami-Aoyama
Minato-ku, Tokyo
107 Japan
IGARASHI
STUDIO
6-6-22 Minami-Aoyama
Minato-ku, Tokyo
107 Japan
Phone 03-498-3621
Telefax 03-498-3669
IGARASHI
STUDIO
6-6-22 Minami-Aoyama
Minato-ku, Tokyo
107 Japan
株式会社
イガラシ
ステュディオ
東京都港区南青山6-6-22
郵便番号 107
電話 03-498-3621
ファクシミリ 03-498-3669
IGARASHI
STUDIO
6-6-22 Minami-Aoyama
Minato-ku, Tokyo
107 Japan
Phone 03-498-3621
Telefax 03-498-3669
TAKENOBU IGARASHI
IGARASHI
STUDIO
6-6-22 Minami-Aoyama
Minato-ku, Tokyo
107 Japan
Phone 03-498-3621
Telefax 03-498-3669
代表取締役
五十嵐威暢
IGARASHI
STUDIO
6-6-22 Minami-Aoyama
Minato-ku, Tokyo
107 Japan

PAOS Inc.
Motoo Nakanishi, President
Tokyo, Japan

"Design for a new PAOS logo began after we celebrated our 20th anniversary in April 1988. As intensifying market and social conditions pose increasingly demanding problems for today's companies, it becomes difficult to pinpoint a client's specific ailments. In such a melange of issues and concerns, it is imperative to help clients establish a clear, solid identity, and a reliable, viable approach to problem solving. For our clients we provide systematic problem solving that is multi-axis and multi-layered, interconnected and synchronic. The set of four symbols reflect this philosophy.

"My own personal stationery plays on the lucky coincidence that my initials—M and N—fall exactly in the middle of the alphabet. I wanted my personal stationery to be lighter, more intimate, and fun than the formal PAOS letterhead. The design picks up the meaning of the first character of Nakanishi—NAKA—which means center or middle. It is an amusing bilingual pun of sorts. Interpreting this idea of 'center' or 'middle' further, it seems an appropriate design for one whose career has straddled traditionally disparate fields—design and management consulting."

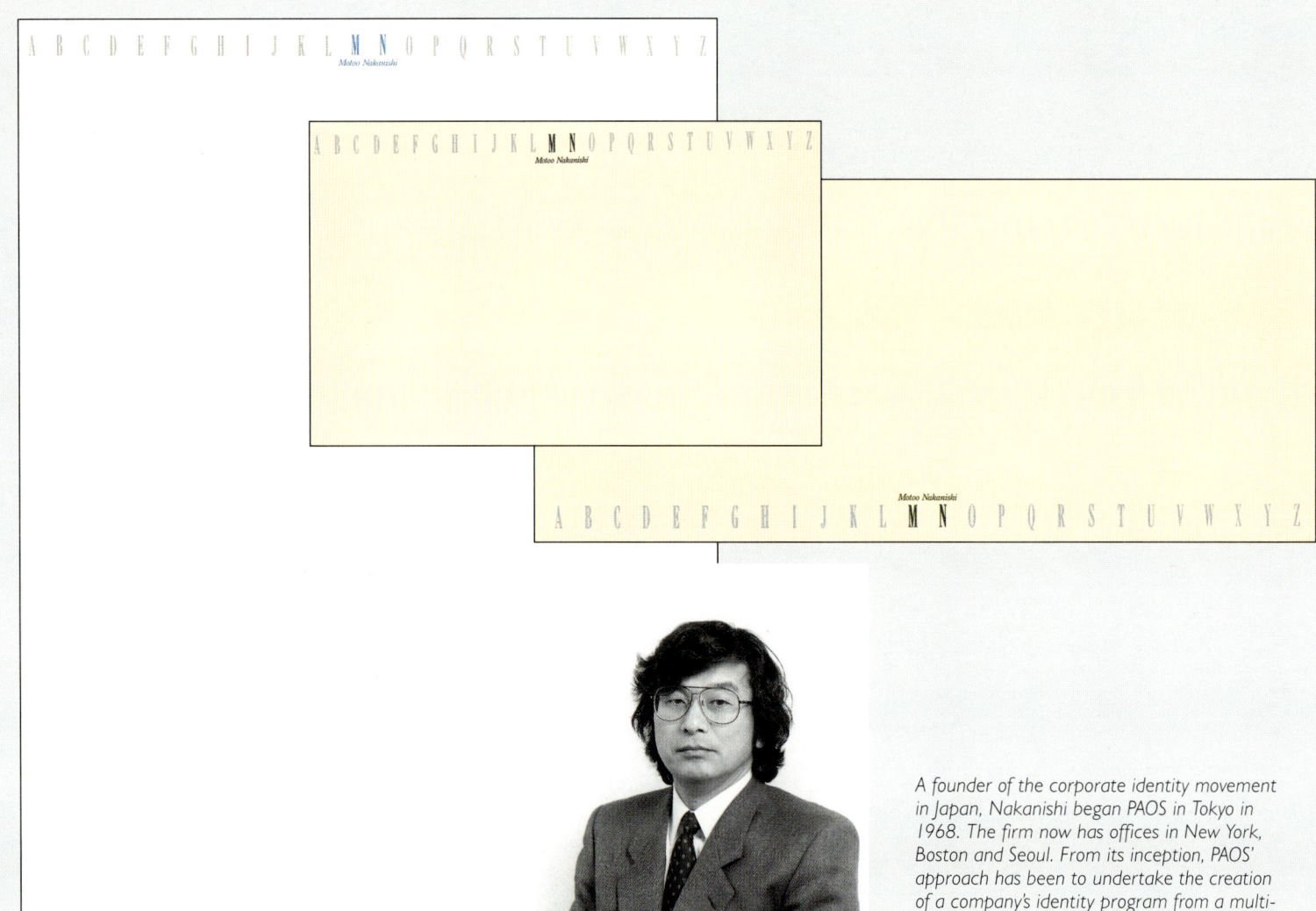

A founder of the corporate identity movement in Japan, Nakanishi began PAOS in Tokyo in 1968. The firm now has offices in New York, Boston and Seoul. From its inception, PAOS' approach has been to undertake the creation of a company's identity program from a multi-disciplined point of view. Nakanishi has expanded his role to include the transformation of a company in all phases including corporate culture, management style, philosophy, employee training, architecture and design. Nakanishi's expression of his identity is expressed through PAOS and its many promotional items.

SIGNAGE

OFFICE INTERIOR

SIGNAGE

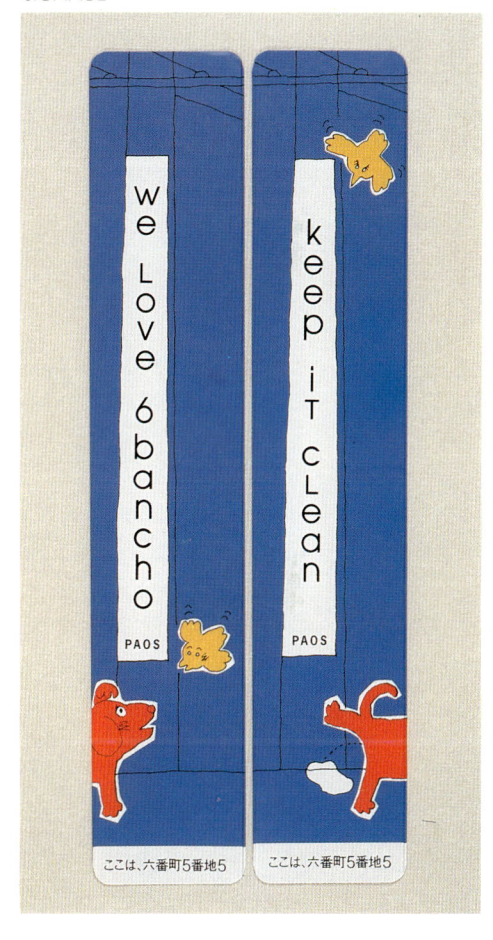

SIGNAGE

OFFICE INTERIOR

CALENDAR

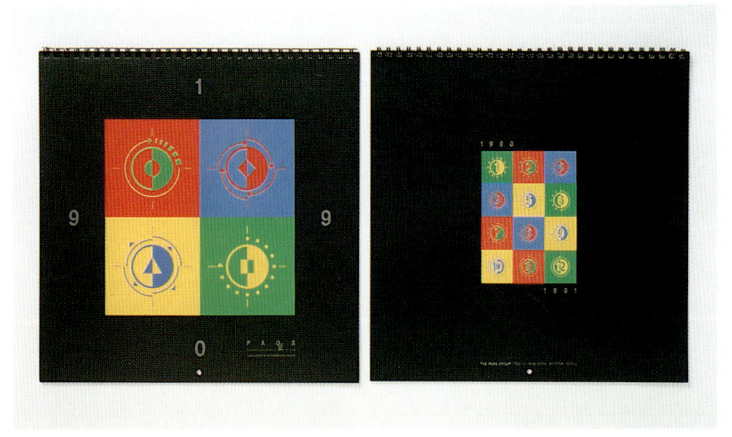

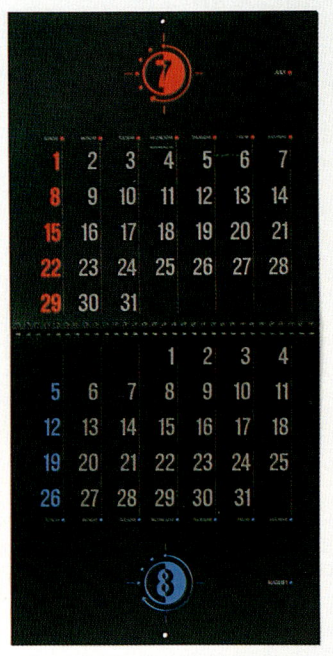

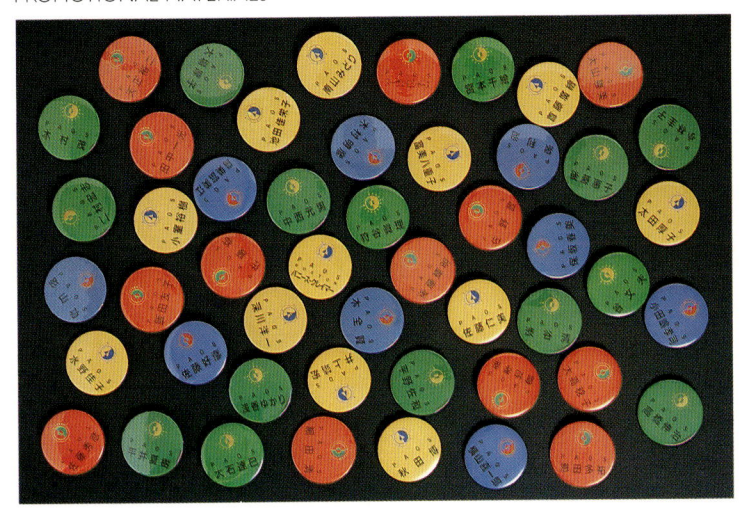

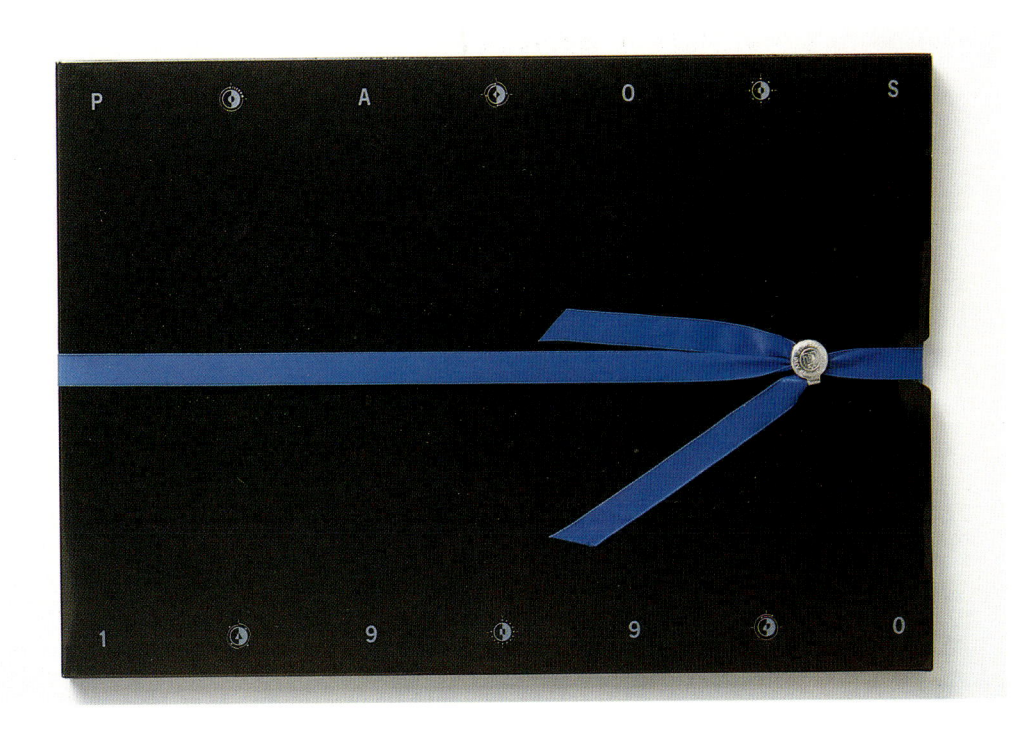

PROMOTIONAL MATERIALS

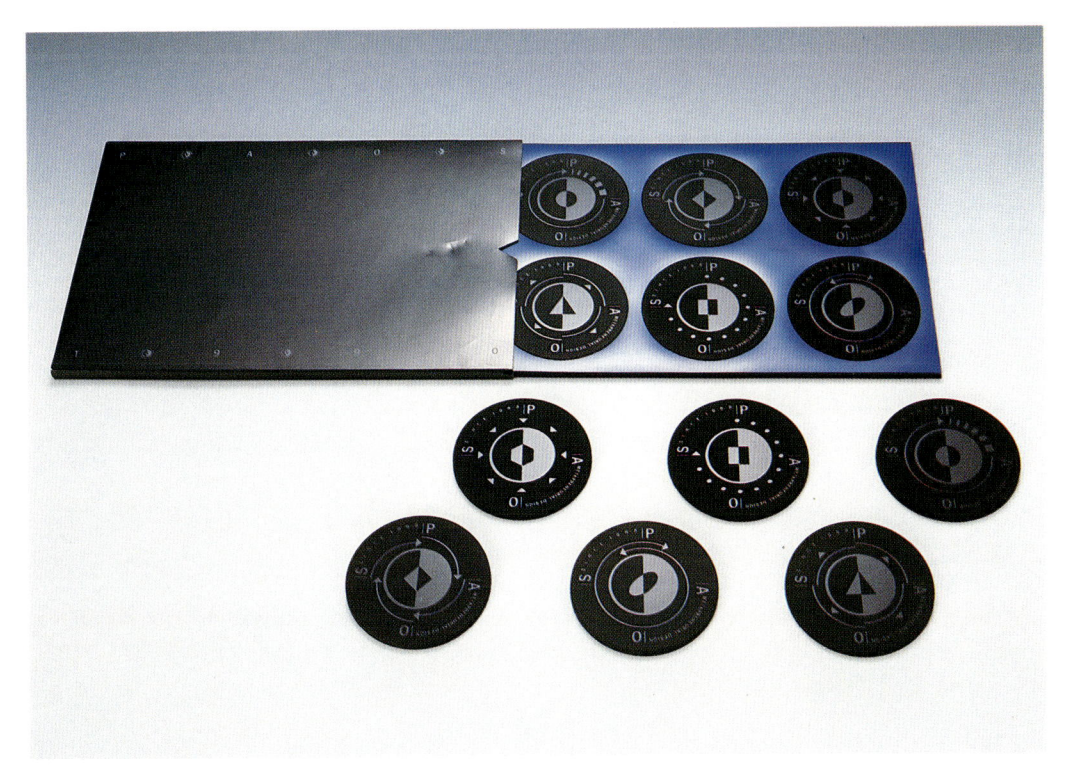

PROMOTIONAL MATERIALS

PUBLICATIONS

188

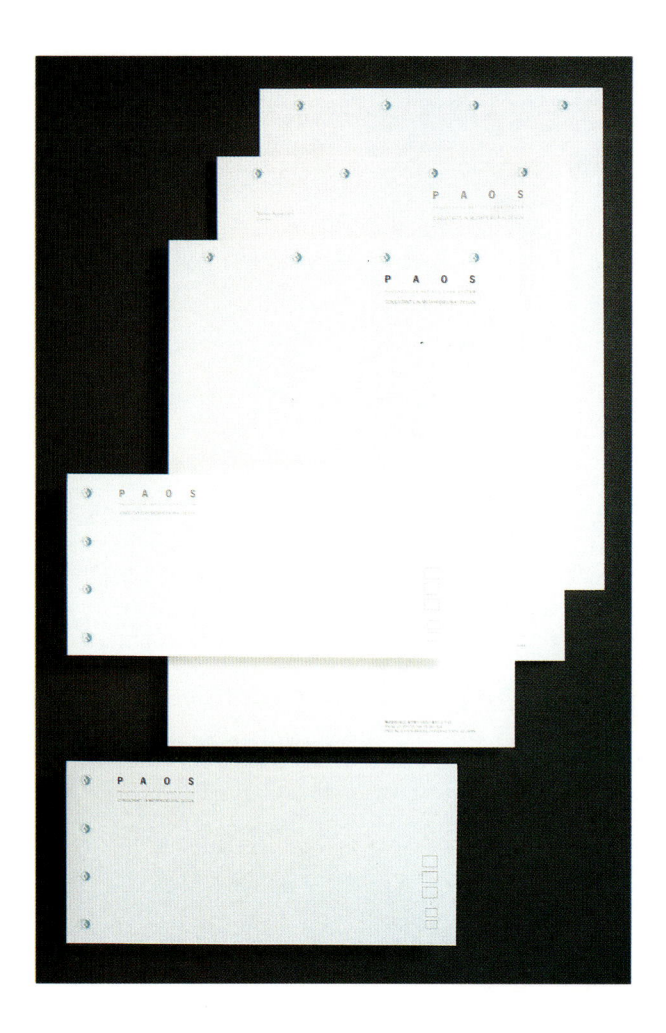

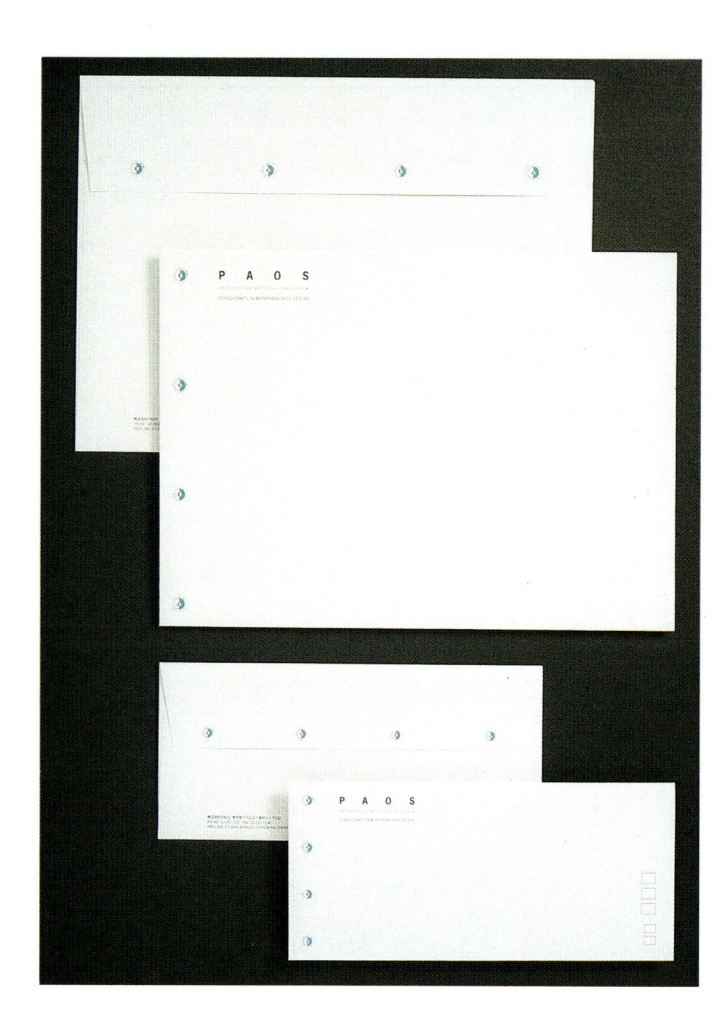

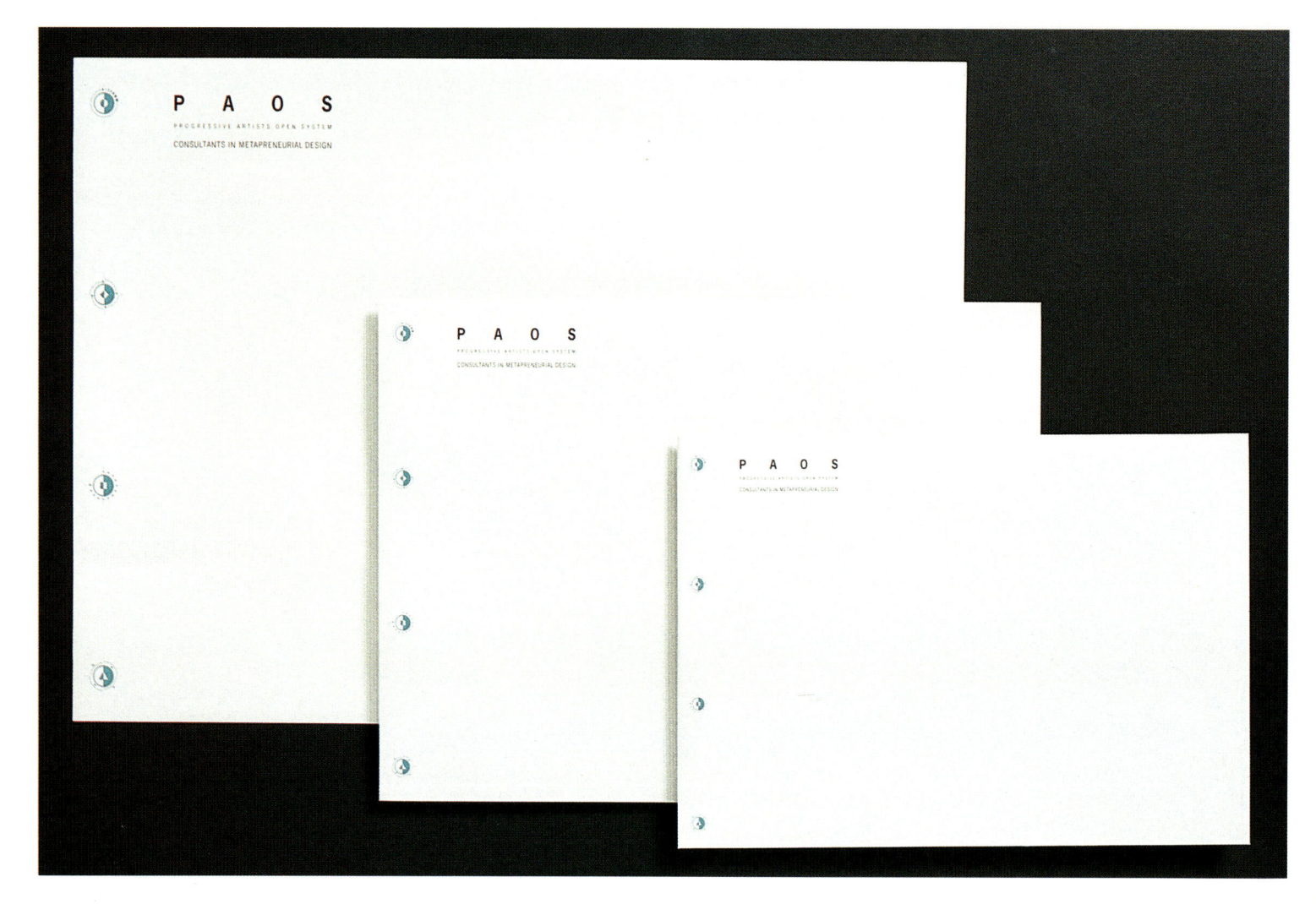

189

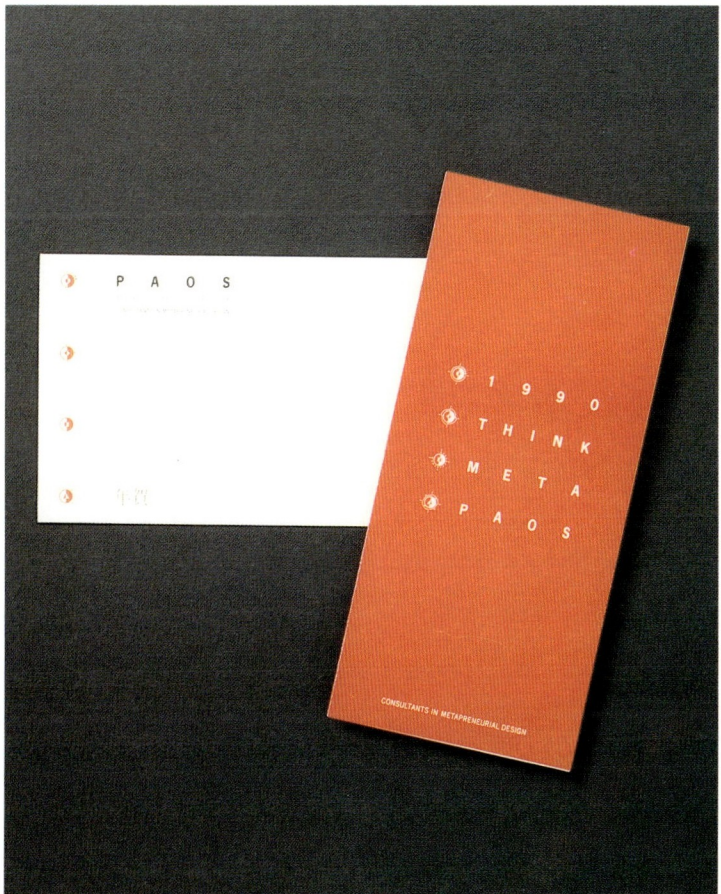

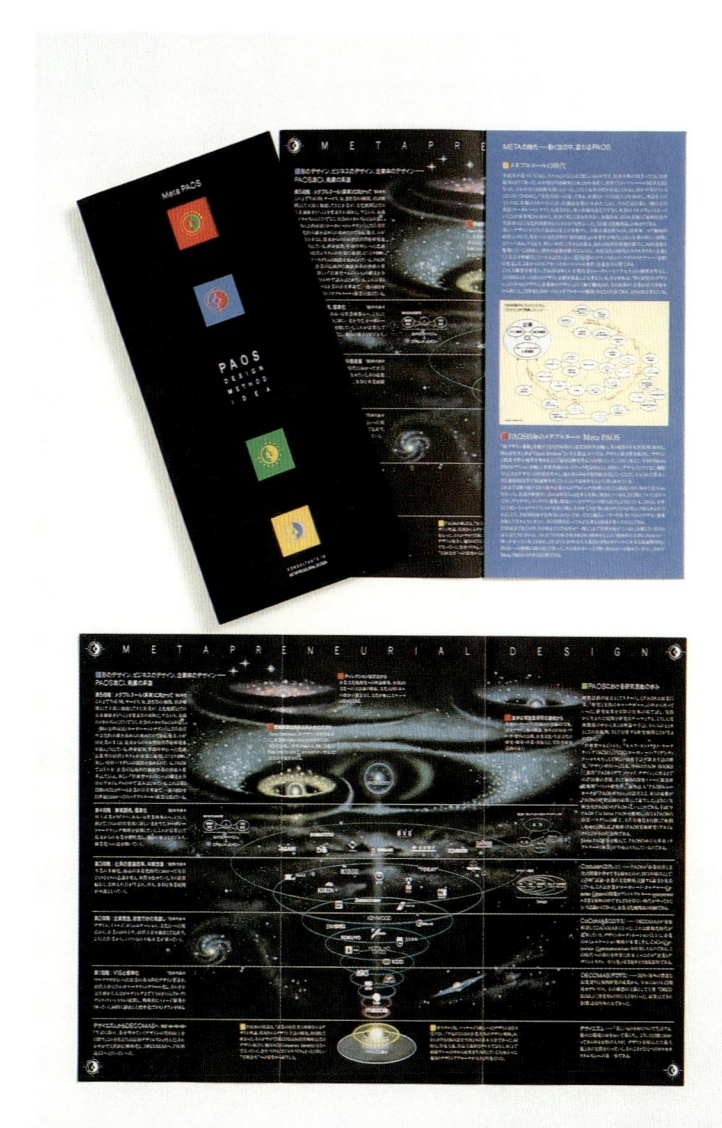

PROMOTIONAL MATERIAL

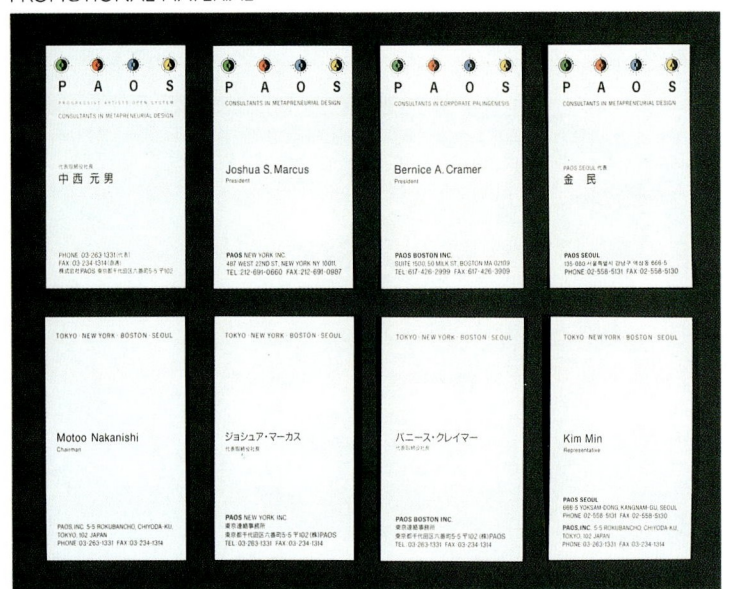

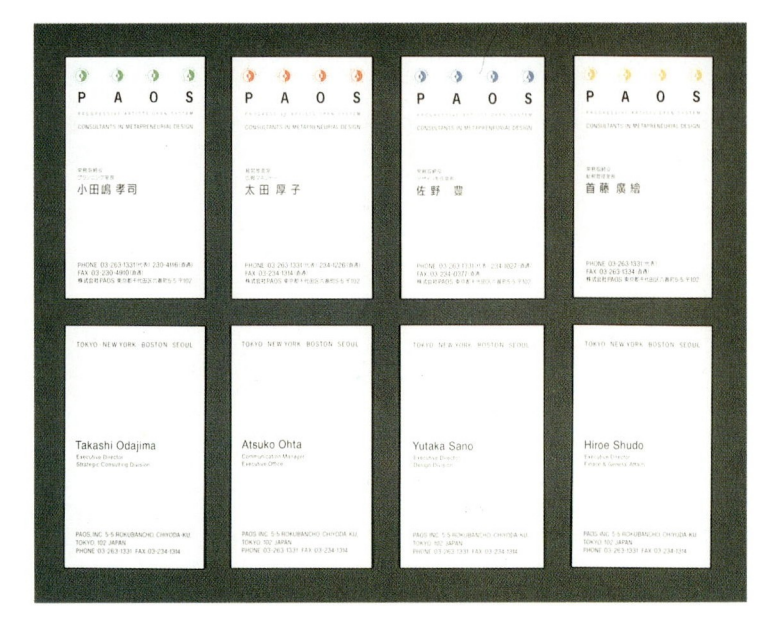

THINK CREATIVE
PAOS

Takashi Akiyama
Graphic Designer
Tokyo, Japan

"The one-eyed owl on my stationery links the eye, which represents vision, to the owl, which represents wisdom. Being both a bird watcher and an illustrator, I take the act of seeing very seriously. The one-eyed owl is both my personal symbol and my office logo; it appears on my business card, letterhead, envelope and seal. Before I invented the one-eyed owl in 1989, my letterhead had only an owl character."

A graduate of Tama Art University, Akiyama is an illustrator and graphic designer known for his work in poster design and for his many design awards.

A COMMUNICATION PORTFOLIO   STICKERS

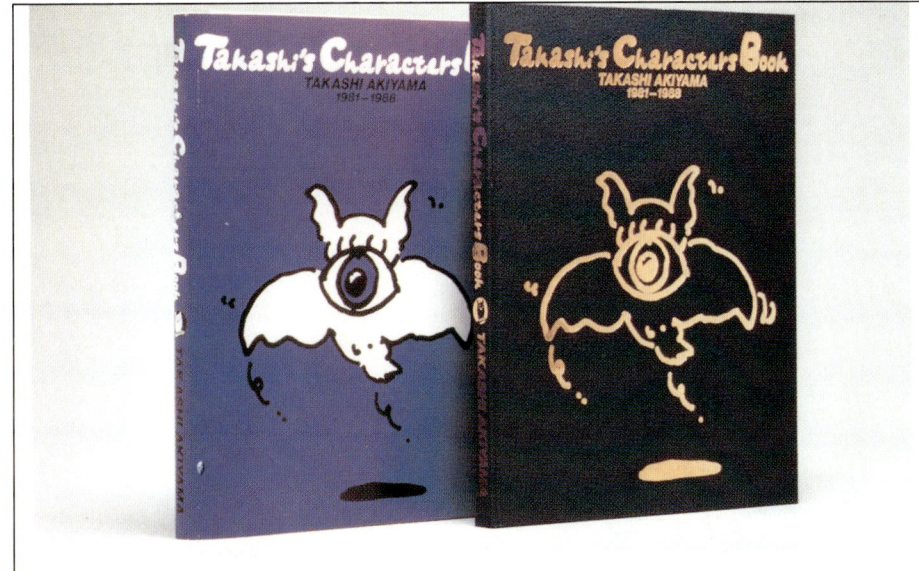

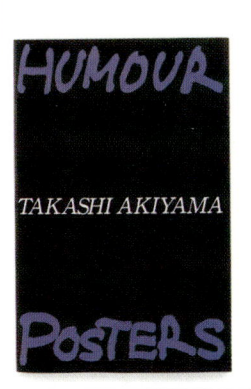

KAN TAI-KEUNG DESIGN & ASSOCIATES LTD.
Kan Tai-keung, *Creative Director*
Hong Kong

"I am a graphic designer and Chinese ink painter, and both are represented in my letterhead which combines a triangular geometric form with a Chinese landscape scene. To further reveal my personal taste and individual style, I utilized a different color scheme in the letterhead, envelope and name card. The choice of paper is Conqueror white, the typeface is serif/Sung style."

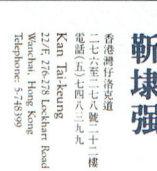

Recognized worldwide as a leading Chinese designer, Kan Tai-keung has won over one hundred and fifty design awards. Following his election as One of Ten Outstanding Young Persons in 1979, he went on to found Kan Tai-keung & Associates where he is currently creative director. His work has been instrumental in several governmental projects.

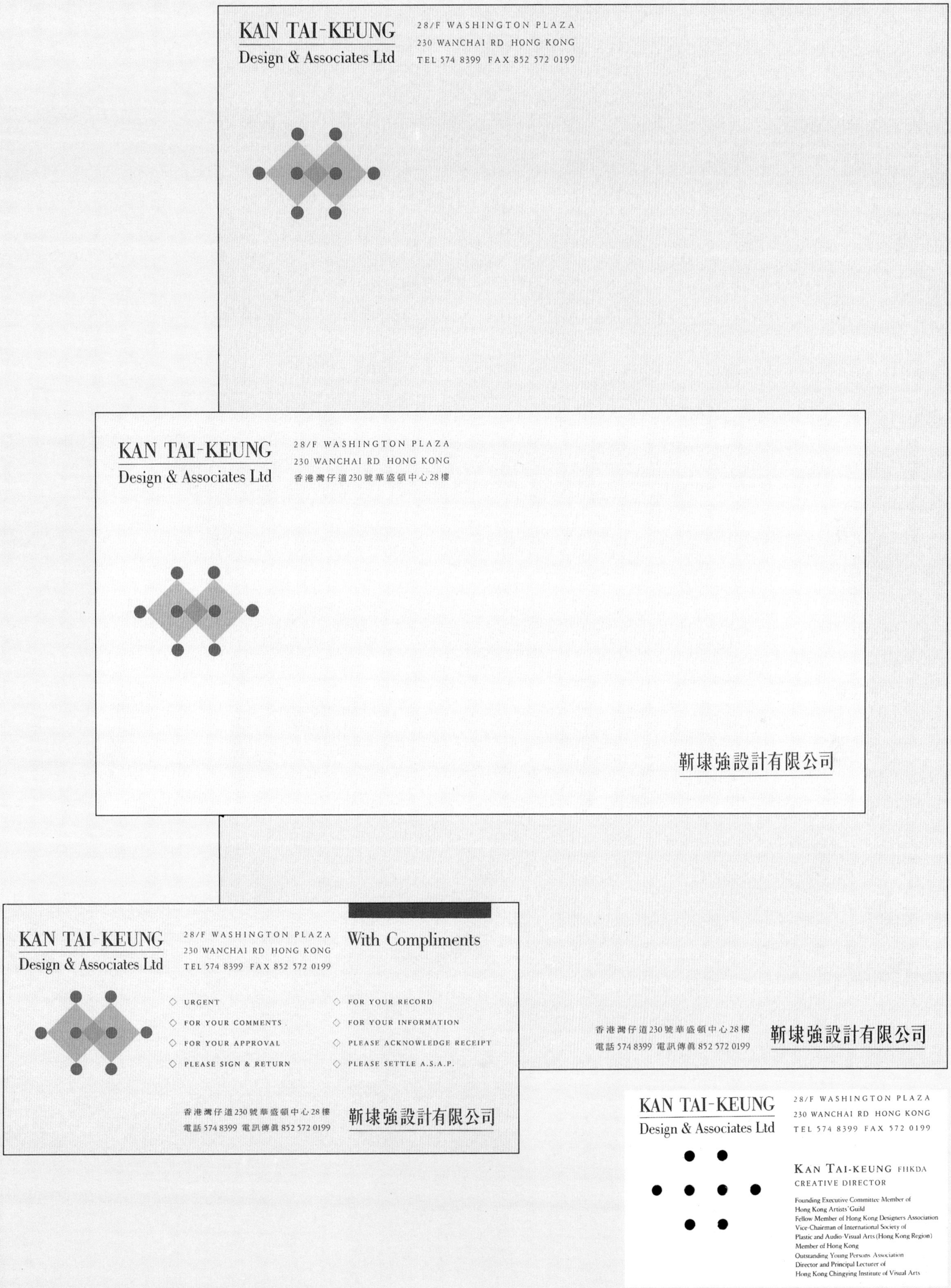

KAN TAI-KEUNG
Design & Associates Ltd

28/F WASHINGTON PLAZA
230 WANCHAI RD HONG KONG
TEL 574 8399 FAX 852 572 0199

KAN TAI-KEUNG
Design & Associates Ltd

28/F WASHINGTON PLAZA
230 WANCHAI RD HONG KONG
香港灣仔道230號華盛頓中心28樓

靳埭強設計有限公司

KAN TAI-KEUNG
Design & Associates Ltd

28/F WASHINGTON PLAZA
230 WANCHAI RD HONG KONG
TEL 574 8399 FAX 852 572 0199

With Compliments

◇ URGENT
◇ FOR YOUR COMMENTS
◇ FOR YOUR APPROVAL
◇ PLEASE SIGN & RETURN

◇ FOR YOUR RECORD
◇ FOR YOUR INFORMATION
◇ PLEASE ACKNOWLEDGE RECEIPT
◇ PLEASE SETTLE A.S.A.P.

香港灣仔道230號華盛頓中心28樓
電話 574 8399 電訊傳真 852 572 0199
靳埭強設計有限公司

香港灣仔道230號華盛頓中心28樓
電話 574 8399 電訊傳真 852 572 0199
靳埭強設計有限公司

KAN TAI-KEUNG
Design & Associates Ltd

28/F WASHINGTON PLAZA
230 WANCHAI RD HONG KONG
TEL 574 8399 FAX 572 0199

KAN TAI-KEUNG FHKDA
CREATIVE DIRECTOR

Founding Executive Committee Member of
Hong Kong Artists' Guild
Fellow Member of Hong Kong Designers Association
Vice-Chairman of International Society of
Plastic and Audio-Visual Arts (Hong Kong Region)
Member of Hong Kong
Outstanding Young Persons Association
Director and Principal Lecturer of
Hong Kong Chingying Institute of Visual Arts

DESIGN FARM
U. G. Sato, President
Tokyo, Japan

"My image is born from the interface between nature and civilization. The outer wall of my office is inlaid with several hundred ceramic replicas of my logo—pencils sprouting forth from a bulb. The same eye-catching image beautifully colors my stationery, designed in 1983 on Spica bond paper in four colors."

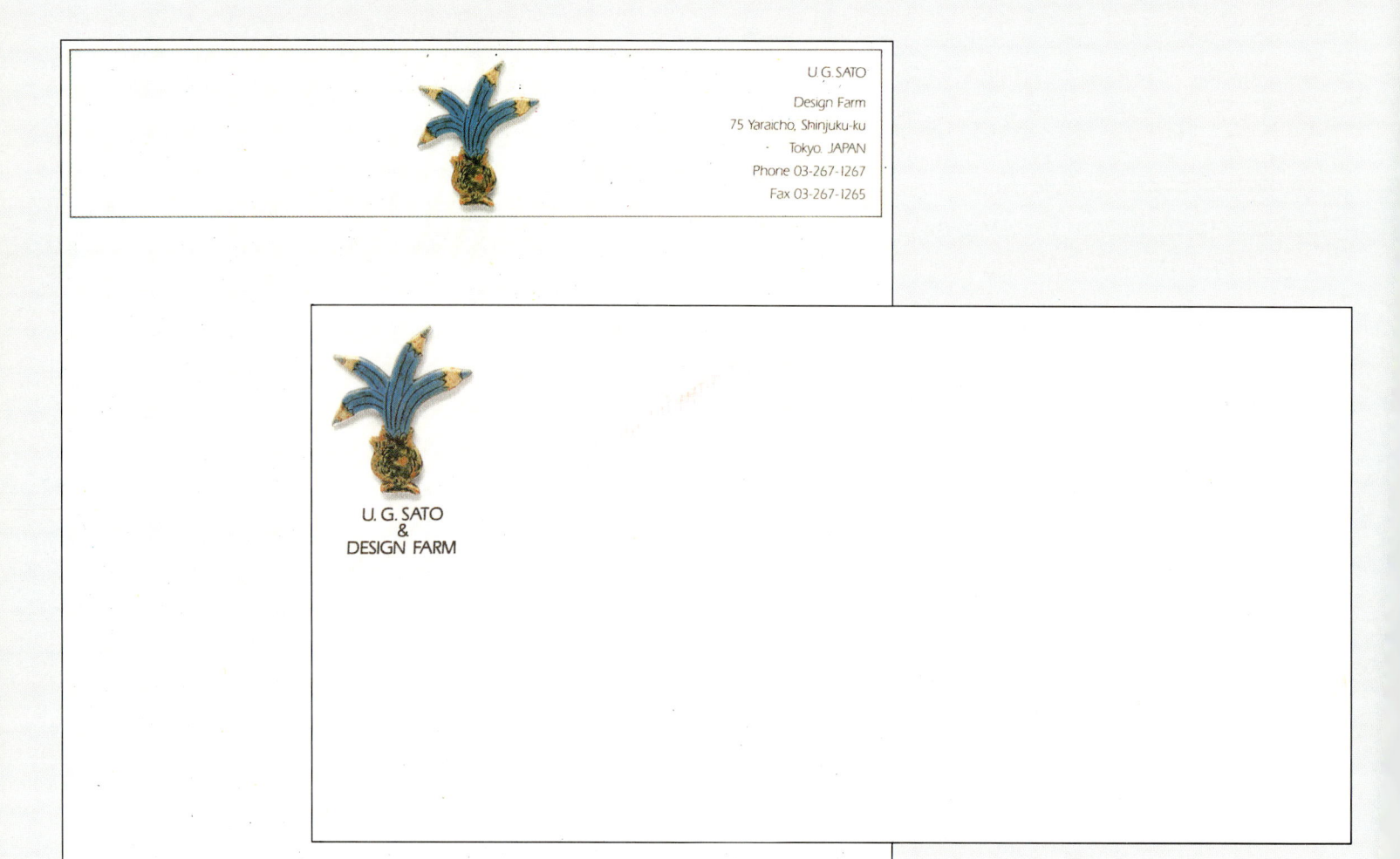

U.G. SATO
Design Farm
75 Yaraicho, Shinjuku-ku
Tokyo, JAPAN
Phone 03-267-1267
Fax 03-267-1265

U. G. SATO
&
DESIGN FARM

Sato studied at Tokyo Gakugei University and graduated from the Kuwazawa Design Institute. He has had numerous one-man exhibits in various countries including Japan, Czechoslovakia, Holland and Finland and has exhibited in the U.S. Among Sato's many design awards are the Gold Medal at the National Commercial Artists Exhibition in Japan, the Gold Prize at the Biennale of Graphic Design in Czechoslovakia, First Prize at the Lahti III Poster Biennale in Finland, and Prize of the Union of Bulgarian Artists in Sculpture.

SIGNAGE

OFFICE EXTERIOR

Susumo Endo
Artist/Graphic Designer
Tokyo, Japan

"The objects that I have been using for my artwork are from everyday life, things people handle and put on the table on a daily basis: eggs, fruit, glass bottles, newspapers, books, light bulbs, pencils…. The pencil is the most familiar item to me as an artist."

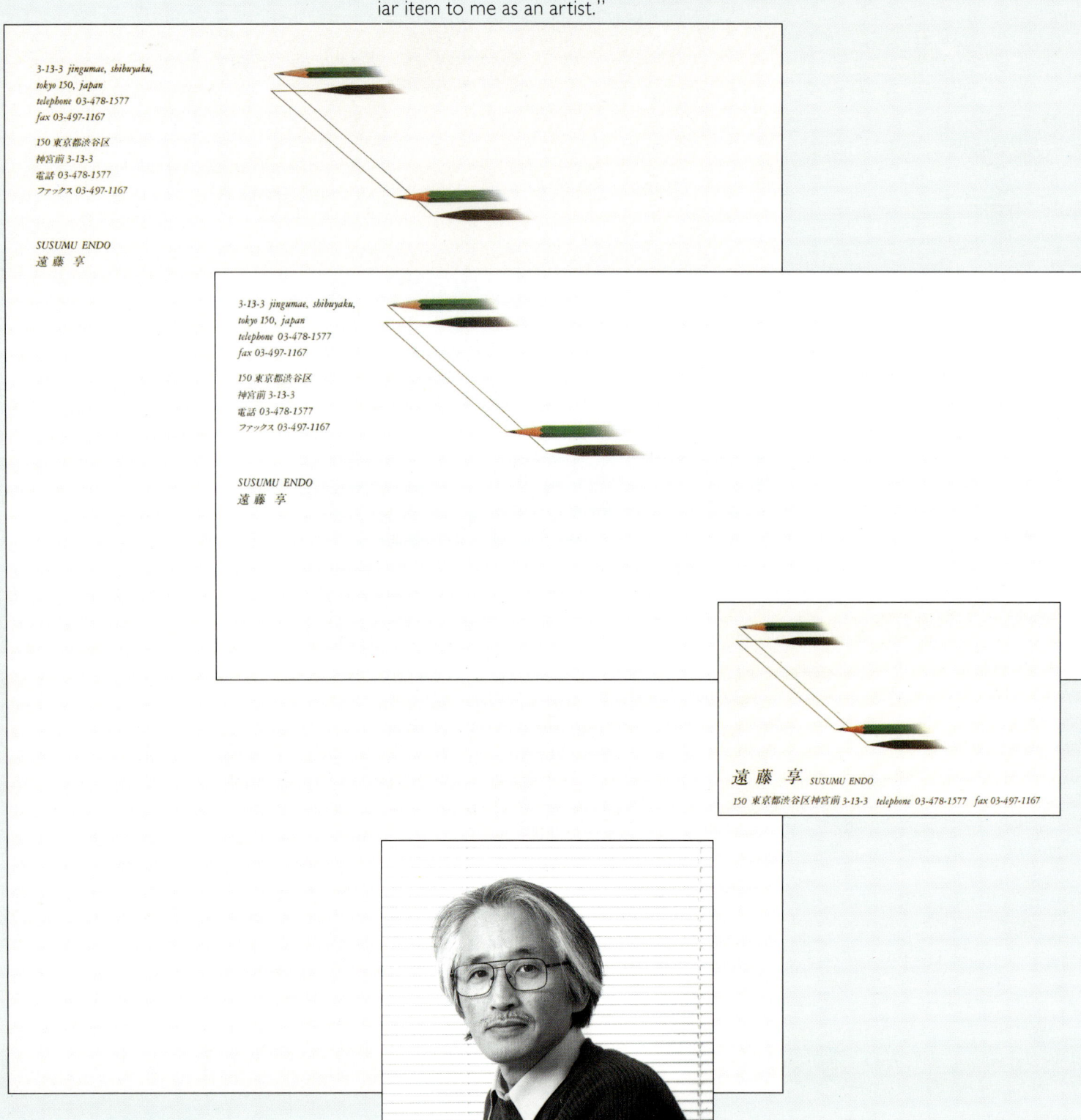

Susumu Endo is known for his beautiful and subtle graphic design work, most notably in posters and packaging. He has received many outstanding design awards, including, most recently, the Purchase Prize of the Agency for Cultural Affairs in Tokyo.

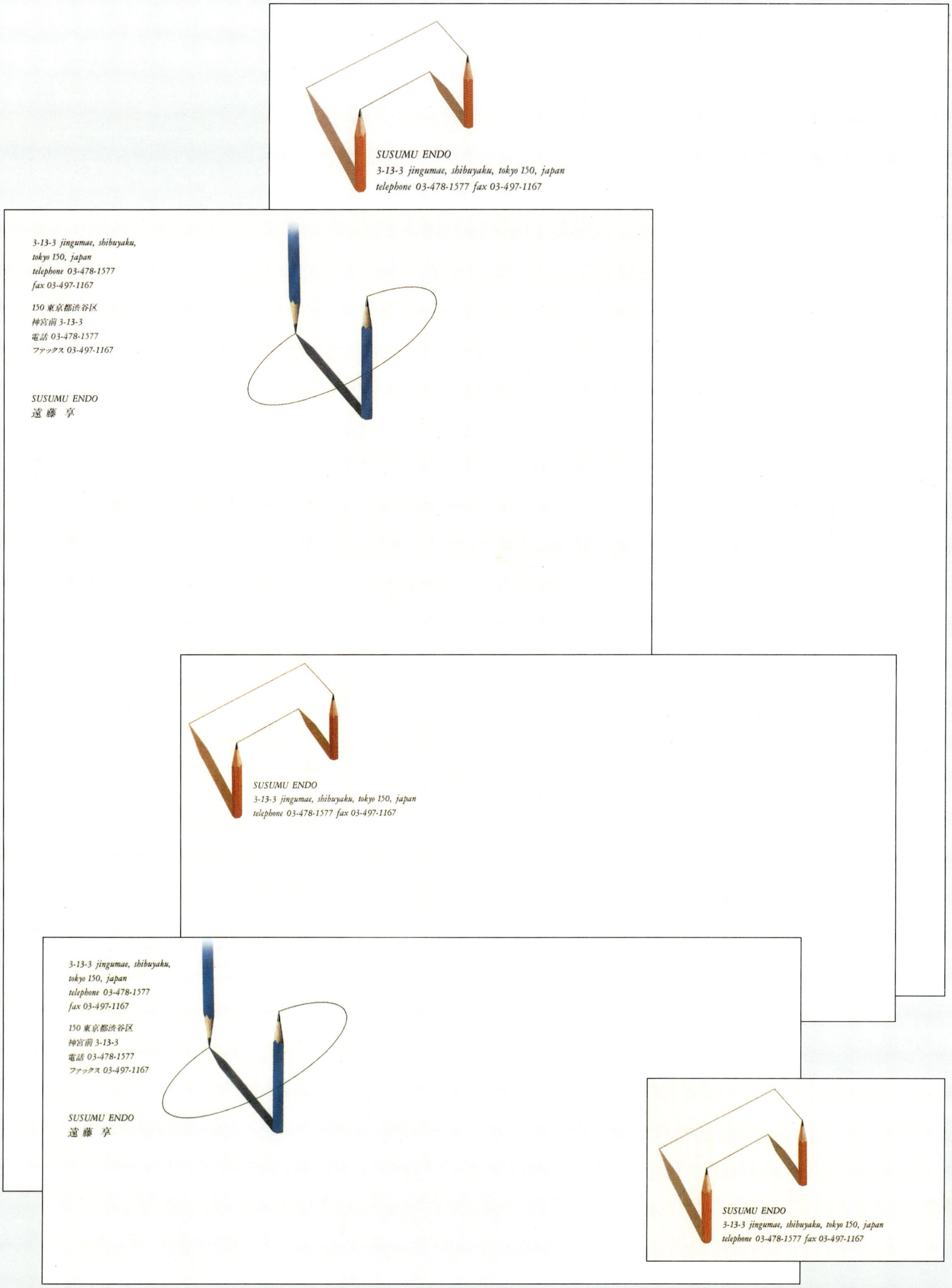

SUSUMU ENDO
3-13-3 jingumae, shibuyaku, tokyo 150, japan
telephone 03-478-1577 fax 03-497-1167

3-13-3 jingumae, shibuyaku,
tokyo 150, japan
telephone 03-478-1577
fax 03-497-1167

150 東京都渋谷区
神宮前 3-13-3
電話 03-478-1577
ファックス 03-497-1167

SUSUMU ENDO
遠藤 享

SUSUMU ENDO
3-13-3 jingumae, shibuyaku, tokyo 150, japan
telephone 03-478-1577 fax 03-497-1167

3-13-3 jingumae, shibuyaku,
tokyo 150, japan
telephone 03-478-1577
fax 03-497-1167

150 東京都渋谷区
神宮前 3-13-3
電話 03-478-1577
ファックス 03-497-1167

SUSUMU ENDO
遠藤 享

SUSUMU ENDO
3-13-3 jingumae, shibuyaku, tokyo 150, japan
telephone 03-478-1577 fax 03-497-1167

Design Room Itoh
Toyotsugu Itoh, *Superintendent*
Nagoya, Japan

"My letterhead combines design with illustration to create a distinctive image. The bold use of red at the bottom of the page serves as a strong accent, contrasting with the pristine white paper. I take great care to achieve a desirable balance in the design, taking into account the lettering and white space and their relationship to the other design elements."

POSTCARD

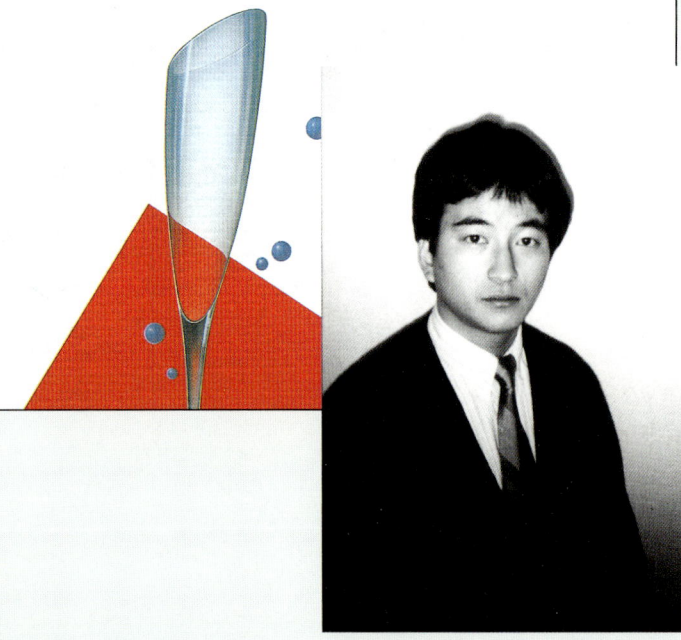

Born in 1958, Toyotsugu Itoh began his own firm, Design Room Itoh, at age 23. As an emerging young illustrator, he is becoming well-known for his refined artwork.

POSTCARDS

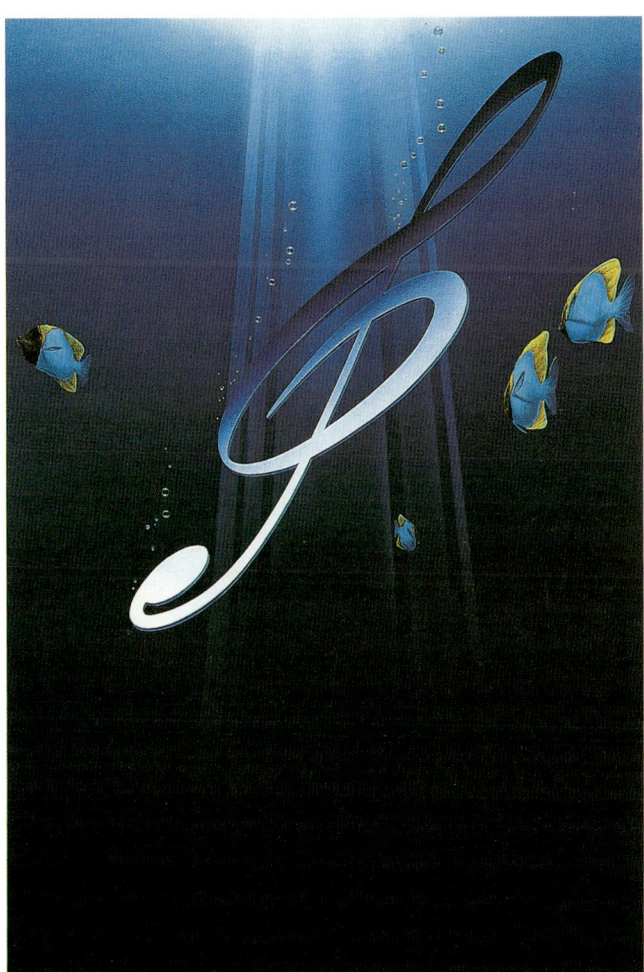

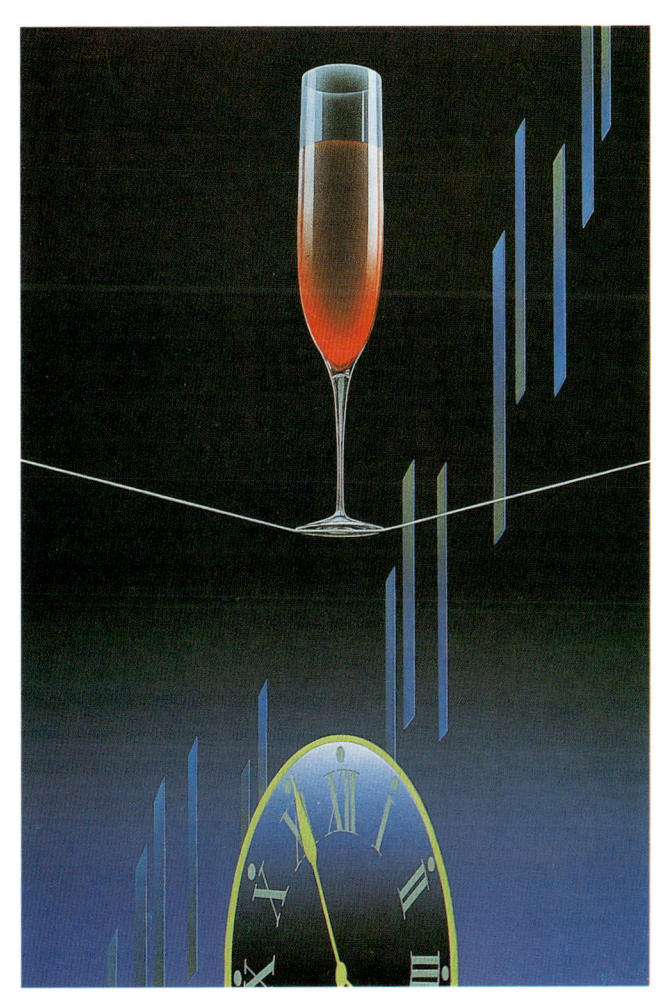

HELMUT SCHMID DESIGN
Helmut Schmid, *Proprietor*
Suita-Shi, Japan

"My stationery expresses the consistency of my design philosophy. For ten years I have been using a letterhead which stresses the bi-lingual address as an informative design element. When my address changed slightly, I retained the basic design, unobtrusively integrating the old address with the new one."

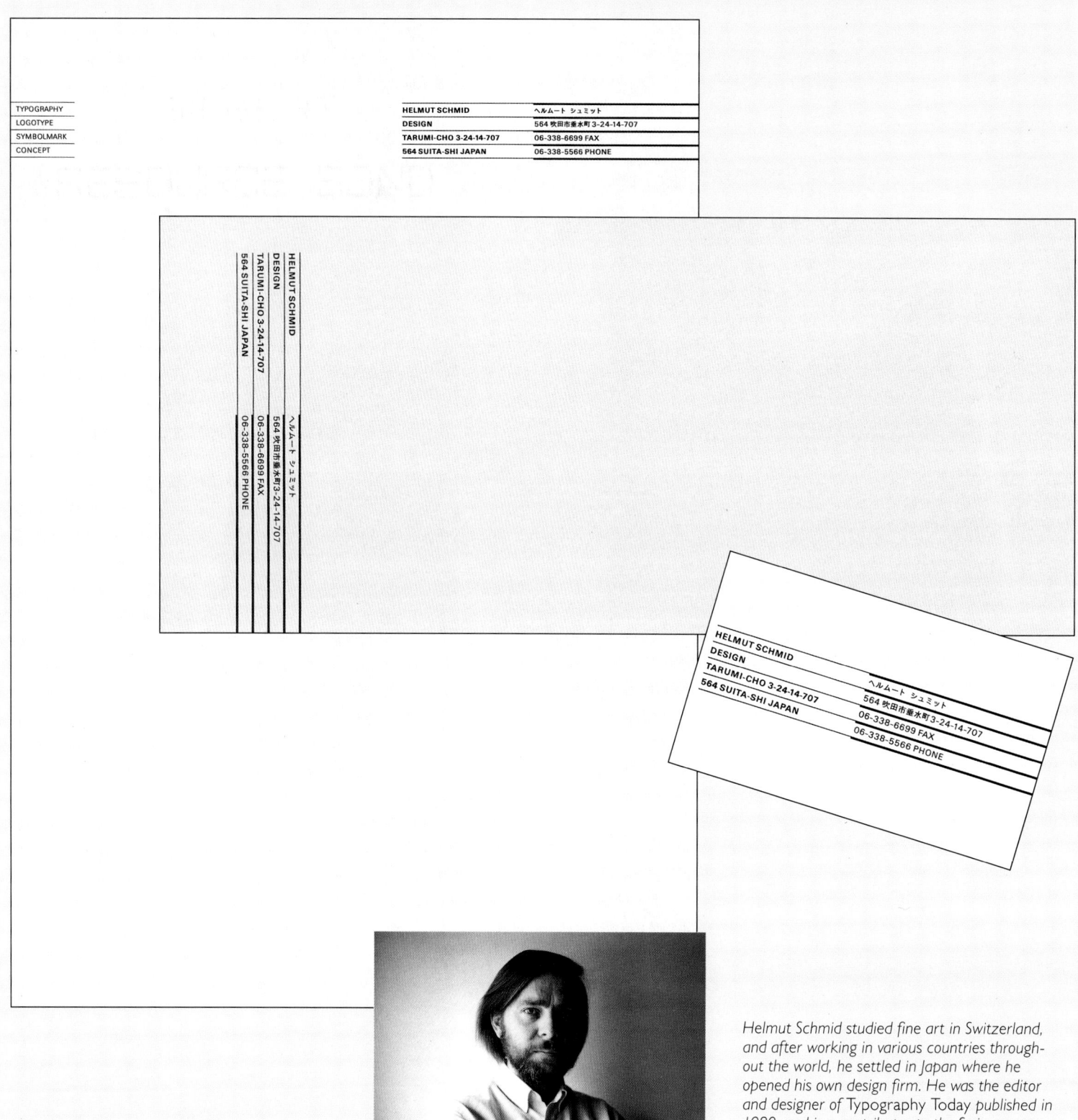

Helmut Schmid studied fine art in Switzerland, and after working in various countries throughout the world, he settled in Japan where he opened his own design firm. He was the editor and designer of Typography Today published in 1980, and is a contributor to the Swiss magazine, Typografische Monatsblatter. He is also a member of several graphic design societies.

Australia

PORTFOLIO

PORTFOLIO

PORTFOLIO

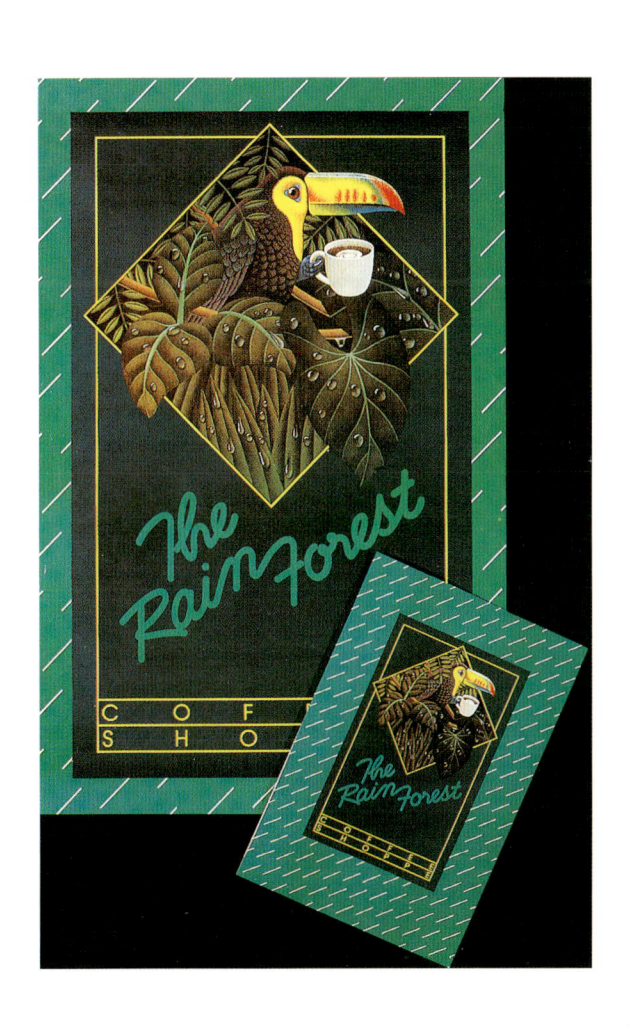

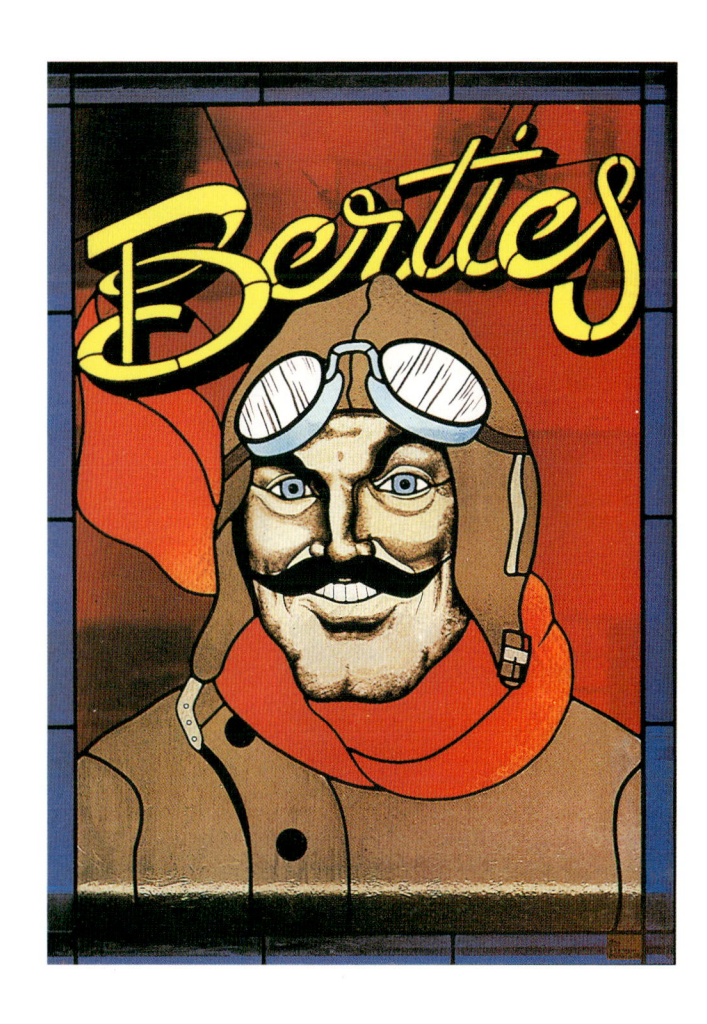

PORTFOLIO

PORTFOLIO

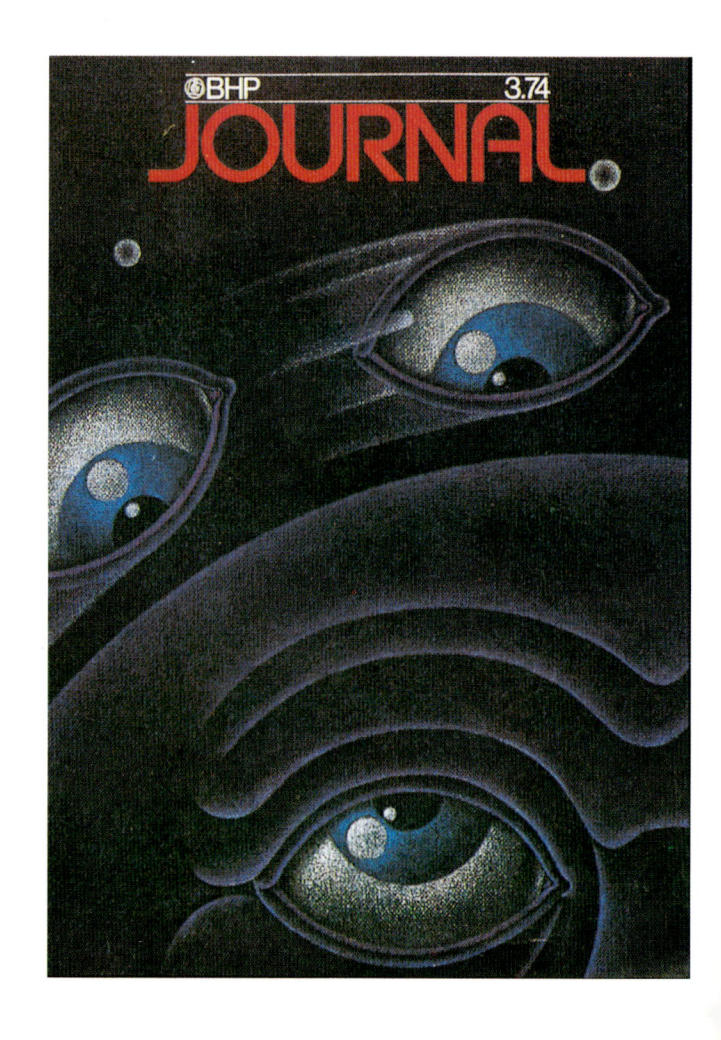

EYMONT KIN-YEE DESIGN
Anna Eymont, Myriam Kin-Yee, *Principals*
Paddington, Australia

"Created in 1987 when Anna Eymont and Myriam Kin-Yee joined forces to establish their present design business, the logo reflects the delicate balance between the formality of the corporate image and the creativity of the designer's art."

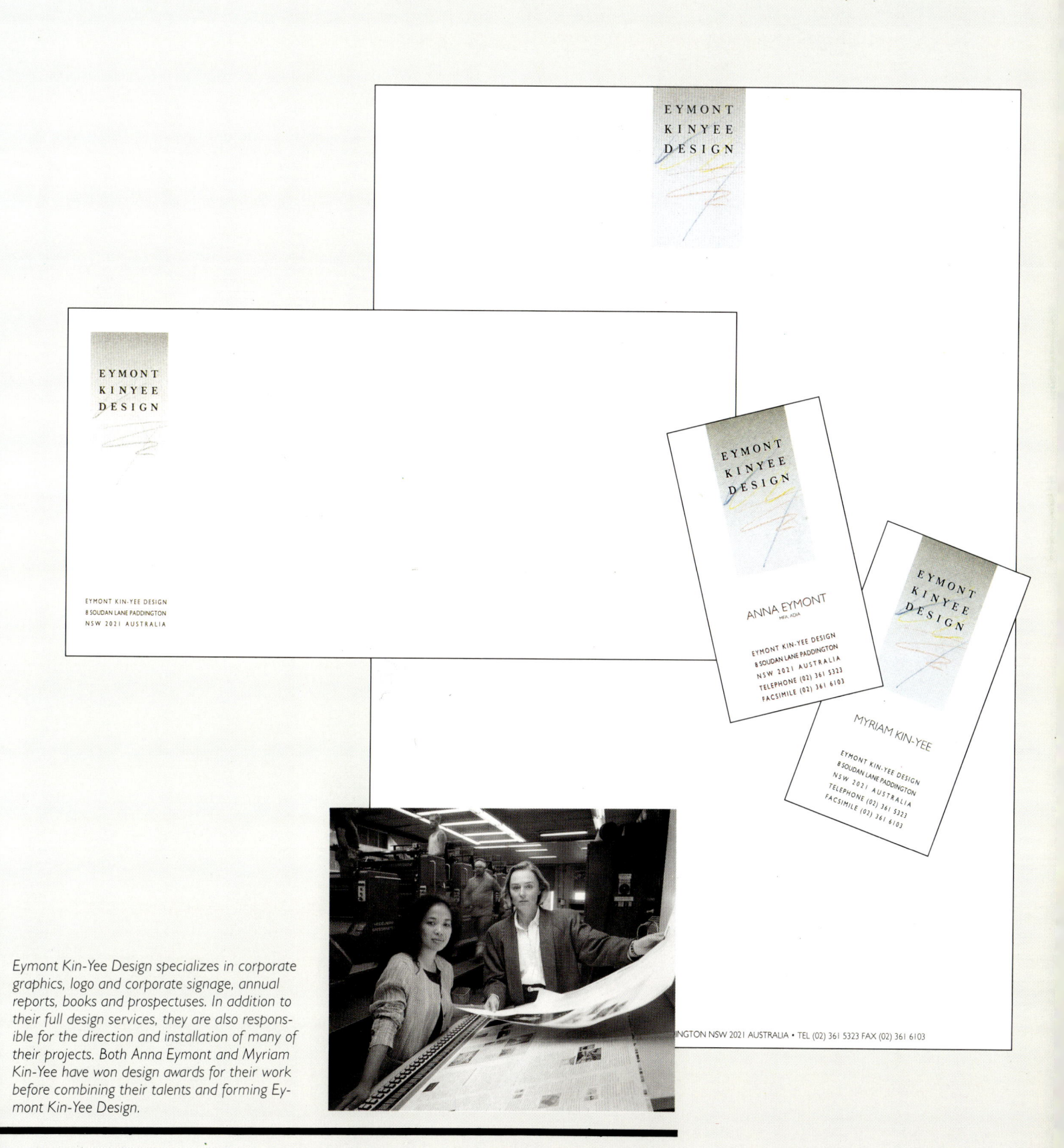

Eymont Kin-Yee Design specializes in corporate graphics, logo and corporate signage, annual reports, books and prospectuses. In addition to their full design services, they are also responsible for the direction and installation of many of their projects. Both Anna Eymont and Myriam Kin-Yee have won design awards for their work before combining their talents and forming Eymont Kin-Yee Design.

COMMUNICATION PORTFOLIO

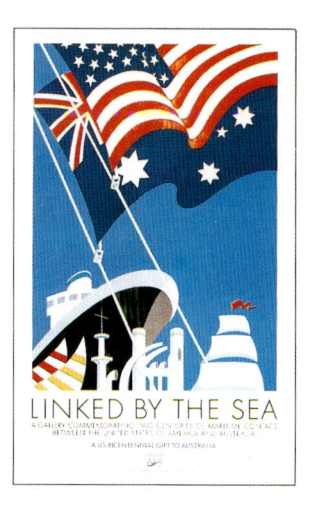

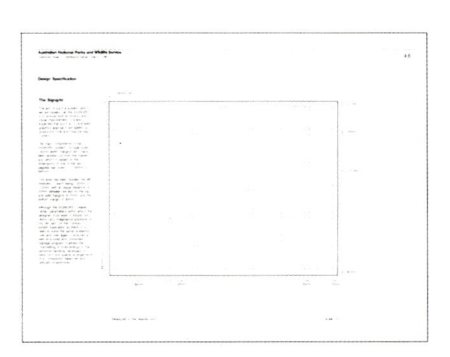

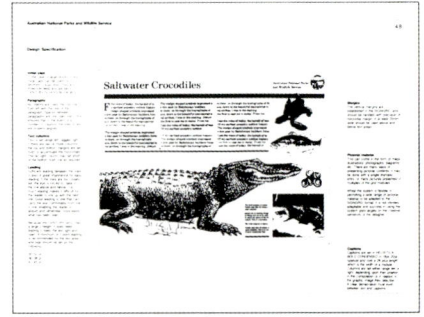

COMMUNICATION PORTFOLIO

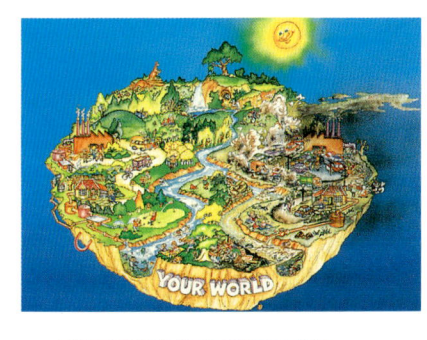

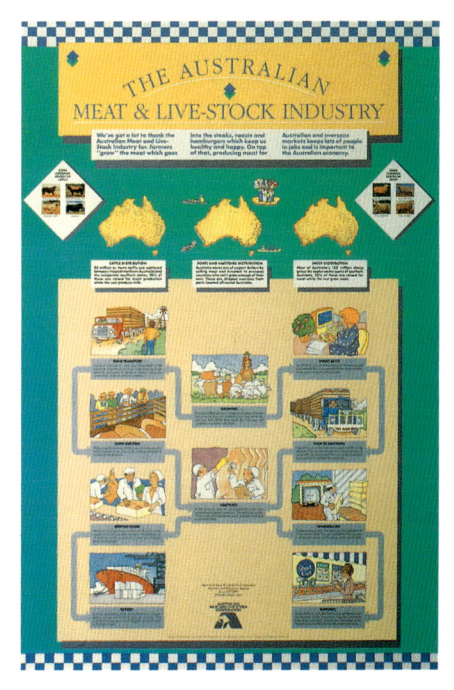

213

COMMUNICATION PORTFOLIO

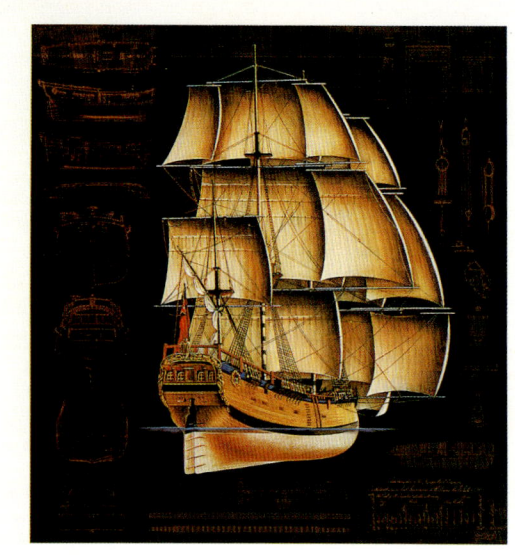

LOGOS

COMMUNICATION PORTFOLIO

COMMUNICATION PORTFOLIO

APPENDIX

DESIGNER DIRECTORY
FROM THE ISRAEL MUSEUM "SELF-IMAGE" EXHIBIT

Entries and addresses listed in this directory are based on submissions to the Israel Museum "SELF-IMAGE" exhibit. The information presented was verified as correct as of January 1989.

2 Associates Inc.
Alter & Dunkelman
198 Walnut Avenue
Toronto M6J 2N6, Ontario, Canada

Aaron Marcus and Associates
1196 Euclid Avenue
Berkeley, CA 94708, USA

Ulla & Tapani Aartomaa
Kelohongantie 7
15200 Lahti 20, Finland

AB&S Grup de Disseny
Avgda. Sta. Barbara 4-6 Entl. F
43870 Amposta, Spain

Lasse Åberg
Fånäsvagen 2
19800 Bålsta, Sweden

ADGFAD
Josep Maria Vallbona
Brusi 45
08006 Barcelona, Spain

Oswald Adler
Ibm Gvirol 179
Tel Aviv 62033, Israel

Advertising Designers Incorporated
818 North La Brea Avenue
Los Angeles, CA 90038, USA

Roland Aeschlimann
11, boulevard du Théâtre
1211 Geneva 11, Switzerland

Takashi Akiyama
2-21-12-301 Nishi-Ikebukuro
Tashima-ku, Tokyo, Japan

Alan Wood Graphic Design, Inc.
274 Madison Avenue
New York, NY 10016, USA

Walter Allner
100 Riverside Drive
New York, NY 10024, USA

Gad Almaliah
Michal 19
Tel Aviv 62361, Israel

Altraforma SA
Sandros & Saenz
P. Manuel Girona, 71, 1er, 3a
08034 Barcelona, Spain

Moshe Amar
Kikar Kedoumim 1
Old Yafo, Israel

Moti Amit
Hallanot 5A POB 5207
Givat Nesher 20300, Israel

Mickey Amit
Sokolov 58
Herzliyah 46380, Israel

Peter Andermatt
Im Buël
8627 Grüningen, ZH, Switzerland

Philippe Apeloig
18, rue de l'Hôtel de Ville
75004 Paris, France

Sarah Arbel
POB 13209
Tel Aviv, Israel

Arcadi Moradell & Associados
Paseo Bonanova 14 Torre A
08022 Barcelona, Spain

Per Arnoldi
Toldbodgade 77
DK-1253 Copenhagen, Denmark

Sherry Arnon
Jabotinsky 133
Tel Aviv 62150, Israel

Santi Artigas
Major, 19
08393 Caldetes (Barcelona), Spain

Atelier Gérard Finel & Associés
3 rue Lacépède
75005 Paris, France

Michael Atteneder
Sebekstrasse 12/2
4400 Steyr, Austria

Ehud Avishai
Cordova 3
Tel Aviv 62487, Israel

Kiyoshi Awazu
1-5-24 Minami, Tama-ku
Kawasaki City, Kanagawa, Japan

Josep Baga
Amigo 42, 2o, 2a
08021 Barcelona, Spain

Bagby Design Incorporated
225 North Michigan Avenue
Chicago, Illinois 60601, USA

Franco Barbon
Viale Vicenza 92
36061 Bassano del Grappa (VI), Italy

Emili Bargués
Ramon i Cajal, 82 2on. 1a.2oN.1a.
08012 Barcelona, Spain

Barnes Design Office
666 North Lake Shore Drive, Suite 1408
Chicago, Illinois 60611, USA

Baró & Vicente
Aribau, 265, 1er 3a
08021 Barcelona, Spain

Gladys Barton
245 Everit Avenue
Hewlett, NY 11557, USA

Andrea Baruffi
341 Hudson Terrace
Piermont, NY 10968, USA

Saul Bass
7039 Sunset Blvd.
Los Angeles, CA 90028, USA

Luis Bassat
Caballeros, 84-88
08034 Barcelona, Spain

Boy Bastiaens
Smissenhaag 74
6228HH Maastricht, The Netherlands

Mark J. Batty
14 Cold Stream Lane
Upper Saddle River, NJ 07458, USA

Ariella Bayer
Struck 15
Tel Aviv, Israel

Justyna Bednarska
ul. Potocka 60 M.1
01-652 Warszawa, Poland

Marat Beljavjev
Candera 7-504
129075 Moscow, USSR

Félix Beltrán
Apartado de Correos M 10733
Mexico 06000 DF, Mexico

Ramon Berga
Portell, 8 Bxos
08023 Barcelona, Spain

Anna Berkenbusch
Witzlebenstrasse 19
1000 Berlin 19, Germany

Beroepsvereniging Nederlandse Ontwerpers
Rob Huisman & Mart. Warmerdam
Het Arsenaal
Waterlooplein 219
1011 PG Amsterdam, The Netherlands

Florence A. Bezrutczyk
The Clock Tower
161 Hollywood Drive
Oakdale, NY 11769, USA

Bruce Blackburn
331 Park Avenue South
New York, NY 10010, USA

Blake + Barancik Design Group, Inc.
1919 Panama Street
Philadelphia, Pennsylvania 19103, USA

R.O. Blechman
The Ink Tank
2 West 47th Street
New York, NY 10036, USA

Bobbye Cochran & Associates
400 West Erie Street, Suite 300
Chicago, Illinois 60610, USA

Egidio Bonfante
Corso Sempione 54
Milano 20145, Italy

Phillipe Boulakia
Mendela 9
Tel Aviv, Israel

Paul + Ann Bowers
6 Bryant Place
Fredonia, NY 14063, USA

Ian Bradbery
125 Hereford Street
Glebe NSW 2037, Australia

Helmut Brade
Hoher Weg 1
402 Halle/Saale, Germany

Pieter Brattinga
Prinsengracht 628
Amsterdam 1017 KT, The Netherlands

Sheila Levrant de Bretteville
8067 Willow Glen Road
Los Angeles, CA 90046, USA

BRS Premsela Vonk
Nieuwe Prinsengracht 89
1018 VR Amsterdam, The Netherlands

Boris Bucan
Ilica 150
41000 Zagreb, Yugoslavia

Stephan Bundi
Thunstrasse 15
CH-3005 Bern, Switzerland

Hartwig Burchard
Wiesenweg 4, Walmsburg
2122 Bleckede, Germany

Feliks Büttner
Dorfstrasse 55, Mühle 2
2520 Rostock 22, Lichtenhagen PF 192
Germany

Mel Calman
Cartoon Gallery
83 Lambs Conduit Street
London WC 1, England

Ezio Campese
via Novi 1
15048 Valenza (Al), Italy

Carbone Smolan Associates
170 Fifth Avenue
New York, NY 10010, USA

Carnase
Thirty East 21st Street
New York, NY 10010, USA

Carol Naughton + Associates Inc.
213 West Institute Place
Chicago, Illinois 60610, USA

Wilhelm Georg Cassel
Kuhdyk 20
4150 Krefeld-Traar, Germany

Ken Cato
254 Swan Street, Richmond
Victoria 3121, Australia

Jim Cave
P.O. Box 5274, Postal Station "A"
Toronto, Ontario M5W 1N5, Canada

Eduard Cehovin
Ljube Stojanovica 35
11000 Beograd, Yugoslavia

Central Institute of Industrial Design
St. Valev
34 Totleben Boulevard
1606 Sofia, Bulgaria

Guillermo Chamorro
Calle Cenicientos, 84. B
28039 Madrid, Spain

Sheryl Checkman
531 East 87th Street
New York, NY 10128, USA

Chermayeff & Geismar Assoc.
Ivan Chermayeff
15 East 26th Street
New York, NY 10010, USA

Hoi L. Chu
39 West 29 Street
New York, NY 10001, USA

Seymour Chwast
215 Park Avenue South
New York, NY 10003, USA

Onésim Colavidas
Passatge Forasté 15
08022 Barcelona, Spain

Coley, Porter, and Bell Ltd.
4 Flitcroft Street
London WC2H 8DJ, England

Communication Design NV
Ray Laenens
Rubenslaan 10
B-2970 Hever, Belgium

Concepts Design
Floor Kamphorst & Anna Stienstra
Kromboomssloot 65
1011 GS Amsterdam, The Netherlands

Contemporain
Lidia van Weenen
Oude Amersfoortseweg 240
1212 AD Hilversum, The Netherlands

Antoni Piñoz Cort
Arquebisbe Pere de Cardona No. 2
Salou, Spain

Creative
Lea Dagan & Tamy Atiya
Sherot Kish 9
Haifa 34721, Israel

James A. Cross
10513 West Pico Blvd.
Los Angeles, CA 90064, USA

Rinaldo Cutini
via Giacomo Favretto 24
00147 Roma, Italy

Roby D'Silva
Botawala Bldg.
7/10 Horniman CRL
Bombay, India

Daley Inc.
234 Brooks Street
Worcester, Massachusetts 01606, USA

Rita & Morgan Daly
233 Harvard Street
Brookline MA 02146, USA

Louis Danziger
7001 Melrose Avenue
Los Angeles, CA 90028, USA

Memy Dar
Prague 10
Tel Aviv 63477, Israel

Paul Davis
14 East 4th Street
New York, NY 10012, USA

Peter Day
Brookhurst Cottage, 89A Virginius Street
Padstow, New South Wales 2211, Australia

Grafikos Design
David Bartlett
17 South Street, Newton
P.O. Box 5375
Auckland, New Zealand

Design
Paul Schuster
Fellnerstrasse 11
Frankfurt 6, Germany

Design Objectives Ptd Ltd
Ronnie Tan
80 South Bridge Road, #04-00
Golden Castle Building
Singapore 0105

DesignSource
Les Holloway
77 Mowat Avenue, Suite 304
Toronto, Ontario M6K 3E3, Canada

Sudarshan Dheer
10 Sind Chambers
S. Bhagat Singh Road Colaba
Bombay 400005, India

di'lect
Kymia Kazemi
Dirklangenstraat 6
261 HW Delft, The Netherlands

Martha Patino Diaz
Colibri 101 Arboledas
Edo de Mexico 54020, Mexico

Andreas Dietrich
Stocklgras 30
A-4910 Ried/I., Austria

Dimension
J.M. Cornu & V. Malcourant
105 Boulevard Pereire
75017 Paris, France

Theo Dimson
96 Avenue Road
Toronto, Ontario M5R2H3, Canada

Branislav Dobanovacki
Partizanka 11
YU 21000 Novi Sad, Yugoslavia

Lou Dorfsman
80 Station Road
Great Neck, NY 11023, USA

Massimo Dradi
via Gaspare Gozzi 6
Milano 20129, Italy

Karl-Heinz Drescher
Am Zirkus 3
Berlin 1040, Germany

Joe Scorsone & Alice Drueding
501 West Avenue, 2R
Jenkintown, PA 19046, USA

Marc Dufour
Moyano 3, entlo. 1
12002 Castellón, Spain

Rod Dyer
8360 Melrose Avenue
Los Angeles, CA 90069, USA

Edigraph Inc.
George Samerjan
Cantitoe Street
Katonah, NY 10536, USA

Stasys Eidrigiewicz
Bednarska 27-11
Warszawa 00321, Poland

Friedrich Eisenmenger
Seilerstatte 16
A-1010 Wien, Austria

Avi Eisenstein
Rav On 6
Givat Savyon, Israel

Bracha Elhassid
Gruniman 4
Ramat Aviv 69972, Israel

Emery Vincent Associates
Garry Emery
80 Market Street
South Melbourne Victoria 3205,
Australia

Susumo Endo
3-13-3 Jingumae
Shibuyaku, Tokyo 150, Japan

Fumihiko Enokido
10-69 Jurigi-Kogen Suyama
Susono-shi, 410-12 Shizuoka Pref.
Japan

Joaquín Sierra Escalante
San Jeronimo 1006-5
San Jeronimo Lidice 102000
Mexico D.F.

Naomi & Meir Eshel
Brachiyahu 5A
Jerusalem 96225, Israel

Esseblu
Susanna Vallebona
via Antonio Cecchi 8
Milano 20146, Italy

Estudi MMJ
Marina Vilageliu
Brusi 39, local 62
08006 Barcelona, Spain

Raphie Etgar
Hirshenberg 7
Jerusalem, Israel

EVE Press
Elsi Vassdal Ellis
1936 Harmony Road
Bellingham, WA 98226, USA

Extra Studio
Armando Cesti & Gianfranco Torri
via Accademia Albertina 21
10123 Torino, Italy

Judith Eyal
Shderot Chen 31
Tel Aviv 84166, Israel

Arnaud Corbin & Eric Fauchère
38, rue Marcel Maillard
92160 Antony, France

Helen & Gene Federico
Eastwoods Road
Pound Ridge, NY 10576, USA

Gina Federico
71 Park Place
New Canaan, Connecticut 06840, USA

Pensar I Fer
Tuset 19-4.° 5.a
08006 Barcelona, Spain

Oscar Fernández
335 E. Sycamore Street
Columbus, Ohio 43206, USA

Antero Ferreira
Rua 5 de Outubro, 293 5.o tras.
4100 Porto, Portugal
Marco Ferreri
Corso Ticinese 10
20123 Milano, Italy
FHK Henrion
35 Pond Street
London NW3 2PN, England
Gilles Fiszman
Avenue Emile Duray 18
B-1050 Bruxelles, Belgium
Jean-Michel Folon
Le Mantegna Port De Fontvieille
MC 98000, Monaco
Normand Fontaine
553 Queen Street W., Suite 300
Toronto, Ontario, M5V 2B6, Canada
Formfabriken
Ninna Jansson & Elisabeth Engstrand
Olof Palmes gata 20B
111 37 Stockholm, Sweden
Franco, Goldberg, Boros
Weitzman 97
Tel Aviv 62262, Israel
André François
16, Rue Robert Machy
95810 Grisy-Les-Platres, France
Lothar Freund
Clausewitzstrasse 62
Erfurt 5080, Germany
Shigeo Fukuda
3-34-25 Kamikitazawa
Setagaya-ku
Tokyo, Japan
Fuorischema
M&M
Viale Verdi 51
61100 Pesaro, Italy
Aviva Furman
400 Slater Street, Suite 1507
Ottawa, Ontario K1R 7S7, Canada

Jacques N. Garamond
La Grange Guainville
28260 Anet, France
Garza & Labarrere
3780 Wilshire Boulevard, Suite 1030
Los Angeles, CA 90010, USA
Ben Gasner
HaMalekh George 52
Jerusalem 94262, Israel
Wolfgang Geisler
Dolgenseestrasse 14
1136 Berlin, Germany
Dan Gelbart
HaTishbi 80A
Haifa 34523, Israel
Marat Genreb
ul. Candera 7/504
129075 Moscow, USSR
Philippe Gentil
2 Avenue Hoche
75008 Paris, France
Daniel Gil
Caleruega 18
28033 Madrid, Spain
Yoel and Orit Gilinsky
Ivshitz 6
Tel Aviv 62741, Israel
Cherry Giljam
46 Cannon Island Way
Marina da Gama
Muizenburg 7951, South Africa
Gips+Balkind+Associates, Inc.
244 East 58 Street
New York, NY 10022, USA

Milton Glaser
207 East 32nd Street
New York, NY 10016, USA
Glazer and Kalayjian, Inc.
301 East 45th Street
New York, NY 10017, USA
Roz Goldfarb
10 East 22nd Street
New York, NY 10010, USA
Pilar Villuendas & Josep Ramon Gomez
PG. Lluis Companys 2, 6e 1aB
08018 Barcelona, Spain
Ayala Goren
Nussenbaum 9/2
Haifa 32808, Israel
Charles Goslin
264 Garfield Place
Brooklyn, NY 11215, USA
Gottschalk+Ash International Design Consultants
Sonnhaldenstrasse 3, Postfach 105
Zürich 8030, Switzerland
Grafik-Design Austria
Severin Filek
Schönbrunner Strasse 38/8
A-1050 Wien, Austria
Graphic Communication Ltd.
Henry Steiner
28c Conduit Road
Hong Kong
Graphic Design
Ophir Paz & Emanuel Rapoport
Ahad HaAm 04
Tel Aviv 65206, Israel
Grapus
Alex Jordan
5 à 7 rue de la Révolution
93100 Montreuil, France
Elena Green
via Marco Aurelio 15
00184 Roma, Italy
Shosh Cohen & Yonah Greenbaum
Israel
Judith Gregory
1081 River Road
Ottawa, Ontario K1K 3V9, Canada
April Greiman
620 Moulton Avenue, #211
Los Angeles, CA 90031, USA
Rosi & Lorenze Grieder
A-2083 Pleissing 28, Austria
Franco Grignani
via Bianca di Savoia 7
20122 Milano, Italy
Group Technic Design
Ethne Hillhouse
41 Dean Street, Newlands
Cape Town 7700, South Africa
Group/Chicago, Inc.
400 West Erie Street, Suite 302
Chicago, IL 60610, USA
Ramis Guseinov
256, Ustinov St., 10-1
Moscow 121360, USSR
Peter Gyllan
Rosenorns Alle 32
1970 Copenhagen, Denmark

Martin de Haas
Svartagatan 8
121 59 Johanneshov, Sweden
Ilan Hagari
Ha Yarkon 177
Tel Aviv, Israel
Albert Hakakian
1460 58th Street
Brooklyn, NY 11219, USA

Ruth Hanani
Sapir 4
Tel Aviv 64359, Israel
Heinz Handschick
Bohnsdorfer Weg 57
Berlin 1186, Germany
Bauch Hannes
Mariahilferstrasse 191/42
Wien 1150, Austria
Zev Harari
Kibbutz Merhavia, Israel
Rolf Harder
1350 Sherbrooke Street W, Suite 1000
Montreal, Quebec H3G 1J1, Canada
Dorit & Shmulik Harel
Moshav Shilat, Israel
David Harel
Pele Yoetz 39
Jerusalem, Israel
George Hartman
304 East 45th Street
New York, NY 10017, USA
Eytan Hendel
Ruppin 38
Tel Aviv 63457, Israel
Henrion, Ludlow & Schmidt
12 Hobart Place
London SW1W OHH, England
Renate Herfurth
Rosentalgasse 17
7010 Leipzig, Germany
Walter Hergenröther
via del Borgo di S. Pietro 52
40126 Bologna, Italy
Lance Hidy
P.O.B. 806 [2 Dalton Street]
Newburyport, MA 01950, USA
Verena Hillairet
19, rue de la République
13001 Marseilles, France
Mike Hodges
3613 Noble Avenue
Richmond, VA 23222, USA
Peter Holzhausen
Theodor-Heuss-Ring 52
5000 Köln 1, Germany
Marvin Hoshino
100 Hudson Street
New York, NY 10013, USA

Dennis Ichiyama
3017 Courthouse Drive West
Apt. 1C
West Lafayette, IN 47906, USA
Takenobu Igarashi
6-6-22 Minami-Aoyama
Minato-ku, Tokyo, Japan
Imagina
Inma Mengual
San Antonio 29
Aptdo. Correos 541
03700 Denia, Spain

Impreso Aqui
Helios Pandiella
Avda. de Colon, 12-2.o Dcha.
33013 Oviedo, Asturias, Spain
Joanne Ingham-Thomas
The Palace, 1st Floor, Suite 4,
42-48 Ponsonby Road
Auckland 2, New Zealand
Integral Design Unit
Robert Schaap
Mr. Pankenstraat 12
5571 CP Bergeijk, The Netherlands
InterDesign
Marc Piel
16, av. du President Kennedy
75016 Paris, France
Irving D. Miller, Inc.
641 Lexington Avenue
New York, NY 10022, USA
Albert Isern
Balmes 333, 4art. 1a
08006 Barcelona, Spain
ITC Advertising
Rebecca Gomez
1740 Ocean Park Blvd.
Santa Monica, CA 90405, USA
Toyotsugu Itoh
605 Heights Hattori
Shiotsuke-dori, Showa-ku
Nagoya, Japan 466
Gregory Izkovich
Bezalel 18
Haifa, Israel

J+M Condon Inc.
126 Fifth Avenue
New York, NY 10011, USA
J.H.B.M. Dijkhuis
Havikhorst 77
6043 RM Roemond, The Netherlands
Jack Weiss Associates, Inc.
820 Davis Street
Evanston, IL 60201, USA
Clive Jackson
80 Wellmeadow Road
Glasgow G43 1JZ, Scotland
Clive Jacobsen
200 East 33rd Street, Mailbox 157
New York, NY 10016, USA
JD Design & Draughting Associates
John Laker
4 Bowman Road, Forrest Hill,
Auckland, New Zealand
Evzen Jecho
Prostredni 424
765 02 Otrokovice, Czechoslovakia
Radovan Jenko
Kamniska 1
63000 Celje, Yugoslavia
Joseph Jibri
Frishman 55
Tel Aviv 64383, Israel

Asher Kalderon
Kehilot Budapest 8
Tel Aviv 69701, Israel
Ron Kambourian
35 A Crescent Road
Newport NSW 2106, Australia

Yusaku Kamekura
Recruit Building
8-4-17 Ginza Chuo-ku
Tokyo, 104, Japan
Ando Kanesato
4-15-7 Sumiyoshi
Hamanatsu-shi
Shiruoka-ken 430, Japan
Kaarina Kari
Saunatie 20
15210 Lahti, Finland
Natan Karp
POB 4048
Jerusalem 91040, Israel
Shemuel A. Katz
Kibbutz Gaton, Israel
Irene Kaufman
153 Mercer Street
New York, NY 10012, USA
Gerd Kehrer
Heinz Herbert Karry Strasse 17
6000 Frankfurt 60, Germany
Gideon Keich
HaMeshurreret Rachel 26
Jerusalem 96348, Israel
Kellogg Design Inc.
West End Avenue
New York, NY 10025, USA
Michel Kichka
Dor VadorShav 8
Jerusalem 93117, Israel
Sanja Rocco Kiiru
Aleja W. Piecka 16
Zagreb 41000, Yugoslavia
A. Eymont & M. Kin-Yee
355 Kent Street
Sydney NSW 2000, Australia
Heinz Kippnick
F.-Engels-Str. 39/40
2792 Schwerin, Germany
Andrea Klausner
Castelligasse 10/7
A-1050 Wien, Austria
A. Klemencov
Kauno 39-28
Klaipèda, Lithuania SSR, USSR
Peter Kneebone
3 Rue Henri Ribière
75019 Paris, France
Manfred König
Wolkensteiner Strasse 10
9048 Karl-Marx-Stadt, Germany
Galina Pavlovna Korbu
8 Sovietit Street
House 44, Apt. 25
Leningrad 193144, USSR
Andrzei Kot
20-112 Lublin
Grodzka 19 m.z., Poland
Jan F. Kovar
5 Kvènta 1555
756-61 Roznov P.R., Czechoslovakia
Kasimir Krastev
Momchil Voivoda
Vidin 3700, Bulgaria

Krog
Edi Berk
Krakovski nasip 22
61000 Ljubljana, Yugoslavia
Shalom Kweller
Gidon 28
Jerusalem 93506, Israel
La Nava
C/San Vicente, 200
46007 Valencia, Spain
Ales Lamr
Valdstejnske namesti 2
11800 Praha 1, Czechoslovakia
Walter Landor
1001 Front Street
San Francisco, CA 94111, USA
Martha Scotford Lange
215 Monmouth Avenue
Durham, NC 27701, USA
Jean Larcher
16 Chemin des Bourgognes
95000 Cergy, France
Jean-Marie Lawniczak
Ramsauerstrasse 28/4
A-4020 Linz, Austria
Alain Le Quernec
Trogour Huella
29136 Plogonnec, France
Vladimir Leder
Herzl 79
Haifa 31071, Israel
Herman C. Lelie
90A Shirland Road
London W9 2EQ, England
Alexander Lembersky
yn. Boichenko 6 k.b. 26
252206 Kiev-206, USSR
Prof. Jan Lenica
Hochschule der Kunste Berlin
Hardenbergstrasse 33
1000 Berlin 12, Germany
Gert Leufert
Apartado 1382
Caracas 1010 A, Venezuela
Michael Levin
13 rue Clavel
75019 Paris, France
Ruth Levin
Megadim 11
Jerusalem, Israel
Benny Levin
Carmiah 1
Jerusalem, Israel
Zvi Levin
Sderot Rothschild 138
Tel Aviv 65272, Israel
Rami Elchanan and Jacky Levy
Yaffo 153
Jerusalem, Israel
T.A. Lewandowski
13 Place E. Goudeau
75018 Paris, France
James L. Lienhart
155 North Harbor Drive
Chicago, IL 60601, USA
Ake Lindstrom
Ehrensvardsgatan 5
11235 Stockholm, Sweden
Leo Lionni
35 East 85th Street
New York, NY 10028, USA

Giuseppe De Liso
via Turati 14
70124 Bari, Italy
ListerButler Inc.
437 Fifth Avenue
New York, NY 10016, USA
Sonsoles Llorens
Aribau 21 bis 1o 2a
08011 Barcelona, Spain
Alberto Locatelli
Corso di Porta Ticinese 76
Milano 20123, Italy
Prof. Uwe Loesch
Kaiser-Friedrich-Ring 38
D-4000 Düsseldorf 11,
Germany
Logo Design
Jordi Serch
Mandri 66 entlo. 2a
08022 Barcelona, Spain
J. De Pas, D. Urbino, P. Lomazzi
Corso XXII Marzo 39
20129 Milano, Italy
Lord, Geller, Federico, Einstein, Inc.
655 Madison Avenue
New York, NY 10021, USA
Lorraine Louie
46 Commerce Street
New York, NY 10014, USA
Reinhold Luger
Badgasse 3
A-6850 Dornbirn, Austria
Luth + Katz Inc.
40 East 49th Street
New York, NY 10017, USA

M&M Graphic Design
Marianne Friedman
339 Fifteenth Street, Suite 204
Oakland, CA 94612, USA
João Machado
R. da Alegria 1714-A AP. 32
4200 Porto, Portugal
Design Machine
Lonn C.A. Beaudry
4415 Warwick Boulevard
Kansas City, MO 64111, USA
Gregie De Maeyer
Doorn 10
2760 Kruibeke, Belgium
Maginnis Graphics Incorporated
540 N. Lake Shore Drive
Chicago, IL 60611, USA
W.M. de Majo
99 Archel Road, W. Kensington
London W14 9QL, England
Marjorie Katz Design
156 Fifth Avenue
New York, NY 10010, USA
Hugh Marshall
37 Stanhope Gardens
London SW7 5QY, England
Mary's River Studio
Rural Route Two, Box 142
Hammond, NY 13646, USA
Mason & Scott
Les Mason
263 Newcastle Street
Perth 6000, Australia
Wlodzimierz Matachowski
Prominskiego 86/10
93-266 Lodz, Poland
Takaharu Matsumoto
5-4-35-608 Minami-aoyama
Minato-ku, Tokyo, Japan
Fernando Medina
Santiago Bernabeu 6
Madrid 16, Spain

Hans-J. Melzer
Appartementhaus Alsterpark
Alsterkehre 2
2000 Hamburg 65, Germany
Frédéric Metz
3445 Rue Saint-Famille
Montreal, Quebec H2X 2K6, Canada
Michael Orr + Associates Inc.
The Hawkes Building
75 West Market Street
Corning, NY 14830, USA
Michael Peters Group, PLC
3 Olaf Street
London W11 4BE, England
François Miehe
94 rue Louise Aglaée Cretté
94400 Vitry, France
Miho
1200 Chateau Road
Pasadena, CA 91105, USA
Armando & Maurizio Milani
815 Park Avenue
New York, NY 10021, USA
Jan Mlodozeniec
3 m. 7 ul. Naruszewicza
02627 Warszawa, Poland
Guy Mocquet
22 rue Agnès Sorel
94130 Nogent/Marne, France
Clement Mok
477 Bryant Street
San Francisco, CA 94107, USA
David Grossman & Yaki Molcho
Israel
Ilan Molcho
Maze 69
Tel Aviv 65789, Israel
Moradell & Vallbona
Paseo Bonanova 14 Torre A
08022 Barcelona, Spain
Morera & Sola-Ser
Aribau 80, átic 2.a
08036 Barcelona, Spain
Josef Müller-Brockmann
Bergstrasse 15
CH-8103 Unterengstringen, Switzerland
Shozo Murase
1-62-1 Yamazoe-cho, Chikusa-ku
Nagoya-city, Aichi, Japan
Martti Mykkanen
Fredrikinkatu 59 C 32
00100 Helsinki, Finland

Zvi Narkiss
Hakotzer 6
Ramat HaSharon 47411, Israel
Barbara Nessim
63 Green Street
New York, NY 10012, USA
Gabi Neumann
POB 402
Herzliya 46103, Israel
Zivit Nevo (Nissilevich)
Israel

Poul Allan Nielsens
Hans Brogesvej 1
8220 Brabrand, Denmark
Rea Nikonova
Su-353660-Eysk
Sverdlova-175, USSR
Nippon Design Center
Nagai
Chuo-Daiwa Building
1-13-13 Ginza Chuo-ku
Tokyo, Japan 204
Marian Nowinski
st. Noway Swiat 34/5a
Warszawa, Poland
Pati Nuñez
Sant Agusti, 5, 4art-1a
08012 Barcelona, Spain

Pierre Mendell & Klaus Oberer
Widenmayerstrasse 12
8000 München 22, Germany
György Olah
Bognar u. 7
1021 Budapest, Hungary
Samerwerkende Ontwerpers
André Toet
Herengracht 160
1016 BN Amsterdam, The Netherlands
Ontwerpforum
Bart Oosterhoorn
Dorpsstraat 28
1182 JD Amstelveen,
The Netherlands
Jacob Oppenheim
Ohel Shlomo 23
Jerusalem, Israel
Asher Oron
Brissmantov 19
Yahud 56101, Israel
Over de Schreef?
Kees Schreuders
Van der Goesstraat 29
3521 TK Utrecht, The Netherlands

Junn Paasche-Aasen
Rosendalsveien 18
1166 Oslo 11, Norway
Charles de Paeuw
Oppeniner Strasse 23
413 Moers, Germany
Ali Partowi
Argentinierstrasse 20A
A-1040 Wien, Austria
Peak Images
John Ewbank & Bruce Madgwick
P.O. Box 790
New Plymouth, New Zealand
Daniel Pelavin
46 Commerce Street
New York, NY 10014, USA
Pen & Paper
Peter Lambert
P.O. Box 33W
106 Webster Street
Ballarat 3350, Australia
Pencil Corporate Art
Achim Kiel
Kuturzentrum Rundbogen
Heinrich-Bussing-Hof
D-3300 Braunschweig,
Germany
Pentagram Design Limited
Alan Fletcher
11 Needham Road
London W11 2RP, England

Perception, Inc.
213 West Institute Place, Suite 602
Chicago, Illinois 60610, USA
Alberte Permuy
Casas Reais 42-1
15704 Santiago, Spain
Supon Phornirunlit
2130 P Street, NW, Suite 327
Washington, DC 20037, USA
Tadeusz Piechura
ul. Zgierska 124/140, m. 168
91-320 Lodz, Poland
Mary F. Pisarkiewicz
72 Charles Street, Suite 3W
New York, NY 10014, USA
Josep Pla-Narbona
Carrer Nou 12, 08939
Sant Vicenç de Montalt
Barcelona, Spain
Plastic Plus Products
Herschenberg
Israel
Peter Pócs
Akadèmia KRT. 35, III/24
H-6000 Kecskemèt, Hungary
Kamen Popov
7, rue Guido Oppenheim
2263 Luxembourg, G.D. Luxembourg
Amram Prat
Mehola 17
Ramat Afal 52960, Israel
Praxis
Roberto A. Dosil
1200 W. Pender, Suite 200
Vancouver, BC V6E 2S9, Canada
Noëlle Prinz & Michel Raby
6 Rue Dumeril
75013 Paris, France
Proforma
Joop Ridder
Slepersvest 5-7
3011 MK Rotterdam, The Netherlands

R. Valicenti Design
213 West Institute Place, Suite 405
Chicago, IL 60610, USA
Robin Rapoport
60 W. 66 St., Suite 31E
New York, NY 10023, USA
Christoph Rau
Box 4208
Lima 100, Peru
Varda Raz
Brenner 23
Tel Aviv 65246, Israel
Barbara Redmond
1006 First Bank West
Minneapolis, MN 55402, USA
Yossi Regev
Emek HaShoshanin 19
Nes Ziona 70400, Israel
Roni Rehow
Kibbutz Mizra, Israel
Dan Reisinger
Zlocisti 5
Tel Aviv 62994, Israel
Guus Rijven
Westeinde 203
2512 GZ Den Haag, The Netherlands
Robert P. Gersin Associates Inc.
11 E. 22nd Street
New York, NY 10010, USA
Roger Black Incorporated
36 Gramercy Park East
New York, NY 10003, USA
Yitzhak Romem
Rosh Pina 12
Netanya 42309, Israel

Sarah Rosenbaum
Lokkeveien 11
0253 Oslo 2, Norway
Abe Rosenfeld
POB 1440 Ramat Hasharon
Israel
Ross Hudson Design
107 East 89 Street
New York, NY 10128, USA
Ambrogio Rossari
via Eustachi 2
20129 Milano, Italy
Michele Rossi
via Val Tesino 52
63013 Grottammare (AP), Italy
Marta Rourich
Mitre, 182, Entlo 3.a
08006 Barcelona, Spain
Andrea Rovatti
via Tantardini 1/A
20136 Milano, Italy
Igal Rozental
Emek Dothan 1
Holon 58486, Israel
Rudolph de Harak & Associates Inc.
320 West 13 Street
New York, NY 10014, USA
Robert Miles Runyan
200 East Culver Blvd.
Playa Del Rey, CA 90293, USA

Michal Saar
HaNetzav 18
Tel Aviv, Israel
Vivian Sahar
Nordau 28
Tel Aviv, Israel
Arnold Saks
350 East 81st Street
New York, NY 10028, USA
Salichs
Bertran, 67 Bajos
08023 Barcelona, Spain
Salpeter Paganucci, Inc.
142 East 37th Street
New York, NY 10016, USA
Roberto Sambonet
Foro Bonaparte 44A
20121 Milano, Italy
Kenichi Samura
Maeda Bldg. 4f, 67-2, 5-Chome,
Yoyogi, Shibuya-ku, Tokyo, Japan
Sara Giovanitti Design
125 Fifth Ave., Studio 206
New York, NY 10003, USA
U. G. Sato
75 Yaraicho, Shinjuku-ku
Tokyo, Japan
Jan Sawka
High Falls, NY 12440, USA
Gila Schakhine
Prug 34
Tel Aviv 63417, Israel
Terry Koppel & Paula Scher
156 Fifth Avenue
New York, NY 10010, USA
Helmut Schmid
Tarumi-cho 3-24-14-707
564 Suita-shi, Osaka, Japan
Prof. Helmut Schmidt-Rhen
Florastrasse 33
D-4000 Düsseldorf 1, Germany

Ward Schumaker
466 Green Street
San Francisco, CA 94133, USA
Serge Segay
Sverdlova 175
353660 Eysk SU, USSR
Segno Associati
Gelsomino D'Ambrosio & Pino Grimaldi
via Arce N. 110
Salerno 84100, Italy
Elinor Selame
2330 Washington Street
Newton Lower Falls, MA 02162, USA
Clifford Selbert
2067 Massachusetts Avenue
Cambridge, MA 02140, USA
Remo Semenzato
via Violino di Sopra 154
25126 Brescia, Italy
Seventeenth Street Studios
Randall Goodall
455 17th Street
Oakland, CA 94612, USA
Weinberg, Karasso, Shamir
Sderot Rothschild 100
Tel Aviv 65224, Israel
David Shapira
Israel
Whitney Sherman
5101 Whiteford Avenue
Baltimore, MD 21212, USA
Hayim Shtayer
Bikurim 36A
Haifa, Israel
Siegel & Gale
1185 Avenue of the Americas
New York, NY 10036, USA
Signo SRL
Heinz Waibl
Via Emanuele Filiberto, 14
20149 Milano, Italy
Skolos, Wedell + Raynor Inc.
Nancy Skolos
529 Main Street
Charlestown, MA 02129, USA
Lex van Soest
Postbus 179, studio Schachtstraat 3
6430 AD Hoensbroek, The Netherlands
Lanny Sommese
481 Glenn Road
State College, PA 16803, USA
Nacho Soriano
Gral. Aranaz, 76-19
28027 Madrid, Spain
Stankowski & Duschek
Lenbachstrasse 43
7000 Stuttgart 1, Germany
Friedel Stern
Yoash 8,
Tel Aviv 63575, Israel
Marie Sterte
Smedjegatan 5
41113 Göteborg, Sweden
Peter Stone
14 Kings Avenue, Bromley
Kent BR1 4HW, England
Dirk Streitenfeld
Lange Strasse 75
637 Oberursel 2, Germany
Strizek & Associates
213 West Institute Place
Chicago, IL 60610
Studio Tecnico
G. Bocchio & G. Palmieri
via Consolata 5
10122 Torino, Italy

Studio Kav-Graph
Tsvika Remetz & Shlomi Amsellem
Canfe Nesherim 31
Jerusalem, Israel
Studio Shtayim
Hana Farhy & Iris Ziv
Shlomo HaMelekh 9
Tel Aviv 64377, Israel
Studio dp(daf)
David Portal
Nathanzon 18 POB 1875
Haifa 31018, Israel
Studio Bubblan
Kari & Jeanette Palmqvist
Sjunde Villagatan 28
502 44 Bor[166]s, Sweden
Studio 77
Franco Bassi
Foro Bonaparte 12
20121 Milano, Italy
Studio Rocca
Via Gimigliano 177
88100 Catanzaro, Italy
Studio 10
Louis N. Donato
Route 17, Tuxedo Square
Tuxedo, NY 10987, USA
Studio HBM
Dan Arnon & Zvi Zelikovitch
Kikar Kedumim 10
Old Jaffa, Israel
Maruska Studios
61A York Street
Ottawa, Ontario K1N 5T2, Canada
Sussman/Prejaz & Company, Inc.
Deborah Sussman
1651 Eighteenth Street
Santa Monica, CA 90404, USA
Alicja Szubert-Olszewska
ul. Miedzynarodowa 46/48 A, m.15
03922 Warszawa, Poland

Walter Tafelmaier
Etschweg 7
8012 Ottobrunn b. Munchen,
Germany
Kan Tai-Keung
276-278 Lockhart Road
Wanchai, Hong Kong
Yukihisa Takakita
601:14-8 Daikan-cho, Higashi-ku
Nagoya, Japan
Ikko Tanaka
A.Y. Bldg, 3-2,2 Kita-Aoyama
Minato-ku, Tokyo 107, Japan
Tangram Strategic Design s.a.s.
Enrico Sempi
via Negroni 2
28100 Novara, Italy
David Tartakover
Shluss 34
Tel Aviv 85149, Israel
Claudia Teller
161 East 25th Street
New York, NY 10010, USA
Telmet Design Associates
553 Queen Street W., Suite 300
Toronto, Ontario, M5V 2B6, Canada
Armando Testa
Corso Quintino Sella 56
10131 Torino, Italy
Rick Tharp
50 University Avenue, Suite #21
Los Gatos, CA 95030, USA
The Mediterranean Fantastic Factory
Ricard Molas
Carretera de les Aigües, 374
08023 Barcelona, Spain

The Understanding Business
Richard Saul Wurman
59 Wooster Street
New York, NY 10012-4349, USA
The Second Oldest Profession
1009 Daniel Drive
Austin, Texas 78704, USA
The Janice Ashby Design Partnership
Werner Prisi
No. 1 Carr Hill Road
Wynberg 7800, Box 7824
Wynberg, South Africa
The Chartered Society of Designers
Patricia Rees Cummings
29 Bedford Square
London WC1B 3EG, England
The New Zealand Society of Designers Inc.
Michael Smythe
Pembridge, 31 Princes Street
Box 3432
Auckland 1, New Zealand
The Jenkins Group
9 Tufton Street, Westminister
London SW1P 3QB, England
Christer Themptander
Vanadisplan 1
11331 Stockholm, Sweden
Nathan Tiberovsky
HaTomar 5
Rishom LeZion 75201, Israel
Trudi van Tilborgh
Singel 109 1
1012 VG Amsterdam, The Netherlands
Siegfried Odermatt & Rosmarie Tissi
Schipfe 45
CH-8001 Zürich, Switzerland
Yusaku Tomoeda
Kumamoto Kamitori 5-20
Central Heights 801, Japan
Hans van der Toorn
Coöperatiehof 16B
1073 JR Amsterdam, The Netherlands
Xosé Maria Torné
La Compañia
Rafael Alberti, 15-1° D
15008 A. Coruña, Spain
Total Design
Ben Bos
Van Diemenstraat 200
1013 NH Amsterdam, The Netherlands
Totalmedia Productions Ltd.
Ran Caspi
Amos 30
Tel Aviv, Israel
Y. Trager
HaNetzav 18
Tel Aviv 67018, Israel
Otto Treumann
Hoogstraat 47
1381 vv Weesp, The Netherlands
Margalit Tsfati
HaNadiv 10
Givatayim, Israel
Barrie Tucker
4 Eastwood Centre
245 Fullarton Road
Eastwood, South Australia 5063
Turquoise
Philippe Sigouin & Mark Timmings
69 rue Vaudreuil
Hull (Quebec) J8X 2B9, Canada
Nils J. Tvengsberg
Holmenveien 20
Postboks 98, Vindern
0319 Oslo 3, Norway

Gad Ullman
Beeri 7
Tel Aviv 64682, Israel
UNA
Will de l'Ecluse
Mauritskade 55
1092 AD Amsterdam, The Netherlands
USP Helsinki Oy
Rita & Viktor Kaltala
Kanavaranta 3.C
SF-00160 Helsinki, Finland

Luc Vanmalderen
Galerie du Roi 18
B. 1000 Bruxelles, Belgium
Yarom Vardimon
Shlomo HaMelekh 87
Tel Aviv 64512, Israel
Anat Vardimon
HaMari 26
Givatayim 53329, Israel
Varis & Ojala Oy
Esa Ojala
Kanavaranta 3 D
00160 Helsinki, Finland
Jonas Varnas
Pranskaus 48-1
Vilnius, 232004, Lithuania, USSR
Thomas Vavrinek
Fasangasse 10
A-2384 Breitenfurt, Austria
Jukka Veistola
Tehtaankatu 34D
Helsinki 00150, Finland
Velko Veldov
z.k. Orel, bl. v-4
7205 Razgrad, Bulgaria
Tomás Vellvé
Rector Ubach 8 E/2
08021 Barcelona, Spain
Verge, Lebel associés, inc.
1039 avenue des Erables
Quebec G1R 2N1, Canada
Xavier Vidal
P.G. del Born 17, 4t, 2a
08003 Barcelona, Spain
Massimo Vignelli
475 Tenth Avenue
New York, NY 10018, USA
Vorm Vijk bv
Bart de Groot
Frederikstraat 501-509
2514 LN 's-Gravenhage, The Netherlands
Hein Vredenberg
Delftweg 27
2289 AK Rijswijk, The Netherlands
WalkerGroup/CNI
320 West 13th Street
New York, NY 10014, USA
Wallace Church Associates, Inc.
330 East 48 Street
New York, NY 10017, USA
Atelier Warminski
Jutta Neufeldt
Borngasse 21
6470 Büdingen 8, Germany
Avi Shapira & Yossi Waxman
Netzach Israel 7
Tel Aviv, Israel

Erdmann Weber
Amselweg 37
D-7900 Ulm, Germany
François Weil
17 rue Corbon
75015 Paris, France
Jean Widmer
126 Bld. Auguste Blanqui
F.75013 Paris, France
Stanislaw Wieczorek
Stowarzyszenie Polskich Antystów
Grafików Projektantów
Ul. Nowy Swiat 7m.6
00-496 Warszawa, Poland
Prof. Bruno K. Wiese
Allhornweg 7
2000 Hamburg 67, Germany
William Hafeman Design
932 W. Washington
Chicago, IL 60607, USA
Henry Wolf
167 East 73rd Street
New York, NY 10021, USA
Worksight
Scott W. Santoro
568 Broadway, Suite 701
New York, NY 10012, USA
Prof. Gert Wunderlich
Moschelesstrasse 1
Leipzig 7010, Germany

Xeno
900 N. Franklin
Chicago, IL 60610, USA

Ako Yehuda
520 N. Croft Avenue, 127
Los Angeles, CA 90048, USA
Nitzah Yogev
Mishol Shnonit 19
Beer Sheba 84738, Israel
Tadanori Yokoo
5-11-5 Seijo Setagaya-ku
Tokyo, Japan
Yoresh
POB 2310
Jerusalem, Israel

Bruno Zaffoni
via Gora 3
38068 Rovereto, Italy
Dieter Zembsch
Waxensteinstrasse 53
8000 München 70, Germany
Deborah Zemke
1830 H Street
Sacramento, CA 95814, USA
Isaokas Zibucas
Zvaigzdziv 23
23205 Vilnius, Lithuania, USSR
Mikael T. Zielinski
127 East 61 Street, 4R
New York, NY 10021, USA
Zoptic
Neus Grabulosa
Bailen 11 5o 2a
08010 Barcelona, Spain
Ami Ravid & Yoram Zung
Herzliya 28
Haifa, Israel

INDEXES

DESIGN FIRMS AND INSTITUTIONS

DESIGNERS

DESIGN FIRMS AND INSTITUTIONS

Aaron Marcus and Associates 22
Antero Ferreira Design 122–126
Atelier Gérard Finel & Associés 96–98

Barrie Tucker Design 204–210
Bass/Yager & Associates 30–35
Basti Brothers 116
Bureau d'Etudes Garamond

Centre Design UQAM 49
Chermayeff & Geismar Associates 12–15
Concepts Design 89–90
Cross Associates 61–66

Daly & Daly, Inc. 16
Design Cornu Malcourant 145–146
Design Farm 196–197
Design Room Itoh 200–201

Esseblu 86–88
Eymont Kin-yee Design 211–216

Fuorischema Design Studio 147–155

George Hartman Design Consultant 59–60
Graphic Communication Ltd. 178–179

H. L. Chu & Company 55–58
Helmut Schmid Design 202
Henry Wolf Productions, Inc. 36

Igarashi Studio 180–181
Illustratørene 161
InterDesign 157–158

Junn Paasche-Aasen Design 95

Kamen Popov Posters and Graphic Design 91
Kan Tai–keung Design & Associates Ltd. 194–195

M&M Communications Agency 147–155
M&M Graphic Design 48
Michael Levin Communication Visuelle 162
Milton Glaser, Inc. 23–26

Natan Karp Studio 170–171

PAOS Inc. 182–191
Paul Davis Studio 20–21
Pencil Corporate Art 127–135
Pentagram Design 69–82
Praxis Design and Consultation 50–53
Prinz-Raby Design Graphique 107–108
Pushpin Group, The 42–47

Reisinger Graphic Communication 169

Samenwerkende Ontwerpers 111–112
Segno Associati 113–115
Seventeenth Street Studios 67–68
Skolos Wedell + Raynor, Inc. 38
Studio de Liso 92–94
Studio KROG 136–137
Studio Tecnico Associato 117–119
Supon Design Group 9

T.A. Lewandowski 138–139
Takashi Akiyama 192–193
Tangram Strategic Design 104
Tharp Did It 28–29
Turquoise Design, Inc. 17–18

DESIGNERS

Akiyama, Takashi 192–193
Almaliah, Gad 166–168
Arnoldi, Per 99–100

Bass, Saul 30–35
Bastiaens, Boy 116
Beltran, Felix 37
Berk, Edi 136–137
Bocchio, Gabriella 117–119

Chermayeff, Ivan 12–15
Chu, Hoi L. 55–58
Chwast, Seymour 42–47
Cornu, Jean-Michel 145–146
Cross, James A. 61–66

Daly, Morgan 16
Daly, Rita 16
D'Ambrosio, Gelsomino 113–115
Davis, Paul 20–21
De Liso, Giuseppi 92–94
Dolcini, Massimo 147–155
Dosil, Roberto A. 50–53

Eidrigevicius, Stasys 120–121
Eisenmenger, Friedrich 105–106
Eisenstein, Avi 175
Endo, Susumo 198–199
Eymont, Anna 211–216

Fernández, Oscar 39
Ferreira, Antero 122–126
Finel, Gérard 96–98
Friedman, Marianne 48

Garamond, Jacques N. 101–103
Glaser, Milton 23–26
Goodall, Randall 67–68
Grimaldi, Pino 113–115

Harel, David 176
Hartman, George 59–60
Hofhuis, Robert Jon 89–90

Igarashi, Takenobu 180–181
Itoh, Toyotsugu 200–201

Kamphorst, Floor
Karp, Natan 170–171
Kichka, Michael 172–174
Kiel, Achim 127–135
Kin-Yee, Myriam 211–216

Levin, Michael 162
Lewandowski, T.A. 138–139
Llorens, Sonsoles 143–144
Loesch, Uwe 109–110

Machado, João 140–142
Malcourant, Véronique 145–146
Marcus, Aaron 22
Metz, Frédéric 49
Miho 27

Nakanishi, Motoo 182–191
Nikonova, Rea 156

Paasche-Aasen, Junn 95
Palmieri, Giulio 117–119
Pelavin, Daniel 54
Phornirunlit, Supon 19
Piel, Marc 157–158
Popov, Kamen 91
Prinz, Noëlle 107–108

Raby, Michel 107–108
Reisinger, Dan 169
Rosenbaum, Sarah 161

Sato, U.G. 196–197
Schmid, Helmut 202
Segay, Serge 163
Sempi, Enrico 104
Sherman, Whitney 40–41
Skolos, Nancy 38
Steiner, Henry 178–179
Sterte, Marie 164
Stienstra, Anne 89–90
Stone, Peter 84–85

Tafelmaier, Walter 159–160
Tai-keung, Kan 194–195
Tharp, Rick 28–29
Timmings, Mark 17–18
Toet, André 111–112
Tucker, Barrie 204–210

Vallebona, Susanna 86–88

Wolf, Henry 36

NC 997 .A4 J46 1991

	DATE DUE	

NC 997 .A4 J46 1991